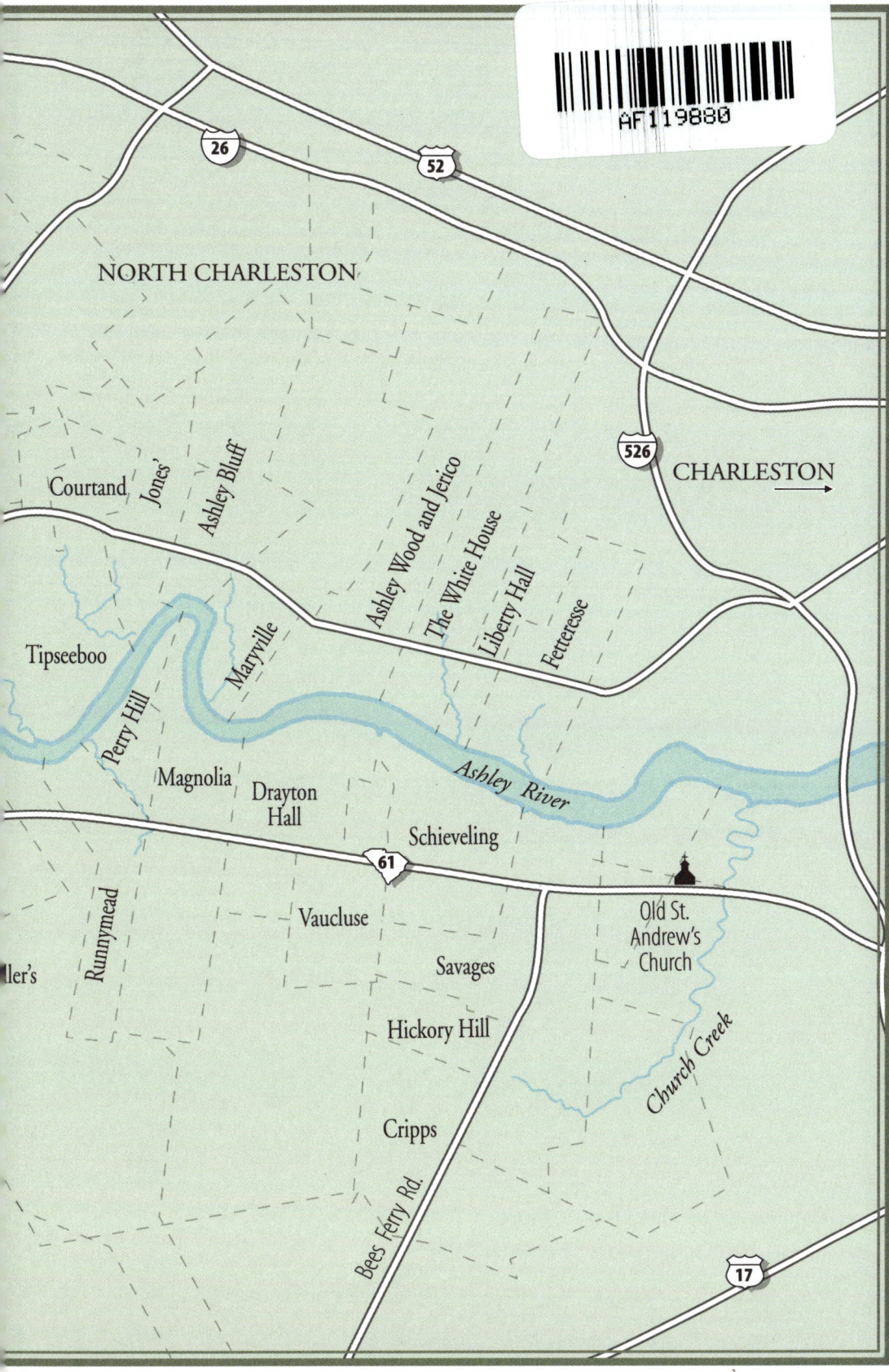

American Landmark

Charles Duell and the Rebirth of Middleton Place

Virginia Christian Beach

MIDDLETON PLACE FOUNDATION

EVENING POST BOOKS

Published by

Evening Post Books
Charleston, South Carolina

Middleton Place Foundation
Charleston, South Carolina

Copyright © 2022 Middleton Place Foundation
All rights reserved.
First edition

Author: Virginia Christian Beach
Editor: John M. Burbage
Designer: Gill Guerry
Photo Editor: Rick Rhodes
Cover Photograph: Rick Rhodes

No part of this book may be reproduced or transmitted in any form or by any means, electronic or mechanical, including photocopying, recording or by information storage and retrieval system – except by a reviewer who may quote brief passages in a review to be printed in a magazine, newspaper, or on the web – without permission in writing from the publisher. For information, please contact the publisher.

Second printing 2023
Printed in the United States of America

A CIP catalog record for this book has been applied
for from the Library of Congress.

ISBN: 978-1-929647-65-1

To

Stephen Frederick Snyder

for his inspiration

and generosity

FAMILY STEWARDSHIP
of
MIDDLETON PLACE

From
JOHN WILLIAMS and MARY BAKER
to their daughter
↓

MARY WILLIAMS, 1721-1761
500 acres as dowry on her 1741 marriage to
HENRY MIDDLETON, 1717-1784
which, with additional grants & purchases, in 1764
passed to their son
↓

ARTHUR MIDDLETON, 1742-1787
from whom it passed to his son
↓

HENRY MIDDLETON, 1770-1846
thence to his son
↓

WILLIAMS MIDDLETON, 1809-1883
and from Williams Middleton to his widow
↓

SUSAN PRINGLE SMITH MIDDLETON, 1822-1900
then to their daughter
↓

ELIZABETH MIDDLETON HEYWARD, 1849-1915
who willed it to her cousin
↓

J. J. PRINGLE SMITH, 1887-1969
(a triple great-grandson of the first Henry Middleton, 1717-1784)
from whom it passed to his grandson
↓

CHARLES H. P. DUELL, 1938-
who in 1974 established the Middleton Place Foundation, which
nonprofit 501 (c) 3 Educational Trust now owns in perpetuity the
Middleton Place National Historic Landmark

CONTENTS

Foreword vii
Preface xi
Prologue: Colorado 1
1: Between Two Worlds 5
2: Empire and Rebellion 27
3: Dreams and Despair 57
4: Where Flowers Bloom 91
5: Heritage Tourism 129
6: Marshaling the Assets 159
7: To Begin Again 181
8: A New Century 219
Acknowledgments 253
Appendix 256
Notes 258
References 262
Index 272

FOREWORD

This is a story of survival against the odds — a testament to one family's struggle to keep their home going despite wars, storms, financial pressures and societal change. It reveals a deep love for a place that has endured for generations. This love has been resourced with ingenuity, determination and at times, pure luck. Or as Charles Duell puts it, "a series of miracles." Every generation has done their bit, and the rebirth of recent times is part of a continuum of reinvention, renewal and reinvigoration. For Charles and his ancestors, it has been their life work.

The book before you is not just about one family. *American Landmark* encompasses some 350 years of American history, from the first Carolina settlers to the present day. Many different people populate the Middleton Place story: from the enslaved workers who built the estate, to the communities that have grown up around it, to the thousands of visitors that come each year to discover and learn about its unique history. It is a profoundly human account — one of beauty, courage and tragedy in equal measure.

At the heart of Middleton Place is the story of slavery. For many, the pain of this history is raw, and healing the wounds is not easy. It should be treated with transparency, humility and, above all, humanity. It is a challenge that the Middleton Place Foundation embraces wholeheartedly. Its mission to use "historic preservation, documented research and interpretation as a force for education, understanding and positive change" provides a clear path for the future and an opportunity for reconciliation. It offers a chance for all Americans to learn and come to terms with their shared history. Middleton Place can be an example of how to unite people and create a positive narrative for the future: one of hope and inclusivity that does not hide the past, but faces it in a spirt of openness and truth.

When talking about family legacy, people are quick to equate feelings of responsibility with a sense of burden and weight. However, this responsibility can also be a source of immense drive and purpose. These attributes feature strongly in this book and through Charles' mission to create a constructive and sustainable future with the Middleton Place Foundation. Building a family legacy also requires long-term, multi-generational thinking. In a world that suffers from "short-termism" — where too often decisions are made for quick wins, or in political cycles of a few years or a few months, to the detriment of lasting solutions — we need reminders of permanence. Middleton Place demonstrates the value of responsibility, preservation and long-term thinking.

One of the most profound changes has been the opening up of Middleton Place to the outside world. What started with small garden tours in the late 19th century has grown into a thriving visitor business. To grow and develop the visitor numbers, Charles had to take big risks early on through loans and investments in the site. This has paid off, and the property can now be enjoyed by many more people than ever before. The confidence and belief he had in his vision is inspiring.

I first met Charles in 2015 during a visit to Charleston with my wife. We took a trip out to see Middleton Place and I was immediately struck by the beauty of the gardens and the majestic oak trees that have stood witness to countless people and events through the years. Charles spoke enthusiastically about his plans and vision for the future. His passion was self-evident. We talked and exchanged notes about the challenges and rewards of maintaining a historic property.

It turns out there are many aspects of our lives that are similar. We both had unexpected inheritances: I with Saint Giles House and he with Middleton Place. And both of us were landed with a family legacy that we had to rebuild and take big risks to do so.

Given neither of us knew we would inherit, we were not encumbered by the weight of expectation growing up. Perhaps that has given us an advantage in approaching the task of becoming custodians — with less pressure and a bit more freedom. There is always a strong camaraderie between owners of historic properties. Despite geographical differences, we share many similarities. I look ahead to where Charles is now and hope that one day I will be able to look back at my own contribution with an equal sense of accomplishment and pride.

We also share a slice of family history. As a direct descendant of one of the Lord Proprietors, Anthony Ashley-Cooper — whose name is associated with the Ashley and Cooper rivers either side of Charleston — I have a strong connection with the early history of the Carolinas. It was one of Charles' ancestors, Arthur Middleton (grandfather of the Declaration Signer), who was responsible for removing in 1719 the Lord Proprietors' control of the colony, frustrated by their lack of action. Thus, my family's local involvement ceased. However, to this day, we feel a close bond with the history of the area.

Reading this book, I find myself full of admiration for what Charles has achieved. He transformed Middleton Place into a thriving business with education at its heart: where history can be learned from and confronted with honesty and empathy, and the natural beauty of the site can be enjoyed and appreciated by the public. The last two years of the pandemic have been challenging, but already there are signs we will emerge out of it soon. Middleton Place has shown it has the resilience to overcome any hurdle; and I am sure, with the great team currently at its helm, the national landmark will bounce back stronger than ever.

Creating a legacy, fighting for something bigger than ourselves, and persevering against the odds are the themes I find most inspiring in this book. There are many more the reader can draw from that can bring us together. *American Landmark* is a fitting tribute to what Charles, his family and the Middleton Place Foundation have achieved. I look forward to bearing witness to the next part of their journey.

Nicholas Ashley-Cooper
12th Earl of Shaftesbury
St. Giles House
Dorset, U.K.

PREFACE

About 30 years ago, I first met Charles Duell when I was a College of Charleston undergraduate working part-time at the Edmondston-Alston House. He was close to my age now (early 50s) and living on the third floor of the museum house. Friends constantly came and went, and Charles traveled often, making a point to stay with acquaintances because he truly enjoyed people and worked hard to maintain relationships. Many times when I arrived in the morning to open the house for the day's visitors, Charles would be returning from a run on the Battery or from windsurfing in Charleston Harbor. He always gave me a kind greeting and took time to ask about my history studies. Athletic and driven, endowed with impeccable manners, and surrounded by friends — these were my early observations of Charles. I had no idea of the life he had led, the accomplishments he had already achieved, or what a profound impact he would have on my life and career.

Later I would learn about his work in preserving and developing Middleton Place as a nationally important historic site, and his leadership role in historic preservation, both in the United States and here in Charleston. As I became more involved with the Middleton Place Foundation, Charles began teaching me, by example, many valuable lessons. Perhaps the most important is the value of stewardship.

Stewardship for most people involves family keepsakes, photo albums or perhaps a beloved car. For Charles, it meant preserving a nearly 7,000-acre-large historical resource that connects to the very fabric of our nation's history. A formidable idea, to say the least, especially considering he had very little money to fund his ambitious plans. But he had an extra helping of steadfast resolve and a penchant for taking risks; sometimes even putting the success and sustainability of Middleton Place over himself and others close to him. He deeply believed and often told me that Middleton Place must survive because it is, at its essence, a microcosm of American history.

In 1998, a job opening allowed me to come out to Middleton Place. I soon began to test Charles' "microcosm" theory with my colleague Barbara Doyle, research historian and genealogist for the Middleton Place Foundation. The foundation has always had an educational mission and a focus on historical research and documentation. Early on, when resources were scarce, Charles placed a high premium on research. He continually encouraged Barbara and me to pursue new discoveries and share them through sound writing and programs.

With so many fascinating Middletons — dating from Elizabethan England and Barbados, to the American Civil War and into the 20th and 21st centuries — it's hard to describe the historical journey I've had; except to say that "the world is my oyster," and to thank Charles for the opportunity of a lifetime. Convinced that Middleton Place is indeed a microcosm of American history, I became a disciple of *Middletonia* (i.e. all things Middleton) and am still working on a PhD, of sorts, in the subject.

Through the years, the research has ranged from the history of camellias to documenting livestock breeds to identifying what the Middletons were reading. Over time, more and more funding was invested in learning about the enslaved people that built and sustained Middleton Place. Supported and encouraged by Charles, the effort gained momentum and resulted in new programs and publications, a PBS documentary, and ultimately joint family reunions of African and European descendants of Middleton Place. The work continues to be transformative for all involved and proves that the impact of history, when it is shared and inclusive, is amplified by the positive good it can achieve.

Charles may not have fully understood how Middleton Place would be relevant in our nation today when his stewardship journey began five decades ago, but he was correctly convinced of its vital importance. Teaching our shared history from inclusive perspectives — where everyone can see and appreciate the trials, contributions and humanity of those that came before us — is a core value of the Middleton Place Foundation. We believe this will result in necessary change and a better future. It is a worthy mission to build upon.

Charles always says "It's been a series of miracles" that has allowed Middleton Place to survive through the colonial era, the Civil War, hurricanes, a major earthquake, economic depressions and unprecedented development.

Of course, he's right. But it was his foresight and fortitude that made Middleton Place a National Historic Landmark and the force for education and positive change that it is today. Many people, Black and White, have had a hand in creating and sustaining Middleton Place; but Charles is the miracle that set it on its current path of excellence and sustainability.

A few years ago, in order to honor Charles — who stepped down after his 80th birthday to assume the new title of Founder and President Emeritus — the Charles Duell Legacy Fund was created. The fund upholds the pillars of preservation, education and sustainability for the Middleton Place Foundation. More than one million dollars has been raised so far. One important donor, Stephen Snyder, a lifelong friend of Charles from Andover and Yale, requested that his contribution be used specifically to record this story. Without Stephen's foresight and generosity, this book would not have been possible.

Charles has continued to teach me and others over his long career in historic preservation. A particularly important lesson, which goes hand-in-hand with stewardship, is knowing that when you devote your energy to a cause, it gives meaning and value to your life. After three decades, I continue to be inspired by my work at Middleton Place and am thankful every day to walk with my colleagues on this hallowed ground where history took place. Even as a young man, Charles saw the meaning and value in connecting to our shared past. For that we should all be grateful.

M. Tracey Todd
President and CEO
Middleton Place Foundation
Charleston, S.C.

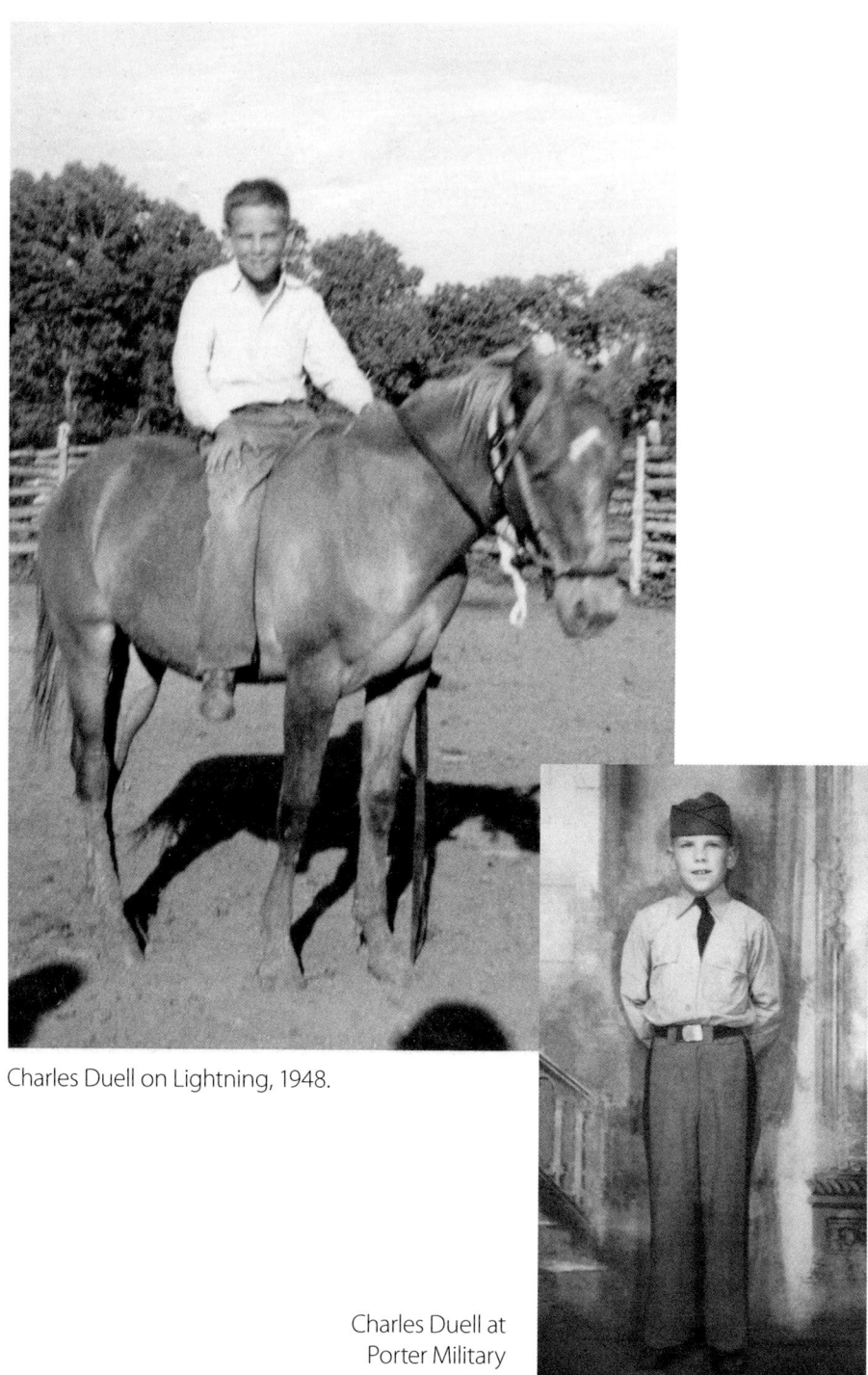

Charles Duell on Lightning, 1948.

Charles Duell at Porter Military Academy, 1947.

Prologue

COLORADO

At the age of 10, Charles Halliwell Pringle Duell was kicked out of Porter Military Academy. Demerits were handed out freely in those days and Charles received more than he could work off. His parents had divorced in New York City a few years earlier, and Charles had moved with his mother to her hometown of Charleston, South Carolina.

When the school suggested he not return, Charles was sent to stay with his paternal grandmother at her Hudson River estate called Ardenwold. From there he was supposed to spend the summer at Great Oaks Camp in Maine, while the family figured out what to do.

By coincidence, Charles' uncles Holland "Holly" Duell and Halliwell "Wally" Duell visited Ardenwold as the boy was packing for camp. They suggested Charles return with them to Colorado and spend the summer on Holland's ranch near the foot of Greenhorn Mountain. Charles' grandmother was all for it, but he was not so sure. Charles was afraid of horses. "In Central Park, I had seen horses running around and looking pretty big and fierce," he remembers. "Ever the negotiator, I struck a deal with my uncles: I would come to Colorado if I didn't have to ride a horse. They said 'OK.' "[1]

It was 1948 and Charles flew to Crow Ranch in a single-engine Beechcraft Bonanza piloted by his uncles. "We had a friend and a cousin on board with us and I'll never forget hearing the air traffic controller at Teterboro Airport in New Jersey calling on the radio, instructing us to come back because we had one too many passengers. My uncles pretended not to hear and kept flying west into the clouds. It was thrilling."

Crow Ranch provided the boy with 8,000 acres of wilderness and an instant, close-knit family. Holland Duell and his wife, Dorothy, had four children with whom Charles fit right in. However, one thing still separated him from his cousins. "They would go out riding every morning, checking on calves and fencing, and other things you do on a ranch," recalls Charles. "Then they'd come back for lunch at the big table, full of energy and enthusiasm and stories about what they had encountered. I would listen to them and then they would get up and go back out; and I would return to reading my book. I couldn't stand it." [2]

"We all have problems. We are hit with them constantly," Charles reflects. "From an early age, I found it good for the heart and mind to embrace one's problems, instead of shying away from them." After a few days, Charles asked his uncle for a horse and riding lessons. Holland was ready. In the orchard where the cousins met each morning to saddle up, Uncle Holly brought out a fat pony named Blackie. Blackie immediately carried the boy under a low tree limb and trotted off, leaving Charles holding on to the branch for dear life. [3]

Soon Charles was riding horseback daily with the others. He accompanied them on a 4-H Club trip to northern New Mexico and joined the youth organization. He also became a Boy Scout and earned the nickname of "Windy," on account of his tall tales. "By the end of the summer, I thought I was the greatest young cowboy that the state of Colorado had ever confronted." [4]

That first summer turned into a year, which turned into three.

As his immediate family broke up back East, Charles found comfort and support with his western relatives — especially his uncle, Holland Duell. So Charles persuaded his parents in New York and Charleston to let him stay and attend Colorado public schools for fifth, sixth and seventh grades (1948-1951). He earned mostly A's and made the basketball team. During his second summer, Holland gave him a Hereford bull calf to raise and a quarter horse colt to train. "I worked with the colt, whose name was Lightning, every day — riding her and brushing her until there was not a speck of dust on her coat. Uncle Holly helped me enter the colt in the 4-H county fair in Pueblo. I didn't win any prizes, but I was gaining something far more valuable: confidence in myself." [5]

The bull calf also thrived. Charles traveled with his uncle and cousins to the Colorado State Fair and entered it in the "fat beef" and "breeding" competitions. The calf was awarded "Grand Champion" and the proud boy with his charge were pictured together in *The Pueblo Chieftain*. Charles was identified in the newspaper caption as Windy Duell. In addition to his temporary name change, Charles had traded his Manhattan trappings for a cowboy hat and rope.

Years later, after Charles completed high school and college and began a career in banking, his uncle lost Crow Ranch. A California developer persuaded Holland Duell to deed the property to him in return for stock in a proposed golf course development and an interest in the company. The development was to be called Colorado City, a revival of the name of the territory's first capital, and championed by local officials as a utopian community where ordinary citizens could enjoy amenities and open spaces typically available to the well-to-do. Colorado City was supposed to offer an innovative civic design and access to a spectacular conserved landscape. [6]

Crow Ranch had been part of a gigantic, century-old land grant from Mexico given in 1844 to French nobleman Ceran St. Vrain, his business partner Cornelio Vigil, and to a member of the Bent clan, one of Colorado's first families. The Duells purchased a portion of the land grant in 1947 prior to Charles' arrival. Before long, shares in the development, once worth $150 each, sank to $3. "The development failed to perform and the whole thing went bust," Charles recalls. "Ever since, I've had an aversion to debt and an appreciation for financial solvency." [7]

In the years to come, land grants and first families, plucky westerners and fine horses, historic properties and cultural archetypes wove an indelible thread through the fabric of Charles' life and work. Crow Ranch's transformational power and its denouement left a lasting impression on the young man.

Crew of the *Obsession*: (l-r) Stuart Walker, deRosset Myers, Douglas Plate, William "Bo" Morrison, Charles Duell, Marion Reid (not pictured: Addison Ingle).

Charles Duell (at left) touring Europe with friends.

Charles Duell (foreground, no. 75) windsurfing in Charleston Harbor.

One

BETWEEN TWO WORLDS

"There is a period near the beginning of every man's life when he has little to cling to except his unmanageable dream, little to support him except good health, and nowhere to go but all over the place" – E.B. White

Hanging in Charles Duell's office at Middleton Place — 15 miles northwest of Charleston, South Carolina — is a portrait of a horse named "Pumpernickel," his favorite mount when he served as Master of Fox Hounds for the Middleton Place hunt in the 1970s, 80s and 90s. By then he had given up his western saddle for a more sporting English one. Charles had come a long way since being afraid of horses as a little boy.

In fact, the equestrian realm was in Charles' DNA all along, as an old photograph attests: his paternal grandfather is shown in full hunt attire and top hat, chasing a fox in Europe. Another painting behind Charles' desk depicts a sleek Herreshoff yacht named "Rowdy" — the New York 40 sailboat owned and captained by grandfather Holland that won more silver than could fill a trophy cabinet. The New York 40 was a premiere class of racing boat popular among wealthy yacht owners on Long Island Sound. When Charles returned to Charleston, he continued the Duell sailing tradition, first as a crew member on a Morgan 41 named "Obsession" — the first South Carolina boat to compete in the Newport-to-Bermuda race — and later as a competitive windsurfer.

While grandfather Holland pursued rarified pastimes, he was also a patriotic, hardworking man. As a colonel in the 306th Field Artillery, he fought in France during World World I, earning both a Distinguished Service Cross and a Silver Star for "gallantry in action." He later was a successful attorney and politician. Charles' aunt Harriet Duell Pierson describes her father:

"It was as if the very genetic coding of Father's family had predisposed

Rowdy, the New York 40 racing yacht owned by Charles Duell's grandfather Holland Sackett Duell.

Holland Sackett Duell.

him to the practice of law and politics. So from a very early age, he knew that after graduating from Yale, he would attend law school and become a lawyer." Specifically, he would practice patent law, of which his own father, Charles Holland Duell, was the foremost authority — having literally written the book on the subject in 1908, and served as head of the U.S. Patent Office from 1898 to 1901. [1]

Holland Duell went on to reconstitute his father's law firm as Duell, Warfield and Duell, and continued its dominance in the field of patent law. Holland twice won election to the New York State Assembly representing Westchester County and championed parklands, truth in journalism, and automobile safety. In addition, Harriet Pierson explains, "his legal representation of various companies gave him the opportunity to be on their boards of directors and acquire stock in those companies . . ." [2]

Charles' grandfather enjoyed the fruits of his labor, as well as those of his wife's family fortune. Grandmother Mable Halliwell Duell was born in 1882 in St. Louis, where her father, C. Eliezer Halliwell, was part owner of Liggett and Myers Tobacco Company. At the same time, James Buchanan Duke had founded American Tobacco and was buying up other tobacco companies around the country. When Duke acquired Liggett and Myers, he made Halliwell a vice president of American Tobacco, prompting Halliwell to move his family to New York where his daughter would eventually meet Holland Duell. On September 29, 1904, Mable and Holland were married. ³

Charles Duell's maternal grandfather, Pringle Smith, with Charles' mother, Josephine.

That same year, Holland's father was appointed an appeals court judge by President Theodore Roosevelt. Seven years later and some 700 miles south, Henry Augustus Middleton (H.A.M.) Smith of Charleston — Charles' maternal great-grandfather — was also appointed to a federal judgeship by Roosevelt's successor, William Howard Taft. Like Judge Duell, Judge Smith was a prominent member of his community. A Greek and Biblical scholar, he was known to be a compassionate arbiter of the law.

 H.A.M. Smith remains a hero to Charles: "He was a true 19th century character, a landowner and historian, and a distinguished federal judge and man of vision." Thus two of Charles' great-grandfathers, on opposite sides of the family at opposite ends of the Eastern Seaboard, were appointed federal judges in the early 1900s. ⁴

But stark differences persist between the two branches of the family. With one foot in the South and one in the North, Charles descends from Confederates and Federals alike, a not so rare reality for many Americans. His genealogical tree includes staunch abolitionists and stalwart defenders of slavery. While his New York clan amassed substantial wealth after the Civil

Josephine Smith Duell. Charles Halliwell Duell.

War — enjoying a privileged world of governesses, chauffeurs and yachts — his South Carolina family became land rich and cash poor, a common trajectory among southern planters. As Yale classmate and friend Chris Seger observes, "Charles belonged to two different worlds, and he had the uncanny ability to travel effortlessly between them." [5]

• • •

Charles' father, C. ("Charlie") Halliwell Duell, followed previous generations of Duell men to Yale and became manager of the Yale Glee Club. It was on a concert tour to Charleston when Charlie met Josephine Scott Smith and fell in love. They were married in 1933 when she was 19. The headline in *The New York Times* read, "Josephine Smith Becomes a Bride — Charleston Girl is Married to Charles Halliwell Duell of New York." Among the groomsmen were poet Ogden Nash and philanthropist Charles Woodward. A Philadelphian, Woodward was smitten by bridesmaid Betty Gadsden of

Charleston. They later wed and began buying property in Charleston, becoming a leading force for historic preservation in the city. [6]

Several years after his marriage to Josephine, Charlie Duell co-founded Duell, Sloan and Pearce Publishing Company in New York, with partners Samuel Sloan and Charles Pearce. Sloan and Pearce had worked for Harcourt Brace, while Duell began his career at Doubleday, later becoming a vice president at William Morrow and Company. Headquartered on Madison Avenue, the new firm published such luminaries as Archibald MacLeish, William Mansfield, Wallace Stegner, e.e. cummings and Benjamin Spock. Dr. Spock served as the Duells' pediatrician when they lived on New York's Upper East Side.

"I grew up in a progressive, creative, book-publishing family in New York that entertained the Frank Lloyd Wrights, the John O'Haras, the Erskine Caldwells and the Alexander Calders of the world," explains Charles, "people who were on the literary, artistic and intellectual cutting edge. And while I had the benefits of a good education, I was something of a Little Lord Fauntleroy — paraded into the living room in my schoolboy grey flannel shorts, jacket and cap; trained to say: 'How do you do? So nice to see you!'

"As soon as I had given the guest a firm handshake and looked him or her in the eye, I would excuse myself because I was bored and because as a child I was really not welcome in that heavy cocktail drinking, smoking, intellectual environment of New York. I grew up to be a fairly glib arguer, and was limited beyond my realization by the asphalt jungle of the big city — a lack of communion with nature in a total urban environment." [7]

In quick succession, Josephine gave birth to two daughters, Anne and Scottie, followed by the birth of Charles in 1938.

Josephine and Charlie Duell divorced in 1943 and a few years later, son Charles and his sisters moved to Charleston with their mother. In 1950, their father and his second wife bought a 22-room mansion in Greenwich, Connecticut, where Charles — having returned from Colorado — completed eighth grade before matriculating to boarding school.

No matter where they were home based, Charles and his sisters would spend holidays and part of every spring and summer in South Carolina with their grandparents Heningham ("Ha Ha") and J.J. Pringle Smith ("Gramps") — traveling south by train and later aboard an Eastern Airline DC-3. Heningham's nickname derived from little Anne's boisterous laughter whenever

(l-r) Anne, Charles and Scottie Duell at Middleton Place.

Anne and Charles Duell picnicking.

her grandmother bounced her on her knee. [8]

"When one arrived in Charleston one was immediately aware of different smells and a different atmosphere; the pluff mud was predominant," recalls Charles. "I can remember how different Charleston looked back then . . . It was pretty shabby. I also remember being impressed by all the electric wires overhead. As you looked down Tradd Street it was like a spider web in the sky. Of course, today those wires are all underground and things are spiffed up . . . [It was] such a contrast from urban New York . . . almost a country village environment that you felt in Charleston." [9]

The family migrated between the Smiths' antebellum house on Charleston Harbor and their plantation along the Ashley River. "I was baptized at St. Philip's Church in downtown Charleston where my parents had been married," Charles relates. "My mother and grandparents were determined that we grow up knowing our family and our history. Gramps and Ha Ha were very much in residence at both the Edmondston-Alston House [21 East Battery] and Middleton Place [west of the Ashley River]. We were land poor,

The Edmondston-Alston house around the time of Charles Duell's birth in 1938.

and still are. Most of our wealth was, and is, in the land." [10]

The merger of Middleton Place and the Edmondston-Alston House under one clan had been consummated by the 1849 marriage of Williams Middleton to Susan Pringle Smith. Susan's ancestor Bishop Robert Smith had arrived in Charleston in 1757 from Norfolk, England. He became a plantation owner and the first American Episcopal bishop of the Diocese of South Carolina. Bishop Smith was also the first president of the College of Charleston, the establishment of which he helped finance. He contributed materials, tools and labor — including capitalizing on the skill of his enslaved workers — to repurpose abandoned military barracks on the Charleston peninsula for the new college. The bishop's children and descendants married into the Middleton and Alston families. Through these intermarriages, the Smith family came to own both Middleton Place and the Edmondston-Alston House. [11]

"During the 1940s and at the end of World War II, one would come

Charles Duell with his mother and grandparents in the Middleton Place garden.

down not for a long weekend (the way you do now), but for several weeks at a time," states Charles, "especially over Christmas and during the spring and summer. My grandparents lived in the surviving south flanker at Middleton Place, which of course didn't have air conditioning. The Middleton Place restaurant was a guest house and we often stayed there . . . it had a screened porch adjacent to the main room, and sofas on either side of the fireplace. Upstairs were the bedrooms." [12]

"When I was a young boy, the plantation gardens were not open to the public year-round, so we often had the run of the place. My grandfather was growing and bailing hay — a stationery bailer sat in the middle of the hayfield where the equestrian center is today — and raising dairy cows and pigs, plus the corn to feed them. He taught me to open and close the heavy iron latch on the entrance gate, a skill which I mastered as a child and took great pride in. During the summers, Gramps and Ha Ha would move into town and take up residence at 21 East Battery. The first-floor piazza on the south side of the house became our living room." 13

When Charles' mother brought her children to Charleston to live with her in the winter of 1947-1948, they resided at 21 East Battery while her parents, Heningham and Pringle, stayed at Middleton Place. The children were enrolled in local schools and spent the weekends with their grandparents in the country. "To us, it was an exotic place," Charles reflects, "and I never, as a child or a teenager, envisioned myself being involved with it because I knew, and it was always made clear, that the land — although thousands of acres — was not worth very much. Yet, the estate taxes could have been crippling." 14

"The thing I remember most," continues Charles, "and that I think had a strong influence on my life,

Mary Sheppard with Charles Duell's sisters, Anne and Scottie, at Middleton Place.

even subconsciously, was the time I spent with my grandmother. She was the driving force behind the restoration of the gardens, and I mean personally. Every time she went out into the gardens, she would carry a pair of clippers with her, pruning camellias and azaleas as we walked the paths . . . There is no question that my grandmother's passion for the restoration of the gardens at Middleton Place [made] a tremendous impression on me."

Charles also admired and adored Josephine: "Mother was beautiful and highly intelligent. She was so positive with me and always sent me letters and books when we were apart. She and I both loved reading. I remember the silver letter opener on her desk that she had won for the writing prize at St. Timothy's School. Somehow I still have it. I'm sure it was her early influence that inspired me to major in English in college." 15

Charles' father was also passionate about books. After graduating from

Yale, he studied English literature at Cambridge. Charlie Duell was a well-read, highly cultured man whose publishing persona was later played by actor Steve Martin in the 2000 film "Joe Gould's Secret," based on the Greenwich Village literary scene of the 1940s. Through his publishing house, his Yale classmates and alumni network, and his numerous affiliations with New York's creative community — including the Century Association — Charlie Duell entertained and associated with some of the great minds of the first half of the 20th century. These connections opened countless doors for his son. [16]

• • •

In the fall of 1952, Charles arrived at Phillips Academy in Andover, Massachusetts. He studied Latin, literature and math, attended concerts and plays, joined the soccer team and served as business manager for the school newspaper, *The Phillipian*. He can still recite (in Latin) Livy 22.49, "Romans at Cannae," the account of Hannibal outmaneuvering the Romans. Andover was a welcome challenge for Charles. He graduated in the top 25 percent of his class, gaining him entry into the Ivy League and instilling a lifelong passion for the liberal arts. He also made important friendships. [17]

"There were 220 boys in our freshman class at Andover," remembers longtime friend Steve Snyder, "and Charles and I were part of the mix. I was a striver out of public schools on Long Island and Charles was a stylish guy from Greenwich. But he had spent those years in Colorado and seemed to be searching for something more in life. We became close right away and remained so through Andover and Yale." [18]

During the summer of 1954 — between Charles' sophomore and junior years of high school — his mother entered Walter Reed Hospital in Washington, D.C. with cancer of the larynx. She had been a heavy smoker. Charles was spending the summer vacation on his uncle's ranch in Colorado and flew to Washington to visit her in the hospital. She died that August. Her second husband — Charles' stepfather — was a navy admiral and thought it impractical to fly the teenager back East again for his mother's funeral. Sixteen-year-old Charles was devastated, and to this day chokes up over her memory. [19]

By the time Charles arrived at Yale in 1956, he had been buffeted by difficult family circumstances: his parents' early divorce, the institutional-

Class of 1960, Jonathan Edwards College, Yale University: Charles Duell (front row, fourth from left), Steve Easter (second row, third from right), Chris Seger (front row, third from right) and Steve Snyder (third row, second from left).

ization of his mentally disabled sister Scottie, and the death of his mother. Nevertheless, Charles was on familiar territory — Yale was a Duell family tradition and the freshman class that year included 54 graduates of Andover.

Chris Seger was another Yale freshman who became a lifelong friend. "Our class had some interesting and exceptional men," says Seger, "such as Bart Giamatti, who became the youngest president in Yale's history 18 years later; Les Aspin, congressman and later Secretary of Defense; William Bush, youngest brother of President George H.W. Bush; diplomat John Negroponte; and Jack Heinz, who came from great wealth to become a U.S. senator from Pennsylvania."

As a public high school graduate from Tulsa, Oklahoma, Seger was a curiosity to his Yale classmates, "many of whom had never been west of the Hudson River," he jokes, "though they might have spent summers in France." As luck would have it, Chris was assigned to a room in McClellan Hall (on Yale's Old Campus), near Charles' and Steve Snyder's room. "I didn't have any pretenses, being from Oklahoma; and Charles had spent time in Colorado and developed a healthy skepticism of the East Coast, so we hit it off immediately."

Steve and Chris visited Charles and his grandparents numerous times in Charleston. They both remember having dinners in the Middleton Place dining room and on the piazza of 21 East Battery, the meals accompanied by mountains of white rice. "J.J. Pringle Smith was a charming southerner and great storyteller, sprinkling his tales with Gullah phrases," recounts Chris. "Once when I commented on a rather flimsy soup spoon I was given to use at dinner, Mr. Smith declared: 'You are referring to original Middleton Place flat silver, buried during the Civil War!' " [20]

"Middleton was in pretty bad shape," Steve recalls, "and after Charles' grandmother died, his grandfather lived on the third floor of 21 East Battery, while the furniture in the drawing room and dining room below stayed shrouded in white muslin." Both friends talk of all they learned from Charles and his grandfather about the Lowcountry and the South.

Chris elaborates: "At a relatively young age, Charles was incredibly interested and knowledgeable about history, and specifically the history of the Edmondston-Alston House, Middleton Place and his family's genealogy."

"Charles and I both studied English at Yale," continues Chris, "and while neither of us was a top student, Yale ignited a serious desire to read books; and the course work required one to question what one was reading, and then demanded that one be able to write clearly on the subject . . . Charles was inclined toward a deeper exploration and understanding of the world and became very well educated and articulate. He prided himself on intellectual achievement and authenticity. These became driving forces in his life." [21]

• • •

Another driving force in Charles' life, and embedded in his DNA, was a yearning for international travel and service. While Chris and Steve joined the navy after graduating from Yale in 1960, Charles aspired to the foreign service. The first time he took the exam he scored a 68 — a failing grade. Surprised and disappointed, Charles was determined to expand his knowledge of the world and redeem himself. So, he bought an "open ticket" on Pan Am Airways for $1,400. As long as he continued heading west, he was good to go for a year — a modern grand tour in the tradition of his 18th and 19th century Middleton forebears, but in the opposite direction.

"Everything that I learned in school and college was based on Greco-Roman and European precedents," says Charles. "In my circle, it was almost as if the Middle East and Far East did not exist. As a result, I was motivated to visit and learn more about parts of the world unfamiliar to me." His first stop was San Francisco, where he spent the summer after graduation studying Japanese before landing a three-month scholarship from Fuji Juko— manufacturer of a popular Japanese motorcycle. ²²

The Rockefeller Foundation's International House of Japan in Tokyo became Charles' home base while he traveled across the island country — from Tokyo to Nagasaki and back — on a Fuji Rabbito Superflow. Characteristically, Charles found himself bridging two worlds,

Charles Duell riding a "saddle bull" in rural Japan on his travels after college.

this time in post-World War II Asia — embracing the Rockefellers' vision of rebuilding cultural and economic ties between the United States and Japan, while astride a machine built by the company that provided Japanese war planes against the United States.

"I had known nothing about the Far East," Charles admits, "and I fell in love with the orderly, structured, minimalist way of Japanese life, as well as their architecture. I also spent time in Hiroshima, which was a powerful experience. This may sound naïve today, but I was sincerely devoted to world peace and diplomacy, versus war. Traveling alone, I made myself available to people. I was able to talk to persons of all persuasions and backgrounds. At the end of my trip, I submitted a report on my experiences as a requirement of the scholarship." ²³

From Tokyo, Charles flew to the Philippines, then Hong Kong and on to

Thailand. In Bangkok (through family connections) he met Jim Thompson — the American who helped revitalize Thailand's silk industry and later mysteriously disappeared — as well as Mary Lord, U.S. representative to the United Nations Commission on Human Rights. In Vietnam, he stayed with U.S. Ambassador Elbridge Dubrow. After traveling by train from Thailand to Cambodia, Charles rode a bicycle from Phnom Penh to Siem Reap to see the great temples of Angkor. He spent most nights in youth hostels and small inns, as well as with friends of his family who were either in the diplomatic corps, international business or academia.

From Southeast Asia, he continued west through Malaysia and Indonesia, visiting the World Heritage Site of Borobudur in Central Java. Upon arriving in India, Charles stayed put for a few months, sharing an apartment with the nephew of Indonesian President Sukarno, whom he had met earlier in the Cairo airport. Charles studied economics and history at the University of Delhi and crisscrossed India by train, sleeping on luggage racks, reading Nehru and swimming in the Ganges. After a trip north to Nepal to trek in the shadow of Mount Everest, Charles contracted a serious case of amoebic dysentery that landed him in a hospital back in Delhi.

Once recovered, he headed northwest into Pakistan, where he stayed with Ethel-Jane and Fred Bunting in Karachi at the mouth of the Indus River. Charles was en route to Chandigarh, the new capital of the northern Indian states of Punjab and Haryana, designed by Le Corbusier. Ethel-Jane, an anthropologist, and Fred, a director of U.S. Aid for International Development, would eventually settle in Charleston.

"Oftentimes, I was able to meet and stay with scholars and dignitaries," Charles relates, "largely due to my father's best friend and college roommate, John H.G. Pierson, who later married my aunt Harriet Duell." Pierson was an economist who helped author the U.S. Employment Act of 1946 and later worked for the United Nations in New York and Asia. He wrote books and essays about his two favorite topics: employment and Eastern mysticism. His brother, George, was chairman of the history department at Yale — a noted authority on Alexis de Tocqueville and promoter of the study of Chinese and Japanese history.

By the time Charles got to Paris in the summer of 1961, he had one month left before his Pan Am plane ticket expired. He spent the next few weeks driving a Volkswagen Beetle (the German "people's car") across Eastern

Europe with Yale classmate Steve Easter. They concluded their journey at the home of Charles' godfather, British historian Sir John Wheeler-Bennett. Wheeler-Bennett lived at Garsington Manor near Oxford, England and was the official biographer of King George VI. His American publisher was Duell, Sloan and Pearce. [24]

Traveling the world had exposed Charles to a fascinating and inspiring realm of people, places and professions. Now it was time to further his study of economics and history. But first, he needed to improve his French. Mastery of a foreign language could earn him five extra points on the Foreign Service exam. He was preparing for a second try.

• • •

That fall, Charles went home to New York and then returned to Paris to enroll in a French immersion program at the Alliance Francaise. Not only did he intend to raise his score on the Foreign Service exam, he also hoped to boost his chances for admission into the Paris Institute of Political Studies, known as "Sciences Po." Headquartered near Boulevard Saint-Germain on the Left Bank, Sciences Po was, and still is, one of the top schools for politics and international relations. It boasts many world leaders among its graduates, including former French President Valery Giscard d'Estaing — who joined Charles many years later for lunch at 21 East Battery, followed by a tour of Middleton Place.

Charles was accepted to Sciences Po in the fall of 1961 and landed lodging in the Le Corbusier building at the Cite Internationale Universitaire de Paris. Described by its architect as *une machine-à-habiter* ("a machine for living") and the first modern building to be built on campus, the dormitory had been sponsored in the 1930s by the Fondation Suisse. The project enabled Le Corbusier — one of the pioneers of modern architecture — to implement his theories of economy and functionality with innovative use of reinforced concrete, cantilevered construction and horizontal windows. Later designated a French historical monument, Le Corbusier's masterpiece deepened Charles' understanding and appreciation for modernist design.

The experience also introduced him to Xuan-Chi Diep, who, like Charles, had a studio apartment at the Fondation Suisse and was a student at Sciences Po. Born into an aristocratic Vietnamese family, Chi was sent to Paris at age

(l-r) Chi Diep, Charles Duell and Peter Manigault riding with the Middleton Place Hounds.

14 to be educated, and never returned to Vietnam. Chi and Charles became lifelong friends, with Chi eventually retiring to South Carolina after a career with the Federal Reserve in Minneapolis-Saint Paul. [25]

While at Sciences Po, Charles met his first wife and future mother of his four children — Carol Wood. Born and raised in Big Horn, Wyoming, Carol was a graduate of Colorado College and an accomplished equestrian. In 1957 her father died, and her mother subsequently married French banker and Ecole Normale de Musique director Rémi Boissonnas. As a result, the family divided their time between Paris and Wyoming. Carol's mother, June Boissonnas, had not only roomed with Charles' aunt at Vassar, she had also been married to his aunt's first husband, Robert Wood. While Carol was not a blood relative of Charles, her father was Charles' uncle and her two half-brothers were his first cousins. Charles' aunt had written to June to inform her that her nephew was studying in Paris and might appreciate an invitation to meet them.

The Boissonnas, who owned an elegant apartment in Paris, invited Charles over. Charles recounts their meeting: "When I first came to France, I eschewed relationships with Americans because I wanted to have a pure French experience. I eased up on that later when I became comfortable in the French language and accepted an invitation to come to a musical event that a friend of the family was having . . . I had heard about Carol, but we had never met. We hit it off immediately and ended up becoming engaged."

In the spring of 1963, Charles passed the Foreign Service exam (thanks to those five extra points). That August, he and Carol were married. "We were well suited," comments Charles, "and because of the marriage situation [between her mother and my uncle], everybody knew everybody. It was one of those weddings where there was not [this separation of] the bride's side of the family and the groom's side. They were all the same people and they all knew each other." [26]

The couple first settled in Washington, D.C., where Charles mulled job offers from the U.S. Department of Agriculture and the Export-Import Bank. He was also courted by New York banks, including Chase Manhattan and Bankers Trust. Ultimately, he joined Morgan Guaranty Trust, first on the French West Africa desk in its international banking division and later in their corporate research department. Charles worked on a computer "the size of a small bedroom," using one of the earliest versions of the computer language known as Fortran. He and Carol rented an apartment on West Ninth Street in Greenwich Village. [27]

A career in finance suited Charles on many levels. New York was his home turf and a place of possibility and potential. "Wall Street loomed for me as kind of a monolithic power structure that I had not been able to understand [when I was] growing up," comments Charles. "I knew there was a lot of economic strength there and maybe it was something that I should get involved with and try to understand." [28]

. . .

A few years later, however, Charles was called back to Charleston to help his grandfather J.J. Pringle Smith, who was in trouble with the Internal Revenue Service. "Having studied economics and become conversant with financial instruments and the tax structure, I had assumed that Middleton Place and its associated lands would eventually have to be sold to pay estate taxes; that there would be nothing left," Charles recalls. [29]

"I knew that my grandparents had very little money because they often talked freely about it. It was also evident that my grandparents in the North were much better off than my grandparents in the South, in terms of their ability to spend and purchase things," elaborates Charles. "My southern grandmother would explain how they really didn't, as she put it, 'have two nickels to rub together' in order to buy chintz to cover the upholstery and such. They just had to make do with what furniture they had, instead of sprucing it up as would have been done in New York. I was well aware of their financial limitations. [30]

"When I came down to help my grandfather Pringle Smith in 1965, my mother had been gone for more than a decade [Josephine Smith Duell died in 1954 at the age of 40] and my grandmother [Heningham] had died in 1957. Gramps was living alone on the top floor of 21 East Battery and managing neither his properties nor his employees very well.

"He had gone through a terrible situation with the Internal Revenue Service because he did not believe in withholding taxes from his workers. He reasoned that if the U.S. government had an issue with some of them, they should settle it directly.

"It was an almost feudal, paternalistic way of life. His employees were paid very little, perhaps a few dollars a day, and they were always paid in cash. At the end of the week on Saturday morning, [my grandfather] would be in his office [at Middleton Place] in what is now called the Cypress Room at the restaurant . . . he'd go in and open the safe and sit behind a desk. His employees would line up outside and file in one by one. He'd say, 'Walter, what have you done this week? Well, I guess you're gonna get paid,' kind of joking with them.

"He would have the payroll all made out and count out what they had earned in one-dollar bills. It was quite an archaic system and a fascinating

Judge Henry Augustus Middleton Smith (1853-1924).

socio-economic vignette to experience as I did as a child. This went on for many years and my grandfather continued to not withhold any taxes until the IRS put a lien on his bank account, preventing him from taking out any money.

"So he was having this crisis and I came down [to Charleston] to help him resolve it. Working with his accountant and lawyer, we determined that my grandfather was paying his workers so little that they did not owe any withholding taxes. Nonetheless, he was responsible if the workers did owe something, which resulted in the lien on his bank account. Eventually he was cleared. But in the process of addressing this problem, I learned that my grandfather did not really own Middleton, [even though] he had always styled himself as the 'owner of Middleton Place.'

"What had happened was that [my grandfather] was left the property by his first cousin Elizabeth Middleton Heyward ('Lillie'), the daughter of Williams Middleton from whom she inherited Middleton Place after the Civil War . . . Lillie had no children of her own and when she died in 1915, she left Middleton and some 6,500 acres to her closest cousin, J.J. Pringle Smith. She determined that because Pringle Smith was triply descended from Henry Middleton through both his mother and his father, and because he was a lawyer and had an interest in agriculture, he should be the family member to receive it [and hold it together].

"The problem was that my grandfather, handicapped by polio as a youth, was neither a good businessman nor a farmer, and he did not know what to do with the property . . . In subsequent years, he dabbled in several business deals, none of which was successful. Finally he went to his father [my great-grandfather], Judge H.A.M. Smith, and asked him to bail him out. We know that Judge Smith had done this before, so when he agreed to bail Pringle out again, he required his son to give him the deed to Middleton as collateral. So [my great-grandfather] ended up taking possession of Middleton Place.

"What Judge Smith did is one of the miracles that saved Middleton Place . . . like his cousin Lillie, he was determined to keep [the plantation] intact and in family hands. So he left my grandfather a life tenancy in Middleton, to be passed on at his death to the next generation — what is tantamount today to a generation skipping trust. I [believe] at the time that my great-grandfather was focused on my mother because she was a favorite of his. [My mother] was very bright, first in her class at school, and I suspect the Judge regarded her as the Eliza Lucas Pinckney of the future [someone who could raise Middleton to new heights, as Eliza Pinckney had done for colonial South Carolina by developing indigo into a cash crop].

"Sadly, my mother predeceased both my grandparents, and then my grandmother died a few years later. So what I learned on this trip south in the mid-1960s was that my grandfather was only a life tenant [at Middleton Place]. This meant that at my grandfather's death, Middleton would be left to my generation . . . This [realization] dramatically changed my attitude about my possible future [in South Carolina]. I spent a lot of time agonizing about whether I should return North and work my way up the corporate ladder, either in New York or elsewhere; or whether I should take an interest in coming down here." [31]

•••

"I don't know what the determining factors were at the time," Charles relates, "but certainly one was that Carol and I wanted to have children. We felt that a rural, less intense urban setting would be more appropriate and healthier than New York. Plus I was working long hours, sometimes from early morning until late at night. So while my grandfather was still alive, we decided to move to South Carolina and start a family there . . . I came not as the heir apparent in any arrogant way, but humbly, behind the scenes. I took a job at South Carolina National Bank in the trust department and gained experience with estates and trusts. I also learned more about taxes, specifically inheritance taxes."

In 1969, Pringle Smith died. Charles and his eldest sister, Anne, sorted out the estate. Anne was a brilliant pediatric surgeon and decided at her grandfather's death to receive all stocks and securities, while Charles would receive the family properties, namely the Edmondston-Alston House (21 East Battery) and Middleton Place. Their sister, Scottie, lived in an institution and was provided for through a trust fund set up years earlier by the family.

Thus, at his grandfather's death in 1969, both Middleton Place and 21 East Battery were left to 31-year-old Charles Halliwell Pringle Duell — a 12th generation Middleton descendant — with any and all securities given to his sister Anne. There were no estate taxes to be paid, because with the life tenancy arrangement, all estate taxes were taken care of by their great-grandfather's executor in 1924. Having worked a few years on Wall Street, Charles made the decision to leave New York and pick up the gauntlet that had come his way in South Carolina. [32]

Inheriting two historic houses and 6,500 acres in the Carolina Lowcountry was no guarantee of financial security for the young banker and his growing family. But Judge H.A.M. Smith had given Charles a good head start.

Arthur and Mary Middleton with their firstborn son, Henry, in the London studio of painter Benjamin West.

Two

EMPIRE and REBELLION

Risk-taking is in the Middleton blood, whether by 20th and 21st century standards, or those of the 17th. So it was in the late 1600s, when Edward and Arthur Middleton — Charles Duell's seventh great-grandfather and eighth great uncle, respectively — departed England to seek their fortunes in the New World. The bachelor brothers were younger sons in an era of primogeniture. They left a propertied, established family and sailed across the Atlantic to the island of Barbados, 50 years after Captain John Powell claimed it for the English crown.

Barbados is the easternmost island in the West Indian archipelago, straddling the Caribbean and Atlantic some 200 miles north of Venezuela. Not much is known about the brothers' brief tenure there except that Edward was described as a "mariner" and Arthur as a "merchant" — ship owner, slave trader and purveyor of other valuable merchandise.[1]

The Middleton brothers arrived in Barbados during an economic boom. The demand for sugar and slaves — fields of sugarcane carpeted the island — exceeded supply, as did the demand for land. Ever entrepreneurial, Arthur persuaded a business partner to go in on a ketch. They used the two-masted sailboat to transport enslaved Africans from port to port, selling them at clandestine auctions and evading the Royal African Company's monopoly on the slave trade.

Their time in Barbados, though brief in duration, had a profound effect on the brothers. As historian G. Winston Lane explains, "They saw firsthand how small investments, if made early, could result in . . . unbelievable wealth." Moreover, they learned how the management of big estates could be organized for maximum efficiency, based in large part on the use of enslaved labor.

But the Barbadians were rapidly outgrowing their island. Within 25 years of settlement, the island was completely deforested and most of the land claimed by a small group of sugar magnates. Before long these planters were sending their second sons to Carolina. Since neither Edward nor Arthur

Sketch of Codrington College in Barbados, the site of a 17th-century sugar plantation owned by Edward and Arthur Middleton's sister, Hester Middleton Browning. The plantation's windmill and boiling houses are seen at right.

appears to have acquired any acreage, and with land prices skyrocketing, moving on made sense.

Arthur's departure ticket to Carolina confirms that he left Barbados in August of 1679 aboard a three-masted, ocean going cargo ship. The vessel was probably laden with sugar and molasses for the English market, in addition to a small complement of passengers to be dropped off in Carolina. A safe arrival was not guaranteed, as boats making the same journey often wrecked or were blown off course. [2]

By the time Arthur landed in Carolina — 10 years after the English colony was established — immigrants from Barbados constituted half the population of White settlers and half the population of enslaved Africans. Walter Edgar elaborates on the Barbados-Carolina connection in his book *South Carolina: A History:* "The Barbadians were seasoned by more than their exposure to and survival of diseases. Either from firsthand experience or from watching parents and relatives, they knew what was required to prosper in a colonial environment, be it political skill, economic opportunity, or plantation management.

"And they [White immigrants] brought with them the Barbadian cultural model . . . Because they constituted the majority of the white population for the first two decades of settlement, the Barbadians set their cultural stamp on the South Carolina society that would evolve during the colonial period . . . they were tough, experienced and driven; they did not care much about how they got what they wanted." [3]

18th century newspaper notice advertising the sale of a slave cargo by Thomas Middleton.

Edward Middleton arrived in Carolina ahead of Arthur, and obtained a land grant in 1678 of 1,780 acres on the headwaters of Yeamans Creek (later called Goose Creek) — a tributary of the Cooper River named for Barbadian Sir John Yeamans. The grant was given jointly to the brothers, listed as "gentlemen" on the deed. Edward later sold his share to Arthur, but Edward continued to receive other land grants. Within two years he had accumulated 4,130 acres, including the Goose Creek plantation he named The Oaks.

Land was the basis for participation in the colony's fledgling government. Under the existing head-right system, the brothers were able to obtain substantial acreage due to the number of enslaved Africans they brought to Carolina from Barbados, as well as those acquired after arriving in North America. For every bondsman imported and/or newly purchased, additional land would be awarded by the Lords Proprietors. Enslavement of Africans was a huge generator of colonial capital and wealth.

As the Middleton brothers accumulated more property, they quickly rose to leadership positions. Edward became an Assistant Justice and Arthur a member of the Grand Council. Their status as Carolina gentlemen was further cemented by the brothers' appointment as deputies to the Lords Proprietors. Eight noblemen made up the original proprietors. They had been rewarded for their loyalty to King Charles II with the charter to Carolina — the territory south of Virginia and north of Florida all the way to the Pacific Ocean. Some of them — including Sir John Colleton and Earl Anthony Ashley Cooper — owned plantations in Barbados. [4]

Historian Walter Edgar explains the rules governing this new landed aristocracy: "A person had to have a stake in Carolina in order to participate in the political process, and the size of an individual's landholdings determined the size of his stake in society. Those with the greatest interest were, of course, the proprietors. Those next in order would have been their deputies or friends . . . Each proprietor would have a voice in the governing of the colony. If he were to reside in Carolina, then he would participate directly; if not, then he would name a deputy to act in his stead . . . The proprietors and the members of the various courts would together form a Grand Council of fifty." [5]

The Carolina colony was also guided by the Fundamental Constitutions — drafted by Lord Proprietor Ashley Cooper and his personal secretary, John Locke — despite the fact that colonists refused to ever ratify it, including four subsequent revisions. Nevertheless, the Fundamental Constitutions became both a governmental framework and "a cleverly written document designed to attract settlers," asserts Edgar.

The document ensured broad religious tolerance to those settling in Carolina, far more than was extended during the colonial era in New England. Jews and Huguenots, persecuted throughout Europe in the 17th century, along with "Indians" and other "idolaters," were welcomed. In that respect, South Carolina had a kinship with the Enlightenment and with the ideals of the nation's founders.

But the Fundamental Constitutions was also a sales brochure, designed to attract a population that would provide the proprietors a handsome profit, under the assumption that tolerance would make the state attractive to the largest number of settlers possible. With financial gain squarely a priority, the document set the stage for the commercial exploitation of enslaved Africans — specifically granting freemen total "power and authority over [their] negro slaves."

Thus, the lucrative, slave-based plantation system of the Caribbean was duplicated in Carolina. But first, the colony was powered by an economy of extraction. Trade in deer skins, free ranging cattle and able-bodied Native Americans generated handsome profits. Timber was also a major commodity, since Europe had depleted most of its forests. Experimenting with a variety of cash crops, Carolinians eventually converted to an agricultural economy. Their governing rules would be neither pure Enlightenment nor pure feudalism. What evolved was a merger of modern civilized thought and ruthless competition, plagued from the start by contradiction and conflict. [6]

• • •

In 1685, the Middleton brothers died: Arthur at age 37 and Edward at 43, both a few years short of the average lifespan of a Carolina colonist. Only Edward and his wife, Sarah Fowell Middleton, left an heir to carry on the family line in America — four-year-old Arthur. Arthur eventually married Carolinian Sarah Amory, and like his father, won a seat on the Grand Council and an appointment as a proprietor's deputy, having inherited thousands of acres.

Arthur also traded in Indian slaves, and at one time served as Commissioner of Indian Affairs. The movement of settlers into Indian lands and the remunerative business of selling enslaved Native Americans — augmented by a built-in incentive to incite warfare to increase the flow of captives — made "Indian affairs" a serious economic and security concern.

According to most South Carolinians' point of view, the Lords Proprietors were failing to adequately protect the colony — whether from Indians, pirates or European rivals. "Neither in the infancy of the Colony or any time since," read a petition to the Board of Trade, "have they . . . soe much as contributed one penny toward the raising of forts or other fortifications." Furthermore, Grand Council members — including the younger Arthur Middleton — were fed up with the proprietors' contradictory and ad hoc directives, vetoes of longstanding colonial laws and reforms, and cessation of new land grants while at the same time reserving large tracts for themselves.

As a result, Arthur presided over a local "Convention of the People" on December 16, 1719 to overthrow the proprietary regime — inviting the English crown to take direct control of the colony. "The proprietors had forfeited their rights to govern through neglect, mismanagement, and abuse of power," writes Walter Edgar. Members of the convention made council member and Indian slave trader James Moore interim governor, pledging to "stand by [him] with our lives & Fortunes, and support [him] in the Honor & dignity of Government." In 1721, the king assented to the convention's demands and dispatched a provisional royal governor to South Carolina. Later, Arthur himself would serve as acting royal governor from 1725 to 1730.

As Edgar concludes in his history of South Carolina: "The Revolution of 1719 was different from many of the other colonial disturbances, such as Bacon's Rebellion in Virginia and Culpepper's Rebellion in North Carolina. It was a well-planned and well-executed coup against a legally constituted government (no matter how ill-advised its actions); not an armed conflict

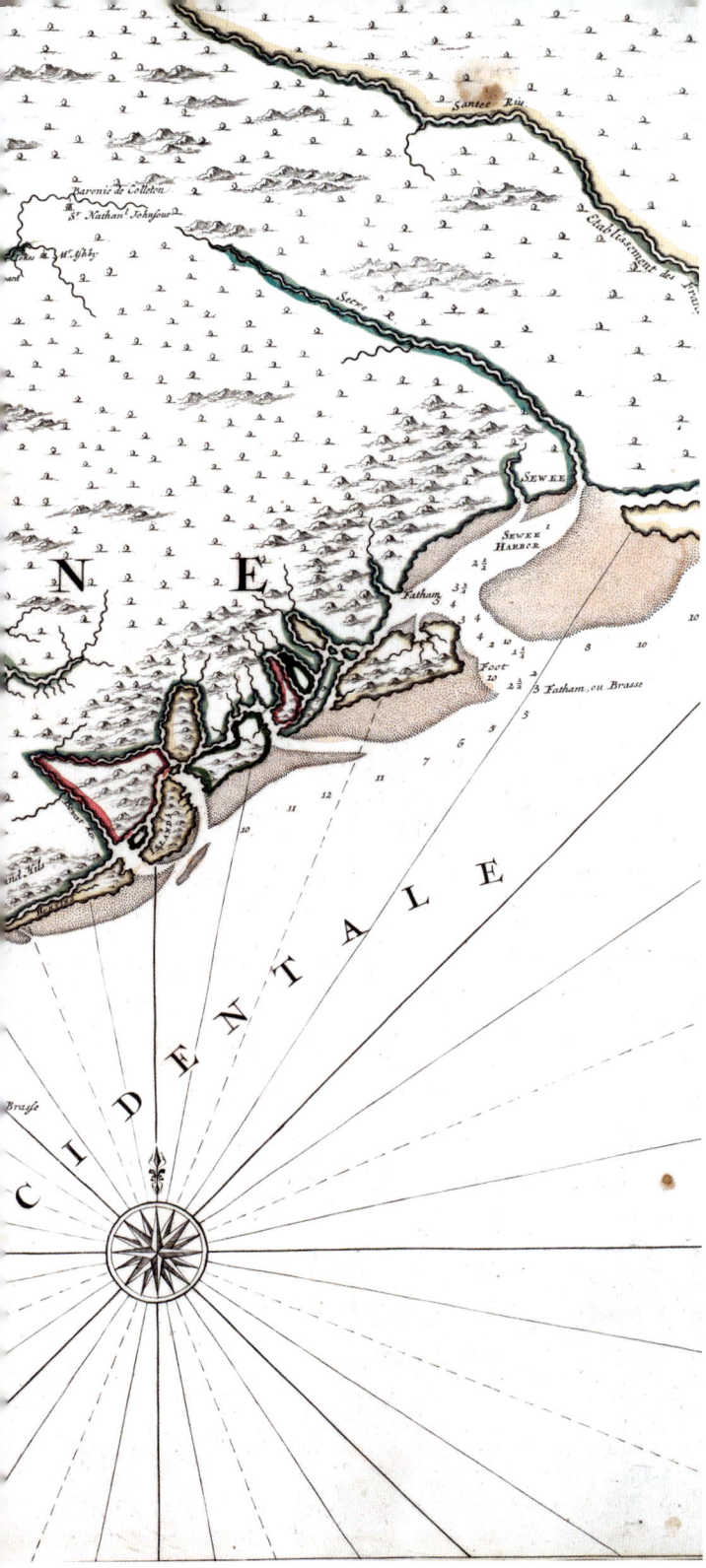

Circa 1698 map showing the South Carolina coast, from the Santee River south to the Edisto River. At center are Charleston Harbor, the Ashley and Cooper rivers, and Goose Creek; with many early landowners identified, including the Middletons.

arising from factional disputes. At its heart was the concept that the revolution was protecting the 'incontestable right' of Englishmen to be governed 'by noe laws made here but what are consented to by them.' " [7]

• • •

When Arthur Middleton died in 1737, he left three surviving sons. According to family historian Langdon Cheves, Arthur bequeathed to 20-year-old Henry "The Oaks [in St. James Goose Creek Parish] and other lands in Carolina," namely 1,600 acres on the Cooper River. Arthur had already provided his eldest son, William, with the bulk of his inheritance when he bought him 1,500 acres on Goose Creek and paid for the construction of Crowfield (named for a family house in England). Meanwhile, younger brother Thomas had settled in Beaufort and become a merchant and planter there. [8]

Four years after claiming his inheritance, Henry wed Mary Williams, daughter and only surviving child of Mary Baker and John Williams. John Williams was a justice of the peace and member of South Carolina's Commons House of Assembly. A wealthy landowner, Williams owned 500 acres on the Ashley River — acquired partly from the father of his deceased first wife, and partly from Mary Baker's father in 1729. Included in the 1729 transaction was a handsome three-story brick house situated on a high bluff overlooking a long, wide curve in the river. Built around 1705 by Richard Godfrey — a cousin of Mary Baker's — the structure afforded one of the most spectacular vistas in the Lowcountry. [9]

Daughter Mary Williams, upon her marriage to Henry Middleton, received 2,248 acres in the form of a dowry from her parents. It included the house and 500 acres on the Ashley River that would form the corpus of Middleton Place — the original brick home and the portion of the property having been conveyed to her father from her mother's estate, with the remaining acreage obtained from the family of his first wife. Thus, it was Mary's inheritance that served as the foundation for Middleton Place; and it was here, rather than at Henry's birthplace on Goose Creek, that the couple made their home in 1741.

A carryover of English law, a woman's dowry in colonial America embodied her right (though not absolute) to inherit property and hold on to it. Few rights were more precious to a South Carolina man or woman than those associated with property, especially land. But for a woman, marriage triggered transfer of her dowry — i.e. her property and inheritance — to the custody and control of her husband. Nevertheless, if she was mistreated or abandoned, or widowed with no children, a portion of the dowry could be reclaimed. If she died with no issue, the dowry was often returned to her family.

In Mary Williams Middleton's case, a proviso in her father's will stated that ultimate ownership of her inheritance and dowry would pass to her oldest son. Thus, while the Middleton men subsequently added thousands of acres to Middleton Place and greatly enhanced the estate, the plantation's origins and its future preservation would be rooted largely in the distaff — i.e. female — side of the family. [10]

• • •

In 1742 Henry Middleton was elected to the state legislature, or "Commons House," representing the area of his new family seat on the Ashley River — St. George's Parish. That same year, Mary gave birth to their first child, Arthur. Mary and Henry also conducted elaborate repairs on the Middleton Place house, transporting enslaved carpenters from other plantations to work on the exterior and interior of the Ashley River estate. As they set about developing extensive formal gardens, the Middletons again depended on slave labor, consulting with English gardener George Newman and following in the grand, classical style of Europe. The gardens were a bold venture, unlike any in America at the time — meshing formal symmetry with the wild woods and waters of the Carolina Lowcountry. Soon the former Williams homestead, under the young Middletons' stewardship, began to be recognized for excellence in design and beauty. A July 1753 issue of London's Gentleman's Magazine offered this amusing couplet: "Here Drayton's seat, and Middleton's is found. Delightful villas! Be they long renown'd."

Over succeeding years, Henry Middleton continued to serve in the Commons House and to build his fortune. Soon he was named Speaker of the Commons House, the highest elected office in the colony. All the while he was adding to his landholdings and work force. Hundreds of enslaved Africans generated ever increasing revenues from indigo and rice — prof-

Henry Middleton (1717–1784).

itable cash crops cultivated on tens of thousands of acres in Dorchester, Goose Creek and Beaufort. In the 1740s, South Carolina planters were exporting more than 20 million pounds of rice annually, a figure that rose to 83 million pounds by 1770. [11]

In the 1750s, Mary and Henry further enhanced the gardens at Middleton Place and doubled their indoor living space by adding two brick dependencies, or flankers, to the main house. According to Middleton Place Foundation President Tracey Todd, "the new additions were likely constructed by enslaved carpenters Hercules, Prince or Stephen, and enslaved bricklayers such as John Baptist." The south flanker, which still stands today, contained the plantation offices and guest quarters. The north flanker housed the family's art collection, as well as a music conservatory and a library of nearly 10,000 volumes. [12]

When his older brother, William, inherited Crowfield Hall (the family estate in Suffolk, England) and moved there in 1754, Henry's status rose. William's departure meant that Henry, age 36, assumed his brother's seat on the Governor's Royal Council and became patriarch of the Middleton family in America. Although William sold Crowfield, he retained his more profitable plantations, and Henry agreed to supervise them in his absence. In return, William looked after Henry's eldest son, Arthur, who was about to begin his formal education in England. The 12-year-old was bound for Harrow and Westminster School, and then on to Trinity College, Cambridge. He later matriculated to the Middle Temple in London for legal training.

Arthur remained with his uncle and English cousins for nine years. Toward the end of his schooling in the winter of 1761, he and his young siblings suffered the death of their mother, Mary, who was 40 years old. Her early death meant that enslaved wet nurses and nursemaids took over the care of

Scholarly rendering of mid-18th century Middleton Place with both flankers intact.

her six small children, ranging in age from one to 10 years. Mary had managed the family's affairs for two decades while regularly giving birth. Five out of her 12 children had died in infancy.

Mary Williams Middleton was buried in a marble tomb within the Bosque — a small forested oasis — at the heart of the Middleton Place gardens. The Middleton coat of arms and crest are etched into one side of the tomb. Etched on top is a long and poignant epitaph, believed to have been written by Henry. It concludes with the phrase, "much beloved and much lamented." [13]

• • •

Soon after Mary died, Henry remarried — to Maria Henrietta Bull, daughter of former Lieutenant Governor William Bull and Mary Quintyne. The following year, son Arthur returned to South Carolina from England. As Tracey Todd speculates, "With five sisters ranging in age from three to thirteen, a 10-year-old brother, and a loving stepmother and father, Arthur's family reunion was likely similar to another returning planter's son, who described 'being kissed and slobbered by all the Masters, Misses, Negroes, Dogs and Cats of your family.' " In 1764 Henry relinquished Middleton Place to Arthur, now 21, as specified by the will of John Williams, Arthur's maternal grandfather. Arthur was ready to start his own family, and on August 19 married Mary "Polly" Izard of Cedar Grove Plantation, located across the Ashley River from Middleton Place. [14]

Suddenly father Henry needed a new country seat of his own. So in 1765 he purchased The Retreat, a 500-acre estate on the Cooper River. But that same year, his elderly stepmother, Sarah Middleton, died. She was 82 years old and considered one of the wealthiest women in the colonies. She had also enjoyed a life tenancy at The Oaks, Henry's birthplace at Goose Creek. So upon her death, Henry was able to return there, all the while managing a large number of other properties and remaining an active member of the Governor's Royal Council (formerly the Grand Council). But his political persuasions were often at odds with his father-in-law, former Lt. Governor Bull. Henry frequently sided with the interests of his fellow colonials, rather than those of the king and his representatives. [15]

Arthur Middleton (1742–1787).

When South Carolina enforced a boycott of British goods and established the Non Importation Association in 1769, a permanent split developed between Henry and other members of the council. The boycott was in response to a series of British taxes, import duties, and other restrictions placed on the North American colonies to help pay down England's national debt. Henry joined the association even though he technically represented royal authority as a member of council. He resigned his seat, ending a Middleton presence on the Governor's Royal Council that had spanned nearly a century.

Plantation and family affairs continued to occupy Henry. Not long after his second wife, Maria Henrietta, died, his oldest three daughters were wed: Sarah Middleton to Charles Cotesworth Pinckney, Henrietta Middleton to Edward Rutledge, and Hester Middleton to Charles Drayton. Later, younger son Thomas married Ann Manigault, and another daughter, Mary, wed Peter Smith. The marriages solidified close kinships of neighboring plantations and properties, and cemented powerful economic and political alliances that bound these prominent South Carolina families for generations. [16]

•••

In 1774 Britain closed the Port of Boston, forced citizens to quarter British troops in their homes, and moved the courts to England. Deeming these acts "repugnant to the rights of people," Commons House delegates from around South Carolina gathered in Charleston to consider sending representatives to a new General Congress being formed "of the several Colonies of North America." Revolution was in the air.

Henry Middleton, brothers Edward and John Rutledge, Christopher Gadsden and Thomas Lynch were elected to attend what became known as the First Continental Congress. In early August 1774, Henry and his son Thomas, along with his daughter Henrietta Middleton Rutledge and son-in-law and fellow delegate Edward Rutledge, boarded the brigantine *Charles-Town Packet* bound for Philadelphia. They arrived on September 5 in time for the opening of the congress.

From the beginning, these Lowcountry planters demonstrated an unshakeable allegiance to their southern homelands and livelihoods, exerting substantial power and influence. When a plan was proposed to refuse all British imports or exports, the South Carolina delegation (with the exception of Gadsden) insisted that exemptions be made for rice and indigo. In a compromise agreement, Congress excluded rice from the embargo. Self-interest prevailed.

Early on, Henry Middleton made a positive impression on delegates from other colonies. Tracey Todd relates how John Hancock described him as being "of first character and fortune of Carolina." John Adams and Silas Deane remembered him as quiet, modest and reserved. In the fall of 1774, when President Peyton Randolph was called back to Virginia, Henry was elected to succeed him, thus becoming the second president of the First Continental Congress. During the last week of the session, Henry authorized and signed a petition entitled "Declaration of Rights and Grievances" that was approved by the Congress and sent to King George III. [17]

Known for his desire to "temper zeal with moderation," Henry hoped the petition letter could achieve redress for the colonies' grievances through a reasoned and measured appeal to the king. It blamed Parliament for creating a "destructive system of colony administration" that caused "distresses, dangers, fears and jealousies that overwhelm your majesty's dutiful colonists with affliction." The king responded by sending a Royal Proclamation to General Thomas Gage, commander in chief of the British forces in North America, calling Henry Middleton, John Adams and others "actual rebels," and directing General Gage "to try and execute such of them as can be got hold of." [18]

In spring of 1775, Henry returned to Philadelphia for the Second Continental Congress. He was re-elected president at age 58, but declined, citing "the infirmities of age" as depriving him "of the ability of rendering so much service to the publick" as he had done in the past. Peyton Randolph agreed to serve as president again, and on June 14 the Congress appointed George Washington to take command of a Continental Army. Henry refused to be re-nominated to the Congress in 1776, and his son Arthur was elected to take his place, allowing Henry to remain in Charleston and serve on the state Legislative Council (successor to the Commons House) and Council of Safety.

Eventually Henry retired to The Oaks with his new wife, Lady Mary Mackenzie, daughter of the third earl of Cromartie and twice widowed. While the marriage with Lady Mary strengthened Henry's ties to the royal government and British aristocracy, his support of South Carolina never ebbed. Between April 1778 and November 1779, he loaned the colony 210,000 English pounds for the war and other expenses — more than $36 million in today's currency. He was one of the largest bondholders of South Carolina debt during the revolutionary period.

When the British captured Charleston in 1780, Henry swore an "Oath of Allegiance to the King" in order to protect his family and avoid being taken prisoner. "Despite this action," historian Walter Edgar notes, "he incurred no penalty after the war, probably because his contemporaries remembered his political service and his generosity to the state." Henry Middleton died in Charleston four years later and was buried in the chancel of St. James Goose Creek Parish church. [19]

• • •

Like many of his fellow congressmen, Arthur Middleton rode horseback to Philadelphia in the spring of 1776. His wife, Mary, and their son and two little daughters followed behind in a carriage, accompanied by Arthur's sister Henrietta and her children. (Henrietta's husband, Edward Rutledge, had gone ahead.) The two young families spent more than a month on the road before reaching the Pennsylvania capital on May 13. Though at a great distance from their southland, they felt quite at home after settling into a rental house in Philadelphia.

On the eve of the American Revolution, Lowcountry South Carolina (Charleston included) was the wealthiest region in British North America. After a single century and four generations in the New World, the Middleton family possessed a rank and status — based on education, wealth and culture — as close to an English landed aristocracy as could be imagined. But the society that Mary and Arthur temporarily left behind in South Carolina was distinctly American: built upon a plantation economy made hugely profitable by an army of enslaved workers. The planters' European heritage, combined with the physical landscape and agricultural opportunities of Lowcountry South Carolina — including the market forces that gave rise to slave labor — created an economic and social framework unique to the region. [20]

Middleton Place served as the family seat and corporate headquarters for dozens of farming operations stretching from the Wateree River to the Savannah. Rice and indigo were the primary cash crops, augmented with livestock, food for home consumption, timber products, and myriad small industries and enterprises. Critical to the Middletons' agricultural empire was their enormous labor force scattered across the Lowcountry.

When Arthur's father (Henry Middleton) died in 1784, his estate comprised more than 50,000 acres and approximately 800 enslaved people — ranging from highly skilled workers and craftsmen to field hands. Managed by paid White overseers and enslaved Black "drivers," enslaved Africans and African Americans were the bedrock of the Middleton fortune — going back to Arthur the slave trader in 17th century Barbados. The monetary value of slaves exceeded the value of all the family's land, houses, crops and other material goods combined. [21]

The material wealth Mary and Arthur accumulated was stunning. Among their many impressive collections was a stable full of English race horses. In addition, there were horses trained for carriages and for riding by family and friends. Prize mounts were housed in elegant stalls and cared for by a team of enslaved trainers, grooms, jockeys, stable boys and farriers — including Toney, Walney and Paul. A groom named Dick and coachmen Jack and Abraham wore Middleton Place livery when traveling to Charleston and

Arthur Middleton's race horse Babraham, standing at stud.

neighboring plantations. Their dark brown cloth coats, worn over pantaloons, were trimmed with black velvet collars and cuffs, and boasted gold buttons embossed with the family crest. Tall beaver hats with gold-colored bands and buckles completed the outfits. [22]

Not long after marrying, Mary and Arthur embarked on a grand tour lasting three years. They traveled throughout England and the European continent, purchasing fine silver, paintings, ceramics and furniture. During this time, their first child, Henry — named for his grandfather — was born in London. Subsequently, Mary and Arthur and their infant son sat for a family portrait in the studio of artist Benjamin West. They were among only a handful of Americans whom West painted during his first decade of royal patronage. Completed in 1772, the monumental oil painting, measuring five by six feet, hung in the main house at Middleton Place.

When Italian traveler Luigi Castiglioni visited Middleton Place after the family's return from abroad, he noted that Arthur, "having traveled in various parts of Europe, has collected a fair quantity of good paintings." The three-story house with its two wings had what Castiglioni termed "the form of an ancient castle . . ." [23]

• • •

As Arthur increased his political involvement during the years leading up to the Continental Congress of 1776, he emerged a leader within the local patriot party. A more radical thinker than his father, Arthur was one of the bolder members on the Council of Safety and its Secret Committee. He organized and led raids on royal armories, encouraged attacks against vocal loyalists, and proposed the confiscation of property belonging to those who had fled the state. "Middleton's enthusiasm," notes historian Walter Edgar, "earned him a position on the panel drafting South Carolina's first constitution, and election as a delegate to the Continental Congress." That fateful summer in Philadelphia, Arthur and his brother-in-law Edward Rutledge joined with the rest of the Congress to declare the American colonies an independent nation and approved a final draft of the Declaration of Independence on July 4. It would be another month before all 13 states signed on. 24

Gold livery button embossed with the Middleton family crest.

Weeks after voting for independence, Arthur wrote to a friend, "I hope I shall be indulged with a Leave to come home as soon as my Time is out, I sigh for it daily . . ." Prophetically he added, "I look upon myself as an Exile . . . my only Consolation is that I am obeying the orders of my Country, & when I cease to be obedient, I shall no longer deserve life." England quickly moved to control her rebellious colonies through force of arms. By late 1776, the British held the City of New York and threatened neighboring Pennsylvania. The assembled congressmen realized they would be wise to move out of Philadelphia. 25

Without delay, the delegates and their families evacuated to the town of Baltimore, 110 miles south. Despite the expense and inconvenience of the move, there was a positive side, as New Hampshire delegate William Whipple wrote: "Congress adjourned from Phila. . . . and we met here the 20th . . . are now doing business with more spirit [than] they have for some time past. I hope the air of this place which is much purer than that of Phila. will brace

John Trumbull's painting depicting the first draft of the Declaration of Independence being presented to the Second Continental Congress. Arthur Middleton is in the middle of the back row, his head leaning forward.

up the weak nerves . . ."

But purer air could not mitigate the fact that the Maryland port town was ill-equipped to accommodate the delegates and their families, and all too ready to take advantage of them. Dr. Benjamin Rush of Pennsylvania wrote his wife from Baltimore: "It will be en[oug]h of the expense of living here to tell you that Mr. Middleton after keeping his family at a tavern for a while at the rate of 100 a week was obliged for want of agreeable accommodations to send them to Annapolis 30 miles from this place." By this time, Mary Middleton had given birth to another daughter, Emma Philadelphia. The growing Middleton family now included a six-year-old boy and three girls under the age of five. [26]

The Middletons' stay in Maryland was relatively short. In February 1777, Congress adjourned and reconvened in Philadelphia. Six months later, again threatened by the British, Congress removed to York, Pennsylvania and convened on September 30. As South Carolina delegate Henry Laurens lamented, "Congress have been hurried from place to place and no business

Trumbull's preliminary sketch of Arthur Middleton, adapted from the Benjamin West family portrait..

done for many days past."

In October, Arthur Middleton made known that he would be leaving Congress. He had signed the Declaration of Independence and helped frame the Articles of Confederation. He had also "desperately tried to get greater military assistance from Congress for the lower South," according to historian Walter Edgar. "His failure in this latter goal, and the counterproductive dissension in the national assembly, encouraged Middleton to return to South Carolina." By winter of 1777, Mary and Arthur found themselves back home at Middleton Place. [27]

• • •

A year later at the close of 1778, British forces brought the Revolutionary War to Georgia, with two campaigns into South Carolina. Arthur Middleton joined the state militia to protect the city. In the spring of 1779, redcoats reached Charleston and lay siege to the capital. Despite turning back the first incursion, Charleston surrendered on May 12, 1780 and was occupied by the enemy.

Unlike his father, Arthur refused to declare loyalty to the king and was placed on parole. On November 15, 1780, British General Cornwallis issued a proclamation confiscating Arthur's estates (with the exception of property in Charleston) and took "the violent rebel Arthur Middleton" into custody. Ten days later, Arthur and a number of other revolutionaries were arrested and sent to St. Augustine to join a group of parolees (including his brother-in-law Edward Rutledge) who had been confined there two months earlier.

Florida, loyal to the king, had been ceded to Great Britain by Spain after the French and Indian War. St. Augustine served as a military base for Britain's southern campaign.

Meanwhile, Mary and their five children (daughter Anna Louisa arrived in February 1778) had taken up residence in the family's Charleston home, having fled Middleton Place the year before as British troops neared the Ashley River. When the city surrendered, its inhabitants became prisoners of war. Five months later, Mary's brother John Izard died. Then, on the same day her husband was arrested, she gave birth to child number six: Isabella Johannes, named for Mary's widowed sister-in-law, Isabella Hume Izard. [28]

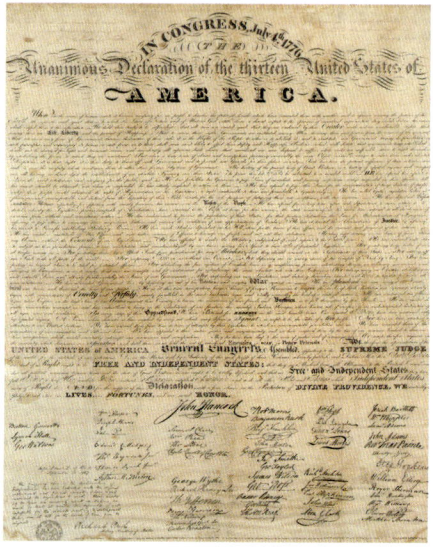

Declaration of Independence as signed by Arthur Middleton, printed on silk.

Thus, Mary was left with the task of fending off both British and American marauders, as well as caring for her many children. Her first major challenge was to escape being banished to Philadelphia as the wife of a rebel. The second was to obtain the release of Middleton Place from confiscation. Succeeding in both, she moved the family back to the plantation and engaged a French tutor to teach academic subjects to the older children.

In St. Augustine, Arthur and his fellow prisoners formed themselves into groups, called "messes," to rent lodging and share provisions for meals. Though confined and deprived, their imprisonment was far from harsh. On December 25, 1780, fellow Charleston gentleman and prisoner, Josiah Smith, recorded in his diary: "Being Christmas day a very good dinner of

Roasted Turkey & Pig, Corn'd Beef, Ham, Plumb pudding, and pumpkin Tarts &c" was enjoyed by the mess he belonged to. No doubt the "Grove" mess, which included Arthur, Edward Rutledge and Thomas Heyward, enjoyed a similarly elegant meal.

On June 25, 1781, news arrived to St. Augustine that "all persons made Prisoners (both Regulars and Militias) in the Southern department, from the beginning of the American War to the 15 June 1781, were generally exchanged." They would be sent directly to Virginia or Philadelphia for exchange with British prisoners held by the American army.

"After taking our last Meal of Breakfast," Josiah Smith wrote on July 17, he and his mess mates boarded one of two ships slated for departure. Aboard the other ship were Arthur Middleton and the Grove mess. Two days later the vessels crossed the bar of St. Augustine Inlet on the way north to American soil.

The terms of his parole prohibited Arthur from returning to British-occupied Lowcountry South Carolina. So the state's wartime government appointed him a delegate to Congress, again meeting in Philadelphia. While Cornwallis' surrender at Yorktown, Virginia (on October 19, 1781) brought renewed energy and hope to the southern patriots, it failed to lessen the risk to exiles if they violated their paroles by venturing home. Some, like Edward Rutledge, returned south anyway. But Arthur remained for another year, until it became clear that the occupation of Charleston was waning and the English were losing control of South Carolina.

With the appointment of a new slate of South Carolina delegates to Congress in the fall of 1782, Arthur was free to leave Philadelphia, no longer an exile. He arrived at Middleton Place in time for daughter Isabella's — the "little stranger's"— second birthday. A greater degree of normalcy returned to the family when the British finally evacuated Charleston on December 14. The Revolution was won. Now Arthur could concentrate on his family and plantations. After six-and-a-half long and painful years, the Middletons set about reclaiming their lives and their war-ravaged estate. [29]

• • •

It is hard to imagine the enormous responsibility and stress endured by Mary as a "prisoner" of the British occupation during Arthur's long absence.

Not only did she have to worry about the safety of her husband, but also that of her children. In the span of two years, she kept the family on the move: first evacuating Middleton Place for a friend's plantation on the Santee Delta; next to a family property near Camden; then to the City of Charleston, and finally back to Middleton Place — all the while raising their sons and daughters and making myriad decisions ordinarily left up to Arthur.

During this time, her brother John Izard of Cedar Grove died and his childless widow, Isabella — Mary's close friend and neighbor — died two years later. While these losses were difficult, they also had a profound effect on Mary's future. Isabella had been granted lifetime rights to the Izard property by her late husband. Upon her death, everything passed to Mary, her sister-in-law. Although as a married woman the land legally belonged to Arthur, Mary essentially became joint owner of several important properties: her family home of Cedar Grove on the Ashley River, the highly profitable rice lands of Old Combahee and Hobonny plantations, and other properties from the Izard family estate.

Also included in Mary's inheritance were some 200 enslaved Africans. Those who served the Middleton family in the late 18th century included Stephen, a steward, and his wife, Daphne, a seamstress. A ledger shows Daphne was valued at five pounds more than her husband. Abram emerges as the name of one of the cooks, and Hercules and his wife, Jenny, are noted as house servants. Caesar and George worked in the house too, as did Sue and Mary. Mary was also a pastry cook. In addition, there was a hairdresser named Ben and another seamstress named Nancy. The list goes on. [30]

After Arthur's return, the family expanded quickly with the birth of daughter Septima Sexta in 1783 and son John Izard in 1785, named for Mary's late brother. On January 1, 1787, Arthur, 45, died of an "unknown fever." Mary was left with eight children, ages 16 months to 16 years, and was pregnant with her ninth. They buried Arthur in the Middleton Place gardens beside his mother. President John Adams wrote later that even though he and Arthur were sometimes on opposite sides of lively debates, "We . . . parted . . . without a spark of malice on either side, for he was an honest & generous fellow, with all his zeal in the cause." [31]

Because Arthur died without a will, inheritance law entitled Mary, by dowry right, to receive one-third of her husband's estate. She chose Izard lands: Cedar Grove, Hobonny and Old Combahee. She also chose not to remarry. By remaining single, Mary retained control of her inheritance and continued to improve and add to her landholdings. In 1793, she hired Jonathan Lucas to construct rice processing mills at Hobonny and Old Combahee. She wrote Lucas requesting directions for ordering millstones from England, informing him that among her slaves "I have a wheel wright, a blacksmith, bricklayers and a number of carpenters to assist."

Slave badge from Cedar Grove.

Mary's other primary role was as matriarch and fierce protector of her family. When 24-year-old Henry wanted to marry, he first asked for his mother's consent. In addition to approving of their spouses, Mary wanted her children close by. While eldest son Henry had received Middleton Place, Mary was concerned for his younger siblings. So she purchased Batavia plantation near Middleton and placed it in trust for her daughter Anna. Likewise, she put 924 acres of Cedar Grove (across the river) in trust for daughter Septima, which kept the property out of reach of Septima's husband. Finally in July 1813, she conveyed the remainder of Cedar Grove to her youngest son, John Izard Middleton.

In June 1814, Mary was visiting Septima in Charleston when she suffered a stroke, never to recover. She was 67 years old. The *Charleston Daily Courier* reported on July 12: "Died at her residence in Mazyckborough, Mrs. Mary Middleton relict of that distinguished patriot the late Honourable Arthur Middleton, esq.: this excellent woman has descended to the tomb endeared to Society by her virtues and her good works." She was survived by five children and 39 grandchildren. [32]

• • •

Other lives were changed by the Revolution, including those of enslaved Africans. Both patriot and British authorities enlisted Middleton slaves to build fortified earthworks around Charleston. Southern revolutionaries also used Blacks, both free and enslaved, as spies and messengers. In addition, slaves were conscripted as construction workers, engineers and sailors. Many of these men and women believed that a British victory would bring them freedom. An estimated 100,000 enslaved people across the South took advantage of the disruption caused by the war and escaped from bondage, with many of them making their way across "enemy lines" to the British forces.

As the loyalists withdrew from southern ports after Cornwallis' surrender at Yorktown, scores of Black refugees sought passage to the British stronghold of New York. But many African Americans who aided the British lost their freedom nonetheless. Some ended up in slavery in the Caribbean, taken off and sold to West Indies traders by British officers, destined for conditions even worse than what they had experienced in South Carolina. Others were prevented from leaving with the British altogether.

Eyewitness accounts describe Blacks swimming out to boats in Charleston Harbor, and British soldiers hacking away at their arms to keep them from boarding. Of the many thousands of enslaved Africans who left the plantations, few actually got the freedom they so desperately sought. Among those who did, however, were a number who voluntarily and legally immigrated to other countries.

At Middleton Place, many slaves found their circumstances altered. Several were taken by the redcoats and some ran away from both British troops and the Middletons. Others died, while numerous bondsmen declared themselves Black loyalists. Of those who perished, the majority succumbed to smallpox, which was rampant in the British camps. Those who fled set out for destinations such as New York, Jamaica and St. Augustine; or in the case of the loyalists, to Canada and Germany.

In November 1782, Britain and America signed a provisional treaty granting the former colonies their independence. As the British prepared for their final departure from the former colonies, the Americans demanded the return of property, including runaway slaves under the terms of the peace treaty. But in New York, the acting commander of British forces did not abandon Black loyalists to their former fate as slaves. With apprehensive Blacks seeking to document their service to the crown, the British commandant in New York compiled a list of claimants known as the "English Book of Negroes." Altogether, some 3,000 to 4,000 African Americans boarded ships in New York bound for New Brunswick, Nova Scotia, Jamaica and England. In a

Governor Henry Middleton (1770–1846).   Mary Helen Hering Middleton (1774–1850).

few cases they fled with the Hessians to principalities in Germany.

Hercules, Tom, Will, Mary and her child — among the enslaved men, women and children at Middleton Place — were released by or escaped from the British and retreated to Indian lands in the upper part of South Carolina. Silvia, Phillis and her child Stephen, another Phillis, Sarry and Gulla died while in British hands, possibly of smallpox. Those who joined the Hessians included Warney; Doctor, who went to New York; John, 25; and George, 30, both described in the Book of Negroes as "stout fellows."

Middleton slaves known to have been loyalists who resettled in Nova Scotia were Charles Middleton (57), Sarah Middleton (25), John Banbury (38), Lucy Banbury (40), Henry Minton (16) and Harry Middleton (50). Lucy Banbury later migrated from Canada to West Africa after Freetown was established in Sierra Leone.   Records indicate that Banbury was born in Africa, making her eventual return to her homeland an extraordinary 18th-century circumnavigation of the Atlantic world. [33]

• • •

Young Henry Middleton II always regretted that his father's premature death prevented him from attending university. Historian Walter Edgar explains that though Henry was well tutored at home, he was nevertheless sent north in 1790 by his uncles Charles Cotesworth Pinckney and Edward Rutledge to obtain "a thorough Knowledge of . . . his own Country." He then went abroad for several years. On November 13, 1794 with his mother Mary's permission, Henry married Mary Helen Hering, daughter of a British army officer, at a ceremony in England. The couple had 14 children, four of whom died in infancy.

In 1799 Henry returned to Middleton Place with his family and took up management of his extensive properties and workforce. Around the same time, he entered the political arena and was elected to the state House of Representatives, serving from 1802 until 1809. In 1810, he won a state senate seat. A few months later, he was chosen governor. Henry's success in public life is attributed to his popularity as a political moderate, support for free public schools, curtailment of the slave trade, and legislative reapportionment to reflect the growing population in the upstate.

Following the War of 1812, Henry was elected to the U.S. House of Representatives. He served four years, representing the Charleston District in the 14th and 15th Congresses and becoming an ally of President James Monroe. On his presidential tour of the South in 1819, Monroe was accompanied by Secretary of War John C. Calhoun and his wife and two children as far as their home in South Carolina. After crossing the Ashley River, accompanied by every military company and society in Charleston, Monroe spent the night at "the country seat of the Honorable Henry Middleton, about 12 miles from town." 34

In 1820 President Monroe appointed Henry Middleton as America's Minister Plenipotentiary to Russia, a position he held for a decade. Edgar notes that Henry was "exceptionally well prepared for such a post," given his knowledge of national affairs, his familiarity with Europe, and his fluency in French. Upon Henry's return to South Carolina in 1830, he became a leader of the Unionists, adamantly opposing the "baneful doctrine of nullification." The Nullification Doctrine was espoused by southern states and conceived by John C. Calhoun (who later became Vice President). It claimed the power

U.S. President James Monroe, c. 1819, painted by Samuel F.B. Morse.

of each state to declare a federal law unconstitutional, and therefore void.

While Henry was devoted to public service and the public good, he also shared his forebears' love of the land and their family seat of Middleton Place. He enlarged the gardens and added many plantings, having befriended Andre Michaux, the famous French botanist who introduced numerous exotic plants to North America. Family history records that Michaux visited Middleton Place when Henry was a teenager, bringing with him some of the earliest camellias to be planted in an American garden.

In 1846, Henry died and was buried at Middleton Place with his father and grandmother. As his descendant Charles Duell writes in the book *A Phoenix Still Rising*, "Throughout the generations, the gardens and the house made up the fabric of the Middletons' lives. Although not their only residence, it was always, more than any other dwelling, the family's home — the one to which they returned with undisguised pleasure and relief."

Six years before Henry's death, Richard Yeadon, editor of the *Charleston Daily Courier*, made a prescient observation: "Here ... we meet with evidence of the taste, wealth and magnificence of colonial times. The mansion ... is constructed of common native brick, although finished off in some parts with more polished material, doubtless of English manufacture ... Although ... considerably more than a century old, it is as substantial and durable as ever, and will probably endure, like the venerable oaks, which shade the adjacent grounds, until the day of final doom, unless deserted, or some uprooting earthquake or tornado shall assign it a shorter term."

"Yeadon could scarcely have known how ironically prophetic his words would be," Duell reflects. "Twenty-five years after his article appeared, the

Circa 1842, color enhanced sketch of the Middleton Place residential complex. Stables are in the right foreground and slave quarters are to the rear.

end of the Civil War found the buildings at Middleton Place burned and looted, the once splendid house only a shell. Yet to come were the 'uprooting earthquake' that felled the gutted walls, and the many devastating storms and hurricanes that compounded the ruin." Aggravating the situation was the fact that Henry Middleton had left behind considerable debt, due to years of borrowing and spending in support of his life as a public servant. [35]

The ruins of Middleton Place after being burned in the final months of the Civil War. The restored south flanker (at left) was reroofed and enlarged in the 1870s.

Three

DREAMS and DESPAIR

"With my orderlies I push on for the Middleton place on the Ashley River . . . Everything was in confusion. The house was strewed with articles and all about the grounds things were scattered . . . Soon found my way to the library, which I think was the largest and most select private library I have ever seen . . . Here met Maj. Smith [commander of the 56th New York Volunteers] who had just come up . . . I sickened at the thought of such pillage as was about to occur and retired begging the Maj. whatever else he might do, to spare the library." – February 23, 1865, Dr. Henry Marcy, Union surgeon

"I have just returned home, and visited St. Andrew's and St. George's Parishes or what remains of them. Everything is completely destroyed, there are but two houses left on our side [of the river] . . . I visited your place, but I suppose you may have heard of what has happened, it is almost too shocking for me to relate . . . I went over on the other side [of the mill pond] . . . everything is burnt and destroyed, dwelling, outhouses, stable, barn and negro houses, nothing but the ruins . . ." – June 2, 1865, John Drayton to Williams Middleton

On the eve of the American Civil War, descendants of Governor Henry Middleton owned more than a dozen large rice plantations (totaling over 50,000 acres) and more than 1,500 enslaved men, women and children, making them one of the largest slaveholding families in the South. But the former congressman and diplomat had also passed on financial obligations amounting to more than $3 million in today's money. As a result, his children were still settling their father's estate at the start of the war in 1860. Because Williams had inherited Middleton Place, his brothers Oliver and John received Hobonny on the Beaufort side of the Combahee River. Old Combahee, also on the west side, was transferred jointly to Williams and youngest brother Edward. Ownership of nearby Nieuport, another Combahee River property, was shared with Arthur and Henry; but it had been mortgaged to help pay off their father's debts. [1]

Day-to-day management of the lands fell to Williams, with assistance from John, who had married into the Alston family and become a rice planter on the Waccamaw River. The rest of the family was dispersed and living elsewhere when war broke out. Older brother Harry and his wife, Ellen, were settled at Heybridge Lodge in Asheville, North Carolina. Edward, who had risen to the rank of captain in the U.S. Navy, chose to remain with the Union. His decades of military service had carried him to ports around the globe. Like other naval officers stationed abroad, his devotion to country trumped his allegiance to his home state.

Dr. Henry Marcy, medical officer, 35th U.S. Colored Infantry Regiment.

Because of this, the Confederate government attempted to confiscate Old Combahee, having deemed co-owner Edward an "alien enemy." Williams and John were able to save the property by showing that, due to a large debt he owed to their brother Oliver, Edward's share of the estate had, in fact, been assigned to Oliver and was therefore no longer under Edward's control; thus, not subject to sequestration.

Eldest brother Arthur had died years earlier in Italy, leaving behind his widow, Paolina, daughter Angelina, and son Henry Bentivoglio ("Benti"). Sister Maria Middleton perished with her husband and children when the steamer they were traveling on — the *Pulaski* — exploded in route to the Middleton summer home in Newport, Rhode Island. That left two surviving sisters: Catherine, who suffered from mental illness, and Eliza, who married wealthy Philadelphian Joshua Francis Fisher in a ceremony at Middleton Place in 1839. Eliza remained in Philadelphia for the rest of her life, later welcoming her widowed mother, Mary Helen Middleton, to live with her.

While Middleton Place would always serve as the physical anchor for the family, the focal point of family communication shifted to Eliza and her mother in Philadelphia. Eliza was exceedingly close to her relatives in South Carolina, visiting them often and becoming a devoted correspondent. Middleton historian Barbara Doyle describes a trip that Eliza made to Charleston in the spring of 1861, just before the Civil War erupted. The bombardment of Fort Sumter on April 12 and President Lincoln's order to blockade Confederate harbors on April 19 caused Eliza to return to Philadelphia earlier than originally planned.

Henry Bentivoglio "Benti" Middleton was among the family members who fought for the Confederacy.

"It was just as well," according to Doyle, "for as Eliza writes a sister-in-law on April 23: 'I returned home three days ago — just in time to escape a detention on the road; for the very next day the bridges for the Railway were burnt down to prevent the passage of troops sent from Boston & Phila[delphia] to protect the Capitol at Washington from the Southern Army & I should have been placed in a most unpleasant predicament if I had remained a day longer in Charleston... I was there during the bombardment of Fort Sumter, & a sad sight it was to me to see the War begun.' "

In the end, the Middleton family was fortunate to have been divided between North and South. Immediately after Confederate General Lee surrendered to General Grant at Appomattox Court House in April 1865, Edward Middleton boarded a steamer to Charleston. As a U.S. citizen and naval officer, he paid the taxes on all of the Middleton family's Combahee River plantations. He would have done the same for Middleton Place, but was unable to meet with the provost marshal for the Ashley River District. Those taxes were paid by the other Middleton sibling living in the North — Eliza and her husband, Francis Fisher.

Thus on November 29, 1865, Old Combahee, Hobonny, Nieuport, Middleton Place and Horse Savanna were returned to Williams, John and Edward Middleton as executors of their father's estate. Thanks to the diligence and determination of these three brothers, most of the Middleton lands survived intact following the war. But it was not until 1879 that Henry's affairs were finally settled, 33 years after his death. [2]

• • •

When news of Abraham Lincoln's presidential win reached South Carolina one day after the election on November 7, 1860, the state's congressional delegation resigned their seats and federal district judges walked out of their courtrooms. The General Assembly immediately called for a special election to choose representatives to attend a South Carolina Secession Convention in the state capital of Columbia. On December 6, brothers John and Williams Middleton were elected to the convention, which met 11 days later.

Ninety percent of convention delegates owned slaves and 27 members, including the Middleton brothers, owned 100 or more. Lincoln had repeatedly claimed that while he opposed slavery's spread, he would not interfere with slavery where it already existed and was protected by the Constitution. Nevertheless, the planters perceived Lincoln and his opposition to the expansion of slavery into the western states as the gravest threat to their livelihood and way of life. His victory electrified South Carolina's political leadership. As Upstate Congressman W.W. Boyce stated, "To submit to Lincoln's election is to submit to death!" [3]

The S.C. Secession Convention delegates spent only one day in Columbia. Due to word of a smallpox outbreak — a rumor that many believe was orchestrated to ensure victory for the secessionists — the convention was adjourned and moved to Charleston. The planter class was clearly in control. As historian Walter Edgar observes, just as their forebears had justified the rebellions of 1719 and 1776, Williams and John and their fellow delegates desired not just action, but a persuasive justification to the rest of the world — "a rationale."

"Fire-eater" Robert Barnwell Rhett and Christopher Memminger (who would later become Confederate Secretary of the Treasury) were assigned to articulate in writing the reasons for secession. Edgar summarizes Rhett's

George W. Bernard

Institute Hall at 134 Meeting Street in Charleston — located between Circular Congregational Church (with columned portico) and TeeTotal Restaurant (with awning) — where the Ordinance of Secession was signed and ratified.

rationale as expressed in his Address to the Slave-Holding States published in the newspaper he owned called the *Charleston Mercury*: "His central argument was based on the right to self-government. He wrote of the history of the North's desire to control the South and thus focused on the struggles of a free government. His political argument was also laced with a discussion of how the North and the South had become two peoples."

Memminger took a more direct approach to the defense of slavery in his Declaration of Immediate Causes: "He listed the northern states' violation of the fugitive slave law, their personal liberty laws claiming that slavery was unjust, and the election of an antislavery Republican president as the reasons why South Carolina seceded; and he stated that the rest of the slave states should follow suit," according to Edgar. [4]

Three days after convening, Williams and John joined the other 167 convention delegates to sign the Ordinance of Secession, declaring that Lincoln's "opinions and purposes are hostile to slavery." Charles Lesser of the S.C. Department of Archives and History describes the scene in Charleston on

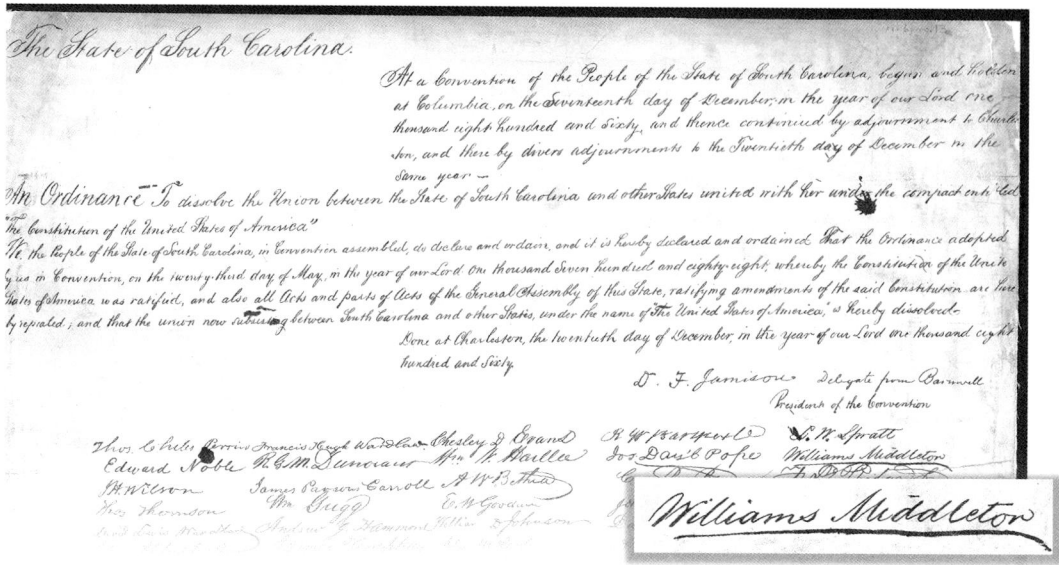

The Ordinance of Secession, as signed by Williams Middleton and his brother John.

the evening of December 20, 1860:

"The delegates eventually agreed that the signing would take place in Institute Hall . . . at 6:45pm the delegates marched in procession from St. Andrew's Hall to . . . the foot of Institute Hall's stairs. The hall [next door to Circular Church and which burned to the ground a year later] with a capacity of nearly 3,000 was filled to overflowing . . . The 'Ordinance of Secession has been signed and ratified,' intoned David F. Jamison [to thunderous applause], president of the Convention of the People of South Carolina. In a loud voice he continued, 'I proclaim the State of South Carolina an Independent Commonwealth' . . . Wild cheering broke out. Order was restored, and at 9:15pm the convention adjourned . . ."

It was an unusually warm night in December as William Martin, clerk of the state senate, went outside to Meeting Street and read South Carolina's new "Declaration of Independence" to the assembled throng. Cannons fired, bands played, people paraded, bells rang, bonfires burned and rockets exploded until past midnight. As other southern states signed on, a government of the Confederate States of America was formed.

John and Williams Middleton, along with the rest of the delegates, put loyalty to South Carolina and the South ahead of loyalty to the United

Williams Middleton (1809-1883).

States — the union their ancestors had helped create a century before. "More than 70 years earlier in 1788," notes Lesser, "South Carolinians in a special convention of elected delegates had ratified the U.S. Constitution. Now the delegates of 'the people' in another convention had again expressed their sovereign power. Fully conscious of the historic moment, South Carolina pronounced the union dissolved."

Lesser concludes, "In the next four years, over 60 percent of the southern white males who were between 13 and 43 years of age on this Secession Day would wear the grey uniforms of the Confederacy." About 18 percent of that age group would die for the Confederate cause. Numerous Middleton family members and cousins were among those who fought, with many wounded and eleven giving their lives. [5]

• • •

At age 52, Williams Middleton was considered too old for military duty. However, his leadership at the S.C. Secession Convention demonstrated his absolute devotion to the Confederacy and the institution of slavery. While his wife, Susan Pringle Smith, and their children retreated to Columbia at the start of the war, Williams remained in Charleston and joined a volunteer company — all the while residing at Number One Meeting Street, the house they purchased in 1855 with what Williams described as "a large part of Sue's property [inheritance]." Susan's brother, J.J. Pringle Smith — whose namesake and grandson inherited Middleton Place — was also a signer of the Ordinance of Secession.

Middleton family house in Newport, Rhode Island.

Williams wrote about the house in a letter to his sister Eliza in Philadelphia: "We are delighted with our new purchase. The situation [is] even more than we had hoped. The view delicious, and everything else as good as any reasonable people could desire," including uninterrupted breezes from the harbor. The 1850s was the last decade of extravagance for the Middletons, as they continued to acquire property and enjoy a rarefied life. Like his forebears, Williams possessed refined tastes, having been educated in Europe and served as his father's personal secretary during Henry's tenure as America's minister plenipotentiary to Russia.

Williams and his family traveled regularly to Philadelphia and to their family house in Newport. Brother-in-law Francis Fisher's first cousin, Sidney Fisher, was often included in the Fisher-Middleton gatherings. On October 30, 1858, Sidney wrote the following entry in his diary, an interesting assessment of Williams Middleton from the point of view of a Philadelphia aristocrat:

"Middleton has really the position of a nobleman, without title, in all the attributes that distinguish such a life. He lives in a state, S. Carolina that is

Eliza Middleton Fisher (1815-1890).   J. Francis Fisher (1807-1873).

practically an aristocracy, as it is governed by planters. He is the owner of hereditary land, descended thro several generations distinguished in public life, his father having been governor, senator in Congress and minister to Russia, and his grandfather a signer of the Declaration of Independence, and he lives on his land, several thousand acres, surrounded by some hundreds of hereditary serfs and vassals. This is feudal, more so, indeed, than nobility now in England." [6]

The Middletons' fertile rice lands on the Combahee River, 50 miles southwest of Charleston, supported this lifestyle. Approximately 575 workers were enslaved there and produced nearly three million pounds of rice annually — resulting in a yearly income from the Combahee River plantations of more than $95,000. The 9,000-square-foot, four-story brick mansion that Williams and Susan purchased in downtown Charleston sat at the corner of Meeting and South Battery streets, facing White Point Garden and Charleston Harbor, with a view of Fort Sumter in the distance. [7]

Many of the bricks that built Number One Meeting Street were made at

Number One Meeting Street.

a Cooper River rice plantation called Medway, owned by the Stoney family. Medway also supplied bricks for construction of the five-foot-thick, 50-foot-high walls of Fort Sumter. Located at the entrance to Charleston Harbor, the fort was 90 percent complete when South Carolina seceded from the Union in December 1860, and when Confederate troops fired on it the following April. [8]

Despite not going into battle, Williams played a key role in defending Charleston and Charleston Harbor. He and Jefferson Bennett led the effort to procure, fill and position many thousands of sandbags to protect Fort Sumter and the wharfs surrounding Charleston. Williams donated the materials and conscripted his enslaved workers to fill the bags and row them out to fortifications around the harbor. In addition, he furnished lumber and railroad ties for the Confederate government and invested large amounts of money in Confederate war bonds. [9]

Williams also campaigned for the procurement of cannons to defend the city's waterfront from Union shelling. He was aware that the Confederacy had purchased two heavy Blakely guns made in England, which by August

1863 had been secretly ferried past the Union blockade. Williams lobbied the Confederate government in Richmond to assign at least one of them to Charleston. His work paid off. In late August Williams triumphantly wrote to Susan in Columbia, "We are to have both the English guns."

The first heavy cannon, drawn by horses, moved slowly through the city to its emplacement. "The great gun is coming steadily down King Street," Williams wrote on August 30. "I suppose that by tomorrow morning it will reach its destination. Heaven grant that it may be put in position in time to do what is expected of it." By the first week of September, Richmond had been officially informed that "the great Blakely" was in position — in view of Number One Meeting and two blocks from where East and South Battery streets meet.

A few months later, Williams' and Susan's 22-year-old niece — "Rie" Middleton, daughter of John — stayed with them at their Meeting Street house. On her last day in the city before returning to her family in Darlington, she went up King Street to buy a comb for her mother and witnessed the bombardment firsthand. Rie wrote in her diary: "I . . . heard someone say 'Look there! Look there!,' turned & saw where a shell had made a cloud of dust — went & got the comb — returning, another shell struck some little way in front of me, and I felt the sand in my eyes — heard one other whirring over the town before I got back to No. 1 . . ." [10]

Williams made another contribution to the war effort. He offered his enormous house as a billet for Confederate soldiers. Because of the unhealthy conditions at the Confederate camps that were guarding the harbor on Morris Island, Sullivan's Island, and Fort Sumter, whenever possible troops stationed at these camps were rotated into the city for two or three days before returning to duty. Despite its exposure to Union shelling, Number One Meeting became a refuge for war weary troops, including two of Williams' nephews: Thomas (son of John Middleton) and Benti (son of the deceased Arthur Middleton). Benti was attending the S.C. Military Academy (The Citadel) when, against his uncles' advice, he left school to join the Marion Artillery. He fought in both South Carolina and Virginia, returning to Italy after the war. [11]

• • •

1863 drawing of proposed expansion of Middleton Place, which was never realized.

By 1864 the bombardment of Charleston had grown more intense and the shelling more threatening to Williams and the soldiers billeted at Number One Meeting. That summer, Williams moved 22 miles inland to the village of Summerville, up the Ashley River from Middleton Place. Summerville was far enough away from the bombardment for Susan and the children to safely join him. He wrote to his sister Eliza: "My house in town [Charleston] was within such easy range of the Yankee batteries that I did not feel justified in keeping my family there, and as I could not hire any other that suited me I established them here [in Summerville] for the summer. The house [on Meeting Street] up to that time, however, has escaped any injury — but will I presume come in for its share ere long."

In leaving the city, Williams returned to the service of a cause to which he was devoted perhaps more than the Confederacy — that of Middleton Place, which lay several miles southwest of Summerville. He went "two or three times a week to spend the day at M. Place," his letter to Eliza continues, where he had a new object of interest, "a recently established brick yard." This was to provide the materials for "the addition to and alteration of the old house. And as this is to be on a pretty large scale, I am likely to have my hands full for some time to come." [12]

Indeed the scale of the proposed expansion at Middleton Place was considerable, as evidenced by the set of 1863 drawings Williams commissioned from Fred Smith, the Confederate States Army engineer stationed at Fort Sumter. Plans called for several new rooms that would have doubled the square footage of the main house, along with the addition of such features as Flemish gables, decorative spires, ornate chimneys, multi-paned windows and porte-cocheres — all in the style of Jacobean and Tudor revival, popular at the time. Like his forefathers, Williams hoped to make a mark upon his ancestral home, even under the cloud of war.

While Williams' sense of optimism obscured the realities of the Civil War, he was not alone in his belief that the Confederacy would prevail and the agricultural economy of the South would rise again, despite the region being split in half during the summer of 1863. Vicksburg had been lost and General Lee's army defeated at Gettysburg. Charleston was under siege from a Union blockade and bombardment, and Port Royal and Beaufort were occupied by Yankee soldiers, busy freeing enslaved Africans and redistributing plantation lands. [13]

Through it all Williams persisted, faced with changing economic conditions evident long before the outbreak of war. Carolina and Georgia had dominated rice sales in Europe all through the 18th century, earning planters a 25 percent return on investment. But several decades before the Civil War, the export market for rice shifted as northern Europe sought cheaper rice to feed its burgeoning labor force. By the 1830s, according to Peter Coclanis, director of the Global Research Institute at the University of North Carolina, rice operations in the English colonies of Bengal, Java and Burma were undercutting South Carolina rice sales abroad and at home.

In 1846 — the year William's father died — South Carolina instituted tariffs on imported rice to protect planters from foreign competitors. As Asia continued to undercut the Lowcountry's rice trade with Europe, the planters proceeded to build up their market share in the United States and Caribbean, including sales to the Spanish colonies of Cuba and Puerto Rico. By shifting their focus to the domestic market and sales closer to home, Lowcountry planters sustained rice production and operated at a profit — albeit reduced — until the start of the war.

At the same time, cotton production had begun to rival that of rice, with mills in the northern states and England buying nearly all the cotton South Carolina could produce. The moniker "King Cotton" was no exaggeration, and rice planters began investing capital and slaves in cotton plantations, in South Carolina and along the Gulf Coast. Cotton production adopted the slave plantation model causing demand and prices for enslaved workers to

View Overlooking the Butterfly Lakes and Mill at Middleton Place, c. 1926, by Alice Ravenel Huger Smith.

rise to unprecedented levels. [14]

Williams tried cultivating cotton at Middleton Place as he continued to diversify and experiment. Ever entrepreneurial, he also amassed 1,000 beef and dairy cattle and planted hay, which became the dominant crop for sale and for feeding the herd. He purchased Cashmere goats and sent their "hair" to France "to have it manufactured by way of curiosity." Hogs, poultry and sheep were also kept. In addition, Williams operated four mills: three rice mills built by his grandmother (Mary Izard Middleton) in the 1790s (two on the Combahee River and one across the road from Middleton Place at Horse Savanna); and a brick grist mill he constructed beside the Ashley River in 1851 at the Butterfly Lakes.

Williams also owned a schooner he inherited from his father: a three-masted, wooden sailing vessel used for transporting rice, cotton, timber, slaves and other cargo — in addition to paying passengers — downriver to the port of Charleston. It was manned by an enslaved captain named Thomas and enslaved crew members Abraham, Tom, Andrew and Sanna, serving not only Middleton Place but neighboring plantations too. On its return from

Charleston, the schooner would bring back manufactured goods, imported wares and specialty items; along with parcels, newspapers and mail.

Williams experimented with a steam-powered water pump for his rice fields, and a team of water buffalos — purchased in Constantinople — for plowing the muddy impoundments. He produced pitch, tar and other naval stores from his extensive pine forests. Perhaps one of his most profitable endeavors was becoming a distributor of the newly invented "barbed wire," used for fencing livestock and also for improving fortifications at Fort Sumter. [15]

• • •

Seven months after surrendering Fort Sumter to the Confederates, northern forces overtook Port Royal Sound and Beaufort in November 1861 — their first step in establishing a blockade of the southern coast that would eventually extend to Charleston Harbor. This early foothold enabled the Union Army to begin occupying coastal plantations south of Charleston, including Middleton family lands. Enslaved Africans, referred to as "contraband" by the Union, were encouraged to enlist in the United States Army. Slaves from Middleton plantations who enlisted included William Middleton, Sando Cavel and Monday Washington, who joined the 2nd South Carolina Volunteer Regiment, renamed as Company G of the 34th U.S. Colored Infantry Regiment.

Not all of the enslaved who fled Middleton plantations became soldiers. One "fine looking black man" named Isaac worked as a waiter and was asked while serving a Union officer who he belonged to. Isaac replied, "I did belong to Williams Middleton who plants on Ashley River, but now I am a free man, Sir." Meanwhile, many enslaved African Americans who remained as chattel were forced to build fortifications and perform other labors on behalf of the Confederacy.

The rice plantations were the most vulnerable to attack, as they lay along the tidal river deltas that Union troops were attempting to enter from the Atlantic Ocean. Once the Yankees penetrated the rivers, they could move overland and destroy the heart and infrastructure of the plantation economy — source of food, raw materials, export crops, labor and revenues so vital to the Confederacy. [16]

As the Union Army moved inland, they offered freedom to the enslaved

Rice field canal and trunk gates at Hobonny Plantation on the Combahee River.

people and the opportunity to control their destiny. On June 2, 1863, three federal gunboats under the command of Colonel James Montgomery made their way up the Combahee River carrying 300 men of the 2nd South Carolina Volunteer Regiment and the Rhode Island Heavy Artillery. Accompanying Montgomery was Harriet Tubman, the heroic Underground Railroad conductor — called "Moses" by her followers — who escaped slavery in Maryland and joined the abolitionist movement in Philadelphia. Risking everything, including her own life and freedom, Tubman returned south time and again to rescue fellow African Americans from bondage.

Disguised as a field hand or a poor freedman's wife, Tubman organized and led undercover trips into the South Carolina Lowcountry where she gathered intelligence and reported it to Colonel Montgomery. Union troops made three landings along the Combahee River that June day: the third being at the Combahee Ferry, owned and operated by the Middleton family and located on the banks of Nieuport — where U.S. Highway 17 crosses the Combahee River.

Upon reaching the ferry, the Union flotilla found earthen fortifications and a pontoon bridge. Montgomery ordered the bridge destroyed and sent one unit to cross the causeway and raid the plantations along the Colleton

Tabby (mixture of oyster shells, lime, water and sand) slave dwelling at Hobonny.

side of the river. Another detachment was dispatched to proceed to Nieuport and "confiscate all property and lay waste to what could not be carried off." In his "after-action" report, Confederate Captain John Lay stated that by 6:20a.m. "the enemy had burned all the buildings at Mr. Middleton's and taken off the Negroes."

Montgomery also landed infantry soldiers in the rice fields to flush out Confederate troops that were hiding and to alert slaves to go to the river. Steamers blew whistles to signal the enslaved people to abandon the plantations and come aboard the Union ships, while Harriet Tubman shouted and sang encouragement. She later described the scene: "I never saw such a sight . . . Sometimes the women would come with twins hanging around their necks; bags on their shoulders, baskets on their heads, and young ones tagging along behind, all loaded; pigs squealing, chickens screaming, young ones squealing."

About 750 enslaved people ran to freedom that day, and hundreds of them joined the new 34th Regiment, 21st U.S. Colored Infantry. Military records and Middleton slave lists indicate that at least three of the runaways could have been from Nieuport. Colonel Montgomery enlisted Adam (Middleton), July

Priscilla Johnson in New England after gaining her freedom.

(Smalls) and Stepney (Grant) in the 34th Regiment in June 1863. The three also appear on the Nieuport slave list and cite Combahee, South Carolina as their birthplace.

News of the raid spread quickly. Yankee Surgeon Robinson reported in *Harper's Weekly*: "We destroyed a vast amount of rice, corn and cotton, stored in the barns and rice mills, with many valuable steam engines. We broke the sluice-gates [sic] and flooded the fields so that the present crop, which was growing beautifully, will be a total loss."

Locally, the Beaufort *Free South*, a pro-Union newspaper, described the destruction: "Large mansions, known to belong to notorious rebels, with all their rich furniture and rare works of art, were burned to the ground. Nothing but smoldering ruins and parched and crisp skeletons of once magnificent old live oak and palmetto groves now remain of these delightful country seats."

It is estimated that about $2 million in private property damage was sustained by planters on the Combahee. Concern over future raids led many to move their remaining enslaved people to locations away from the river. In the Middleton Place archives is a document titled, "List of negroes brought down from Combahee after the yankee raid at Nieuport, June 7th 1863." The list contains the names of 40 enslaved workers from Hobonny, Nieuport and Old Combahee plantations who were brought to Middleton Place. Later in 1865, General Sherman's forces captured Combahee Ferry before pivoting inland to Columbia. [17]

• • •

Six days after Charleston surrendered to General Quincy Gillmore on

Moro Brewer beside the Middleton family tomb following his emancipation.

February 17, 1865, Dr. Henry Marcy, a Union medical officer with the 35th U.S. Colored Infantry Regiment, arrived at Middleton Place. Williams Middleton and his overseer were nowhere to be found, and pillaging was well underway. Dr. Marcy recorded the scene in his diary: "All here was in confusion — [the slaves] had heard the news from their friends and they were making ready to leave . . . The colored people flocked around me and gave various demonstrations of joy . . . All wanted to 'shake hands' — guess this is a custom of theirs. The driver [Isaac], a very intelligent man, said he was placed in charge of a party [of slaves] and team [of horses] to go up country [at the behest of his Middleton owner], but he had contrived to get away with the whole party and return."

Also at Middleton Place was a detachment of the 56th New York Volunteers who, under the orders of Major Eliphas Smith, proceeded to burn the property. The next day Dr. Marcy was ordered by his commanding officer, Colonel Charles Van Wyck, to return there as he put it, to "do what I can to repair the damage done by Maj. S. and 56th yesterday . . . the col. [ored] people were robbed indiscriminately . . . My first object was to get the col. people together and advise them what to do — find there is a schooner and

1810 marble Wood Nymph statue, sculpted by Rudolph Schadow.

several flats here and as they are all determined to leave, I advise them to load the boats and proceed to the city."

Dr. Marcy found that "all the principle buildings were burned and are a mass of ruins. Tis very sad. Yesterday, it was the finest place I ever saw, now all destroyed . . ." Even for someone like Dr. Marcy — a White Boston surgeon serving a Black brigade, who held abolitionist tendencies — the allure of beauty and riches overshadowed the reality that Middleton Place was built on the backs of enslaved men and women.

"Accompanied by the driver [possibly Isaac]," Marcy continues, "I rode down to the [Horse] Savanna estate [owned by the Middletons across the road] five miles away. Here found about 150 slaves. Called them together and made them a little talk . . . The col. people seem happy and are making ready to leave for town."

That same year, Dr. Marcy hired Isaac's niece Priscilla Johnson — who had been born into slavery — to return north with him to care for his aging mother in Cambridge, Massachusetts. [18]

Some of the enslaved men and women may have cooperated with the 56th New York Volunteers in burning Middleton Place. Others helped save some of their Middleton owner's belongings. One was Moro Brewer, whom Williams inherited from his father. Brewer was born into slavery at Middleton Place around 1820 and served the Middletons as their trusted butler. Around 1840 he married Rachel, a laundress, and together the couple had 12 children: Betsey, Ann, Jane, Rosa, Daniel, Castle, Moro, Celia, Parker, Moses, Rebecca and Mary. Their son Moro, Jr. later followed the Union army north. [19]

Brewer helped Williams hide many family treasures, including burying china and silver, securing the Benjamin West portrait in a false wall in one of the outbuildings, hiding a portrait of Czar Nicholas, as well as the Schadow marble Wood Nymph statue and the Cerrachi marble bust of George Washington. Williams' cousin Alicia Hopton Middleton recounted the tale told by her brother Russell of the night they hid the valuables ahead of the Yankees' arrival:

"About midnight the old butler Moro, appeared, according to arrangement, with spade and shovel in hand and the three together [Williams, Russell and Brewer] took the box of china [gift from the Czar to Governor Henry Middleton], a remarkable piece of statuary in marble (a girl putting on her sandal) [the Wood Nymph] . . . and several other articles of great interest and value. A large excavation was made in the earth to receive these things, which were then covered securely and the spot marked for future recognition and carefully concealed from the eye of the enemy."

As Williams departed Middleton Place, he left Brewer in charge of the property. When the Yankees arrived, they hung him by his neck until he revealed where some of the valuable items were hidden. But he did not betray the burial site. Later Brewer would help his former enslaver locate many of the family heirlooms, including enough furniture to help restore their lodgings at Number One Meeting Street. Once freed, he took the surname of Brewer and lived at 10 Limehouse Street in Charleston, while continuing to work for the Middletons in town and on the plantation. [20]

Williams had fled Middleton Place for the safety of Springville (a summer community about 90 miles northwest in Darlington), where he rented a cottage for his family near where his brother John had brought his wife and children. It is unclear exactly when Williams and his wife, Susan, learned of Middleton's destruction. However, Susan's sister Emma wrote to her on March 11, 1865 stating that she had received Susan's letter the previous day which verified rumors she had heard previously and "could not bear to mention it to you nor had I the heart to believe it . . . Deeply do I feel for you, Mr. M. & the children, knowing how your happiness was bound up in it & its associations & well can I imagine what you must endure at the wanton desecration of the tomb of Mr. M's ancestors. It is too monstrous to dwell on & yet dwell on it we must."

The devastation of Middleton Place was felt beyond those who were immediately affected. Emma went on to write, "Our love & reverence hover round those places & memory will cling only the more tenaciously to them, because lost & irreparable." Even Dr. Marcy, who had no personal connection to the property, voiced his dismay after revisiting the property in June 1865. He wrote in his diary, "A spot once so lovely, so full of life, rich in treasures gathered from all parts of the world now so desolate and in such utter ruin! It was sad in the extreme." [21]

Meanwhile, Number One Meeting Street survived Union bombardment and more than one fire that swept through Charleston during the course of the war. But by early 1865, the house had been commandeered by Yankee officers. Once the surrender of the Confederacy was official, Williams Middleton took the Oath of Allegiance to the federal government and returned to Charleston. Later that year with the help of his brother Edward and sister Eliza, he was able to reclaim the family's Combahee River properties, his downtown mansion and his Ashley River plantation. While the buildings at Middleton Place suffered the most damage, the gardens endured their share too.

In early 1866, Williams wrote his brother-in-law Francis Fisher in Philadelphia: "As I was too lame to walk I rode round what was the garden, but which is now in most places covered with a growth of broom grass nearly three feet high. Here and there, Anthony [Anthony Alston, the gardener] had burnt round the spots where the choicest plants were growing, and I was able once more to get a look at my old pets. There were but few that did not bear witness to sufferings inflicted either by the hands of our conquerors or the feet and horns of cattle roaming about." [22]

Another sad homecoming occurred in April 1867, when Williams took his son Hal and nephew Russell to Middleton Place while they were on spring break from the College of Charleston. Williams described the scene in a letter to his sister Eliza: "We set out for M. Place, they full of their anticipation of shooting, riding & country sports generally. We crossed the river in a row boat... The carrying of our baggage for a pretty long distance on foot in our own hands threw a little shade on the glow of spirits at starting, but on arriving there the sight of the desolation all around was too much for them & evidently much more than they had been prepared for. There was no thought of frolicking after our survey of the localities."

No one in the North, complained Williams to the Fishers, could appreciate how the war had overturned "our institutions, rules, regulations, habits

Phosphate mining near Charleston after the Civil War.

& opinions & indeed everything." At the same time, he was humbled by the responsibility he personally felt for leading the South into war, observes historian Daniel Kilbride in his book *An American Aristocracy: Southern Planters in Antebellum Philadelphia* — a war whose result, Williams wrote, "was to bring ruin to four or five millions of whites, misery to almost an equal number of blacks, & loss of liberty to a whole continent full of human beings." [23]

• • •

Amid the despair and destruction, a rice planter several miles downriver from Middleton Place turned a hobby into a profitable discovery. Francis Holmes was an amateur paleontologist and had long collected fossils in the marl beds of the Ashley River. He noted that the sediment was full of ancient bones and teeth, and thus rich in phosphates. He began experimenting with the marl as a natural fertilizer and published his findings in various

Susan Pringle Smith Middleton (1822-1900), painted by Thomas Sully.

agricultural and scientific papers. Soon new technologies developed that could make water-soluble plant fertilizer out of crude phosphate. At the same time, ancient deposits of the mineral were discovered in vast fossil beds up and down the South Carolina coast.

Soils everywhere were exhausted, particularly across the South where healthy farmland and regular labor were scarce. With fewer fertile fields in operation and a greatly reduced workforce, farmers needed to extract more yield per acre. But chemical fertilizers were prohibitively expensive and difficult to obtain. Moreover, so much livestock had been lost during the Civil War, there was no longer a ready supply of manure to replenish nutrients in the soil.

In 1867 Holmes and chemist Nathaniel Pratt set out to find investors for a fertilizer plant on the Ashley River. At first they couldn't convince local businessmen to back the venture due to the uncertainty and upheaval of postwar Reconstruction. And many planters were reluctant to rent or sell their farmland for an industrial enterprise like strip mining — perceived by some of the landed gentry to be at odds with their once grand agricultural tradition. So the following year, Holmes and Pratt took their proposal north. They subsequently secured $1 million from investors in Philadelphia to establish the Charleston Mining and Manufacturing Company.

Cash-strapped plantation owners quickly got on board and sold or leased the mining rights to more than 10,000 acres of land on the Ashley River. Before long, there were a dozen phosphate mining and processing operations on the Ashley alone, including Ashley Phosphate Mining Company — formed in 1868 by Williams Middleton in partnership with investors from Baltimore. Within a few months, Williams had extracted 100 tons of phosphate rock. As Tom Shick and Don Doyle write in their history of phosphate mining, "Middleton Place began to take on the look of an industrial site as wharves, washers, drying sheds and a tram railroad were constructed on the property." [24]

Middleton Place's ample phosphate deposits gave Williams hope for future income and security. But phosphate mining and processing was an unfamiliar, grueling and dangerous business. For the first time, Williams had to pay wages and negotiate with a newly emancipated workforce. Several of his former slaves, along with other freedmen on the Ashley River, were employed at the Ashley Phosphate Company. Williams' letters from 1868 reveal the challenges he faced as well as the hardships endured by his workers: "Not easy to find labor . . . Available hands entirely without experience . . . Our mining during the recent hot spell has not been carried on as well as I should desire. The men kept at work, and many of them fainted in the pits . . ."

Williams further observed that digging phosphates "is wet work & the objection of miners to it is that it looks like times of slavery . . . our laborers are so destitute that we have to furnish them with tools and let them pay for them in labour. So, also, with regard to commissary stores — a large portion of our labour is paid for in these . . ." Enduring enormous hardships during the postwar era, the formerly enslaved who remained had to navigate a complex and capricious world of ever changing laws and labor relationships, with chronic indebtedness built into the system to ensure de facto servitude. [25]

A personal benefit of Williams' phosphate enterprise was that it required him to spend more time at Middleton Place, although he and the family had settled back at One Meeting Street after the war. Ever optimistic, Williams wrote his sister Eliza in the fall of 1868: "I am beginning to look forward to making my headquarters pretty constantly in the country. The mere going there for a few hours at a time does not enable me to carry on my business as I should desire." He hoped to put a roof and floor "to the North outhouse [the north flanker]," which would allow him to give up "the mere shell which has hitherto sheltered me."

But it was not until the spring of 1869 that Williams was able to begin even rudimentary repairs, and his plan to convert the north flanker to living quarters failed to materialize. Meanwhile the south flanker stood firm in spite of smashed windows, missing doors, broken plaster and other damage. As historian Barbara Doyle explains, "It would be necessary to nail rough boards over the window openings upstairs in order to keep it moderately warm; but the walls, although unplastered, were very thick and if fires were kept going all night, the downstairs rooms were not uncomfortable." [26]

• • •

In October 1870, mounting debt forced Williams to sell Number One Meeting. Susan Middleton wrote their son Hal, "I don't know whether we shall retire to the shades of Middleton Place or hire a small house or rooms in Charleston . . . we must go where it costs least." Should they finish the first floor of the south flanker, or stay in town? It would cost about as much to repair the lower story of the south flanker and put in sashes and doors in the upper story as to rent a house in the city for a year. The decision was finally made: they would rent hotel rooms "in that delightful village, Summerville" until they could move to Middleton Place.

Apparently little progress was made in repairing the south flanker during the next several months. Nevertheless by November 1871, Susan told Hal that his 22-year-old sister Lillie "is so anxious to go to M. Place as soon as the country is healthy [once a hard frost made it safe from malaria] I think we shall go there instead of going to Charleston and shall probably remain there until cold weather drives us out of the unfinished house. L. cannot bear the idea of returning to Charleston — she feels so much better in the country."

Two weeks later, with a wagonload of baggage and provisions, and a borrowed buggy for themselves, the Middletons moved from their hotel in Summerville to "the dear old wreck" of Middleton Place. Assisted by one of his phosphate workers, Williams immediately set about securing the south flanker. Doors were installed, cracks were filled, and floor boards put down. "As for the 'dear old muzzy,'" Susan related to Hal, "she is knocking about as usual with a finger in every pie sometimes overwhelmed with the recollection of the past in contrast with the present and then working bravely on with the hope of preventing the dear old place going entirely to ruin."

Lillie was delighted to be once more at Middleton Place. She informed brother Hal of their father's fruitless efforts to spear a particular trout in the reflection pool, but "its life is not in <u>immediate</u> danger as Papa has undertaken to put a seat round the oak tree [the Middleton Oak] by the Rosary, & seems quite absorbed in his work." More serious was the damage being done in the garden at night by a herd of feral hogs. "The wild animals in these parts are quite too smart for us."

Lillie continued:

"You ask how we amuse ourselves here . . . We walk about the garden, trim the overgrown shrubs, pick up [Spanish] moss, and occasionally when the weather is fine I rake the leaves or collect camellia seeds. The house is very much as you left it. Papa has ordered window sashes for the North room, but the man promised them three weeks ago, and they have not yet 'put in an appearance.' We are thinking of whitewashing the bricks inside to look like plaster for the walls. Mamma advises that the lower story be made close, and boards be put over the staircase opening, as we cannot afford to put sashes in the upper story. It is not at all necessary for our small family to have any more rooms.

"You need not worry yourself about our suffering from cold, as Anthony keeps us well supplied with wood, and Papa builds roaring fires. I am very actively employed in killing spiders in the house . . . Papa is waiting for a good day to burn off the lawn and the slopes. Sometimes it is too cold, sometimes too wet, so I do not know when we will have a chance. The garden looks very well, but the frost has burnt up all the camellias which were so beautiful when we first arrived." [27]

• • •

Between 1872 and 1873, the Ashley Phosphate Mining Company burned to the ground. Williams was tempted to finally let go of Middleton Place, but his brother-in-law, Francis Fisher, convinced him to hang on to the property and lease it to an outside phosphate operator named Julien Fishburne. Though short-lived, mining on the Ashley River laid the groundwork for industrialization and new economic development in postwar Charleston. And while phosphates failed to bring Williams personal riches, "the prospect had caused him to hold on to his property," notes Barbara Doyle, "and make it habitable again, instead of selling it as he at one time planned to do." Thus, according to Doyle, phosphates produced a result of arguably far greater consequence: the conservation and preservation of Middleton Place. [28]

Combined revenues from mining, farming, timber cutting and milling continued to provide modest employment for the freedmen on the place. A

A camellia allée at Middleton Place.

few formerly enslaved persons — including Chloe Brown, her husband, Ned, and their daughter Catherine, along with gardener July Wright — returned to Middleton Place to work in exchange for housing and token wages. Ned had been a "driver" or field supervisor for the plantation and Chloe a nursemaid. She was one of 30 enslaved workers whom Susan brought to the estate as part of her dowry when she married Williams in 1849. Others, such as Hercules Prioleau, found work on neighboring lands. Before Prioleau died, he chose to be buried at Horse Savanna across from Middleton Place.

One of Williams' early endeavors following the war was to build "Negro houses" to replace those burned by Union soldiers. Around 1870 he completed construction of a two-family, frame dwelling now known as Eliza's House — named for Eliza Leach, the last person to live there and which today serves as an African American interpretive center. Eliza's House was home to several African Americans, some of whom were born into slavery and others who were born free.

Ned and Chloe Brown appear to have been early occupants. Ansel Horlbeck, who tended the gardens and served as general caretaker from the late 1800s until after World War I, probably lived in the house too. Gardener Anthony Alston also stayed on at Middleton and worked for wages. However, he chose to establish a home in Summerville where he founded the First Baptist Church. [29]

Following the sale of One Meeting Street, Williams undertook a full restoration of the south flanker at Middleton Place — the least damaged of its structures. Archival papers show that the family occupied the building while construction work was in progress. Neither money nor labor nor materials were readily available; thus, it took more than a season to complete.

The gardener July served as a carpenter on the project, as recorded in a letter Williams wrote to his son Hal in 1871: "Though this is slow work with July as carpenter to help me, still we have made considerable progress." A few years later, Williams wrote his sister Eliza that "by dint of hard work in another line we have been able to make habitable another room in our house..." By 1875, tax records show a total of nine structures at Middleton Place. Except for the sun porch (added in the 1930s), the south flanker — now a house museum — appears today much as it did following Williams' restoration. [30]

• • •

The year 1870 was when the Reverend John Grimke Drayton opened his gardens to the public at nearby Magnolia Plantation in order to generate much needed income. Northerners had begun wintering in Florida, and on their way home in spring, would step off the train in Charleston and board a small steamship to travel up the Ashley River. Amid ruin and decay, Magnolia Gardens would appear like an apparition, beckoning visitors to come ashore. *Harper's New Monthly Magazine* contributor Constance Fenimore Woolson described the scene in 1875:

"The garden, in its present beauty, has been in existence only 10 or 15 years, although Magnolia had, of course, the usual garden and live oaks of the Ashley plantations . . . seven persons, touching fingertips, can just encircle the trunks of some of the live oaks here; there are camellias 18 and 20 feet high . . . There are also many rare trees and shrubs . . . But the glory of the garden is the gorgeous coloring of the azaleas, some of the bushes 16 and 17 feet through by 12 feet high, others 19 and 20 feet through by 13 feet high — solid masses of blossoms in all the shades of red, from palest pink to deepest crimson, and now and then a pure white bush, like a bride in her snowy lace. It is almost impossible to give a Northerner an idea of the affluence of color in this garden when its flowers are in bloom."

In the same article, entitled "Up the Ashley and Cooper," Woolson encounters Middleton Place, not yet open to the public: "A few miles above Magnolia are the ruins of Middleton Place, once one of the most beautiful plantations in South Carolina. This was the home of Arthur Middleton, a signer of the Declaration of Independence. Here he lived and here he died. The old oaks, the hedges, the elaborate terraces and ponds, still remain, but the place is deserted, and the spirit of melancholy broods over it." [31]

By the 1880s, Williams had signed a contract with the *Silver Star*, a "fast and safe steamer." It left Charleston's Central Wharf every Tuesday morning at 9a.m. in the spring to take visitors to Middleton Place and Magnolia Gardens. Neither Susan nor Lillie liked having boatloads of strangers wandering around the grounds. Lillie writes in 1883: "I see the steamboat is to go every Tuesday to M. Place, or as they call it, the 'Middleton Barony,' those celebrated gardens, etc." Later as the tours expanded, she comments, "I am sorry Papa intends to have Sunday crowds at Middleton Place, but of course

19th century brochure advertising steamer tours up the Ashley River.

there is no use arguing the point if he is bent upon it. He is so anxious to have 'company' it is quite useless to say anything."

For Williams, the gardens had become as great a passion for him as the house. He also hoped that tour revenues would help maintain the 16 structures now populating the plantation. His letters to his sister and her husband in Philadelphia frequently mention improvements he intends to make, or has already made; but he confesses in a lament any gardener can understand, "Oh Lord, there is much yet to be done." Williams wanted others to enjoy the azaleas, camellias and myriad plant specimens, both native and exotic; and most of all, to have the fame and beauty of the celebrated gardens once again acknowledged. But he had little time left to enjoy his garden or the excursionists. His health was deteriorating and on August 23, 1883, Williams died at the age of 74. [32]

• • •

Through tremendous effort and sometimes miraculous circumstance, Williams, Susan and Lillie held on to their storied family seat. They prevailed with the help of financial and moral support from Eliza and Francis Fisher and numerous relatives, combined with income from phosphate mining, timbering and other endeavors — and sustained by the labor and loyalty of the African American workers, and the Middleton family's own indefatigable spirit. While despairing at times of being able to repair and maintain what generation after generation viewed as their legacy, the Middletons recognized an obligation to preserve their ancestral property for the sake of family and posterity.

Moreover, without the ingenuity and steadfastness of the formerly enslaved African Americans — men and women such as Moro and Rachel Brewer, Ned and Chloe Brown, Ansel and Molsey Horlbeck, and Annette Mayes and her husband — Middleton Place would surely have been lost. The plantation owes its continued existence as much to the Black families and their descendants as to the Middletons themselves. They all had a hand in its survival. [33]

"Reine des Fleurs" is the last remaining of the four *Camellia japonica* planted at Middleton Place by André Michaux, according to family history.

Four

WHERE FLOWERS BLOOM

Two decades after the Civil War, Middleton Place and Charleston suffered another upheaval — this time of seismic proportion. On August 31, 1886, an earthquake between 6.9 and 7.3 magnitude on the Richter scale erupted at 9:51p.m. along a fault line between Summerville and Charleston. The quake was felt as far away as Boston, Chicago and Cuba, but an area from the Ashley River corridor to Charleston took the brunt of its destruction. Eighty-three people died and almost all the city's buildings experienced damage. An estimated 14,000 chimneys fell, multiple fires ignited, water lines and wells ruptured, and railroad tracks split apart. Total damage exceeded $5.5 million, or about $112 million in today's dollars. It was the strongest earthquake to ever strike the Southeast. [1]

Ironically, the aftermath of the Great Shock of 1886 presented an opportunity for reconciliation and rebuilding in the wake of the Civil War. In their book *Upheaval in Charleston,* authors Susan Millar Williams and Stephen Hoffius describe how many 19th century Blacks and Whites of Lowcountry South Carolina had been somewhat accustomed to living side by side; but the events of 1886 brought them into even closer physical and economic proximity. In the days following the earthquake, integrated tent camps popped up in Charleston's parks, and free food and shelter were provided to the poor. The widespread destruction also enabled the city's Black craftsmen to command higher wages and better working conditions.

Aid and funds poured into Charleston from the northern states. Hundreds of African Americans fled the impoverished countryside seeking assistance in the city. Abolitionist John Greenleaf Whittier exhorted northerners to give generously: "New England in this matter knows no North and no South, and if . . . any old jealousies and resentments remain they should be swept away in the flood of practical sympathy for our afflicted fellow countrymen." One Union veteran stated, "We were her bitterest enemy a quarter of a century ago: let us be her most earnest friends now."

The enormous relief effort, however, infuriated those Whites who feared any measures that might empower Blacks. Instead of seizing on an opportunity for renewal, most of South Carolina's ruling elite reverted to the old ways, having regained their ascendancy in the 1876 election deal that ended federal occupation and the prospect for reform. Within a decade, South Carolina passed a new constitution legalizing segregation and disenfranchising Black voters, laying the groundwork for more than a half-century of what became known as Jim Crow laws. As bestselling author Pat Conroy observed, Charleston's "collective unconscious [was still] simmering with angry memories of bombardment and Reconstruction." [2]

• • •

Up the Ashley River, the ruins that remained of Middleton Place had been gradually eroding since being torched at the end of the war. In 1874 Williams wrote his sister Eliza, "The elements are fast doing their work [on the main house] . . . the walls are falling pretty rapidly." In 1881 he reported that the sun porch had been blown down in a storm. Five years later, the earthquake delivered its blow, with the epicenter at Middleton Place.

Geological Survey team member Earle Sloan visited Middleton Place three weeks after the quake and documented the damage: "The ceilings in the remaining south flanker were severely cracked, and the chimneys were badly injured. The power of the earthquake was evident . . . destroying what little was left of the burnt-out walls of the main house." [3]

The Middletons were not in residence when the "Great Shock" struck. Williams had died three years earlier in Greenville, South Carolina. His widow, Susan, remained in the upstate to live with their daughter Lillie and her husband, Julius Heyward, who had been married at Middleton Place in 1881. Meanwhile Lillie's brother, Hal, had settled permanently in England since entering Cambridge University in 1878. With everyone scattered, the plantation was the family's anchor.

Irishman Patrick Dolan — hired to manage Middleton Place — was probably not there either. He and his wife and daughters left every summer to escape the threat of malaria. But it is likely that formerly enslaved workers Ansel Horlbeck and July Wright, as well as Ned and Chloe Brown and their daughter Catherine, were on site for the great upheaval. July's daughter

The family pictured in front of the south flanker is believed to be that of Patrick Dolan, manager of Middleton Place in the late 1800s. The south flanker was the sole surviving building of the house complex after the earthquake of 1886.

Annette Mayes, who remained at Middleton after emancipation to work as a cook and maid, also might have experienced what one observer termed "the night of Sodom and Gomorrah." Annette had married Smart May, and with their five children were living in a tenant house on Middleton property along Ashley River Road.

Middleton descendant and artist Alice Ravenel Huger Smith was 10 years old at the time of the earthquake. She and her parents and siblings were living with her grandmother at 69 Church Street in Charleston. In her *Reminiscences* of 1950, written at the age of 74, she recalled that fateful evening: "The walls vibrated in dead earnest on that terrifying night of August 31st [1886] . . . When the roar of the earthquake, and the menacing movement of our friend, the solid earth, began — when the big, square brick house

Alice Ravenel Huger Smith at Middleton Place. She painted Josephine Smith Duell as a young girl in this same tree, on the opposite side.

which had always seemed to us akin to the Rock of Gibraltar began that disconcerting tremor and thud, there was instant reaction, a recognition of a hitherto totally unexpected and unknown force... The earthquake shook only its walls, but the war just past had shaken the souls of those who were now sheltered by them." [4]

• • •

Buildings and souls were not the only entities impacted by the mighty rupture, which burst some 12 miles below the earth's surface and shook Middleton Place for approximately one minute. Geologist Earle Sloan noted

Miss Josephine Smith [mother of Charles Duell] *in Oak with Peacock,* by Alice Smith.

"indications of increased violence on the grounds. The earth was severely disturbed and innumerable craterlets had appeared. Some were eight feet across . . . still actively spewing water." Sloan also observed that when the quake hit, "large fissures appeared in the earth, ripping open the garden's terraces. The landscape rolled like a flag waving horizontally; and the Butterfly Lakes at the bottom of the terraces were sucked dry." [5]

Six years later in 1892, teenager Alice Smith would walk to Middleton Place and back with her father, Daniel Huger Smith, and cousin Julian Wells. In her memoir, Smith reflects on that visit: "All the world goes there now, bowling along a paved road. It is a mere nothing as a trip, but then it was something. The girls of my generation were not 'athletic,' we had no golf or tennis, but we could walk. So with my Father and cousin I did 15 miles there and 15 miles back, with the good earth and grass under foot. Sometimes we toiled through sand that made us really work over every step . . .

"Middleton Place was beautiful — a jewel thrown down in the green woods. We strolled through its paths under the great oaks looking out across the fields and the river. We had no lack of history there. The settlement of the Colony and the growth of its laws and government brought one noted figure after another to walk those paths with us, and the Revolution brought another group for me to imagine. There was many another plantation that could match it in history and romance, but I had walked a long, long way to take part with these especial gatherings under these especial oaks, and I did not waste the opportunity."

In the ensuing decades, Alice Smith returned to Middleton Place time and again to sketch and paint. She captured its riotous blooms, primeval trees and haunting landscape like no other artist. As she put it, "I have painted this country. I have loved this country; painted it the better because I have loved it, and loved it the more because of those dear days when slowly jogging down the quiet roads one had to be intimate with the grass on the ground and the trees overhead; because each blade of grass, and each branch of the tree was so definitely a companion, and yourself not a hasty, careless passerby." [6]

Not long after young Alice Smith's long walk, her cousin Lillie (nearly a generation older) pasted in her copybook a well-known poem of the era titled "Everybody's Garden," by William Zachary Gladwin. Published in Henry Ward Beecher's *Christian Union* magazine, Gladwin's lines must have reflected the joy and hope that family and friends derived from the Middleton gardens in those days of turmoil, depravation and decay:

"... *Come out, with hearts of gladness, ye big and little children,*
Into our Father's garden, made for our strolling feet.
The flitting butterfly,
The fragrant winds that sigh.
The tiny clouds that hover above us in the blue,
The bird's song high and clear,
Make heaven draw more near.
In everybody's garden the world once more is new!"

• • •

Pilgrimages to "the dear old place" were an important ritual for both immediate and distant relatives. No doubt Lillie longed for the comfort of Middleton Place when her mother, Susan, died suddenly in 1900. Estranged from her brother Hal and somewhat isolated in the Upcountry, Lillie (age 51) suffered from poor eyesight and other afflictions. But like her father, Williams Middleton, she persevered, especially when it came to the management and reputation of Middleton Place — which she now owned with Hal and oversaw from Greenville.

Lillie continued phosphate mining and lumbering operations on the plantation into the early 1900s, signing a lease agreement with the United Timber Company. She also allowed hunting parties to shoot deer, fox and other wild game on the property. Before long, brother Hal, perpetually strapped for cash, sold his portion of the estate to his sister for the sum of $10,000. In doing so, he relinquished all claim to his ancestral home, making Lillie the sole owner of Middleton Place and approximately 8,000 acres. [7]

Ansel Horlbeck, manager of Middleton Place in the early 1900s.

By this time former enslaved worker Ansel Horlbeck had been hired to manage the plantation, as indicated in a letter that Lillie penned from Greenville to her first cousin Emeline Middleton in the spring of 1902: "I heard from Polly Coxe that you and your mother and brother were in Charleston, and thought it possible that you would like to go to Middleton Place to spend the day. I therefore enclose you a card [decorated with ribbons and signed by Lillie] for you to give to Ansell Horlbeck, the negro who is at present in charge of our Place. If you will tell Ansell that you are the daughter of my

1928 photograph of the butterfly lakes by Frances Benjamin Johnston.

Uncle, I think he will show you every attention."

Lillie went on to advise the party how to reach the plantation and the best time to visit: ". . . in order to get to Middleton Place [if not by boat], you must take an early train to Summerville, hire a carriage at the Pine Forest Inn (or some other livery stable) to drive 10 miles to Middleton Place. You must also be sure that the driver knows the way, as country roads are very confusing to strangers . . .

"If you expect to be in Charleston for a week or two you had better postpone your trip to Middleton Place as long as possible because the camellias are now over, and the weather has been so cool that the azaleas are just now beginning to bloom. I should like you to see the garden when it is in its full beauty, as the flower-show is then very fine. We have hundreds of azalea plants but Polly said that the azaleas in Magnolia were not in full bloom, and ours come out even later in the season." [8]

Clearly caretaker Ansel Horlbeck had his hands full. He and his wife, Molsey, lived on the plantation in the two-family, frame cottage built by

Williams Middleton after the Civil War. At the time, it was located just steps from the south flanker, where Lillie stayed while she was in residence and where former slave Annette Mayes served as housekeeper. While managing the farming operation — which included a dairy — and maintaining numerous buildings and structures on the property, Ansel also tended the gardens. Lillie came down from Greenville periodically to do what she could, but inevitably nature began to overtake the paths and terraces, creating a "jungle of overgrowth."

• • •

In spite of the distressed appearance of the gardens, Lillie continued to answer more and more requests from people wishing to visit Middleton Place. She fielded inquiries from horticulture enthusiasts, writers, artists and curious northerners. According to landscape designer and historian Virginia Lopez Begg, such intense interest reflected an American phenomenon called "garden fever" — an obsession that began in the 1890s and continued until World War II. "As Americans recoiled from a machine-dominated way of life," Begg explains, "many developed a new interest in nature and expressed it in a variety of ways: the founding of national parks, the Audubon movement and, above all, gardening. Old gardens, their roots deep in American history, seemed to weave together many of these cultural threads. Where better to find old gardens than Charleston?" 9

Country Life in America and *The Century Magazine*, popular periodicals with broad circulation, were sending authors south to write about Charleston gardens. Magnolia Plantation was already a well-known destination among horticulture enthusiasts, having been open to the public since 1870. Magnolia's gardens had become a major business venture of owner John Grimke Drayton and his descendants, the Hastie family. In contrast, Middleton Place had received minimal care due to meager finances and the fact that no family members lived there. Many of the paths were overgrown, the Butterfly Lakes silted in, and the old shrubs and trees desperately in need of pruning.

Lillie was sensitive to the way in which Middleton Place would appear to the rest of the world and careful about whom she granted access. In 1906 *Country Life* sent photographer Herbert Angell to the plantation, but Lillie disliked the results and refused to allow his photographs to be published.

She explained to editor Wilhelm Miller: "I do not think that any pictures taken when the azaleas and the camellias are not in bloom could do the garden justice, and under such circumstances would always object to their being published. I told Mr. Angell so when he was at M- Place, and I certainly understood him to say that he had been sent too early in the season. I asked him if he could return, but he said he did not think so as he had other engagements. He said also that the azaleas at Magnolia were in full bloom and I am sure if photos were taken at Magnolia when there were no flowers in the garden, that Mrs. Hastie would not wish to have them published."

Again, like her father, Lillie dreamed of restoring Middleton Place to its former grandeur. In her same letter to Miller, she states, "Since Mr. Angell took those views of the house, a new room has been put on, every window in the house has been taken out, changed and painted, so it does not look at all like those pictures, now. In the Fall the open terraces and balustrades, will be added, and the ornaments, put on the top, to make it look as much like an old English house as possible. I have also a plan for building on top of the ruins so the whole Place will be changed . . . In the meantime, I trust you will continue to take an interest in the old place, and believe me with kind regards, Very cordially [yours], E. M. Heyward."

In a postscript at the end of her letter, Lillie admonishes Miller for breaching an important point of etiquette: "As I am not a widow, pray do not write to me as Mrs. E. M. Heyward. My name is Mrs. Julius H. Heyward." Despite the "many gardens belonging to millionaires" in the North, Lillie — even in her reduced circumstances — could proudly assert her standing as a southern aristocrat, and as owner and steward of an "old fashioned garden." [10]

• • •

Another visitor that year was poet Amy Lowell, who took a sympathetic and rather melancholy view of the destitute Lowcountry. As *South Carolina Historical Magazine* editor Elise Pinckney writes, ". . . it remained for the Massachusetts writer Amy Lowell to articulate more than gloom — an abysmal negativeness — no better for being poetical. She came to Charleston in the spring of 1906, and wrote of 'O loveliness of old decaying, haunted things . . .' and 'There is no dawn here, only sunset.' "

According to Pinckney, the poet's excursion to Middleton Place "released

THE CENTURY MAGAZINE

Vol. LXXX   OCTOBER, 1910   No. 6

AN OLD-TIME CAROLINA GARDEN

BY FRANCES DUNCAN

Author of "Charleston Gardens," "The Gardens of Cornish," etc.

WITH PICTURES BY ANNA WHELAN BETTS

QUITE alone among American gardens stands the rare old estate in South Carolina known as Middleton Place. It represents a phase of colonial life which has vanished completely, and belongs to the days when South Carolina was a royal province and, like the mother-country, had its hereditary and wealthy aristocracy.

Beside the Ashley River, some seventeen miles above Charleston, past Runnymede, past Magnolia of the famous azaleas, past Drayton Hall, and opposite where once was the town of Dorchester, lie the old pleasure-gardens, as elaborate in form and beautiful in line as when, before the Revolution, the "gardens of Mr. Middleton of Carolina" were of note in England, and ranked with the foremost English estates of two centuries ago.

There is something refreshing in the serenity with which the early Southern colonists, menaced constantly by the Indians, annoyed by growing disaffection with the home government, established themselves. It was in no tentative fashion: they made stately homes, goodly and extensive gardens, in the wildernesses of the new country, building for themselves and their children's children.

In the early colonial days, the wealth and luxury of the South was concentrated at Charleston, or Charles Town, as it was then called. Crèvecœur, who visited the city in 1765, was astonished at the elegance and affluence of the life and at the sumptuousness of the entertainments. Charleston was the social and political center, while within a radius of about twenty miles, beside the Ashley and the Cooper rivers and along the sinuous curves of the lovely little stream known as the Goosecreek, were the country estates of the planters, many of them with large and much-embellished gardens, such as "Crowfield,"[1] on the Goosecreek, with its spacious walks, bowling-green, and "fish-ponds properly disposed which form a fine Pros-

[1] The estate of Arthur Middleton, President of the Council and Royal Governor of Carolina. It was called Crowfield after the place of that name in Suffolk, the seat of the English Middletons.

Copyright, 1910, by THE CENTURY CO. All rights reserved.

The Century Magazine 1910 feature article on Middleton Place, by Frances Duncan.

her imagination," as evidenced in the oft quoted line:

"Step lightly down these terraces, they are records of a dream . . ."

Lowell became infatuated with "The Middleton Place" — the title she gave her subsequent poem — and vowed to return. In 1922, then quite famous and on a lecture and poetry reading circuit, she visited Middleton again.

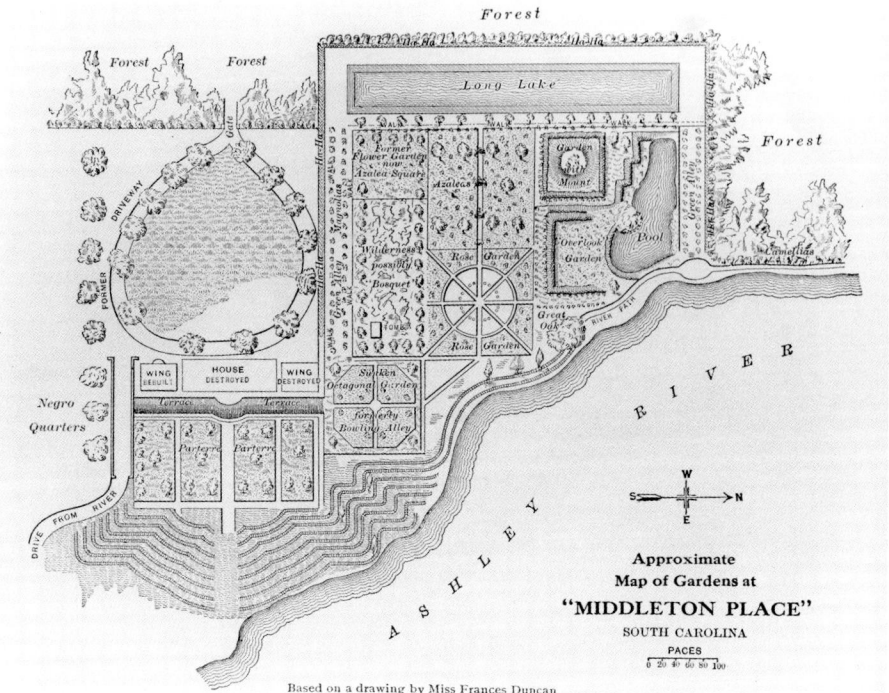

Frances Duncan's garden diagram.

As Pinckney relates, "She found the [Middleton] Place cleared of its jungle of overgrowth and as lovely as ever. A ride in the country was described in an emotional poem: 'Do anything to drown the screaming silence of this forest . . . What mystic adventure is this/In which you have engulfed me.' " Still, Lowell held to her mournful theme:

"Sunset wanes along the quiet river.
The afterglow is haunted and nostalgic,
Over the yellow woodland it hangs like the dying chord of a funeral chant;
And evenly, satirically, the mosses move to its ineffable rhythm,
Like the ostrich fans of palsied dowagers
Telling one another contentedly of the deaths they have lived to see." [11]

That same spring of 1906, a second northern woman of letters found her way to Middleton Place — prominent garden writer Frances Duncan. It was her idea to write a series of stories on "old Southern gardens," appealing to *Century Magazine* editor Richard Watson Gilder, an advocate of reconciliation between North and South. Gilder was attuned to the growing interest in Charleston and the area's gardens. Their mystery, beauty and deterioration were products of a grand and tragic chapter of American history — a source of intrigue for *Century*'s cosmopolitan readership.

In her proposal to Gilder, Duncan explains: "This magnificent old estate lying forgotten among the wilds fascinates me . . . I don't know a place in this country which touches it. Of course, it is now in a state of decay. The house with its splendid library & art treasures was destroyed by Sherman and is now desolate except for a wing left; much of the garden has gone back to the wild, some obliterated, but you would be as fascinated with the place as we were.

"Today Miss Betts [illustrator Ann Whelan Betts] & I went lunchless until five o'clock, she sketching & I working out a plan of the original garden. What I want to do is this: Reconstruct the place, show it in the days when it was really a barony — when it was noted as a garden even in England . . . The present Middletons have no money, the owner of Middleton Place [Lillie Middleton Heyward] will not allow visitors nor cameras — nor Northerners!! . . . You can imagine the wires to be pulled in order to see Middleton Place, for its present owner Mrs. Hayward [sic] is very peculiar. Even her near relations thought we might not be allowed to land . . . in fact it has taken all this time [nearly three weeks] to make the thing possible."

Indeed, Frances Duncan persevered and was able to win Lillie's permission to visit Middleton Place. Duncan then persuaded Charleston harbormaster Colonel Armstrong to ferry her and Miss Betts up the Ashley River and deposit them at the plantation on April 29. It would be several years before Duncan's story — "An Old-Time Carolina Garden" — would appear in the October 1910 issue of *Century Magazine*. Not only was it the lead article, according to landscape historian Virginia Lopez Begg, it was also the first full account of the Middleton gardens in a national publication. [12]

• • •

Frances Duncan had worked and studied at Long Island's renowned Parsons Nursery, a concern responsible for propagating and introducing many Asian shrubs and trees to American gardens. She was also well versed in the

The garden's main axis begins at the Ashley River Road (top), then intersects the main house complex and descends the terraces to the river.

classic texts of landscape design. Thus when she arrived in South Carolina, according to Begg, "she knew what she was seeing."

"Quite alone among American gardens," Duncan begins her *Century* article, "stands the rare old estate in South Carolina known as Middleton Place. It represents a phase of colonial life which has vanished completely, and belongs to the days when South Carolina was a royal province and, like the mother country, had its hereditary and wealthy aristocracy . . . To this day, the lines of the original gardens have been kept and Middleton Place is essentially as it was in 1750."

She continues, "The story is, that in 1740 Henry Middleton put 50 men [enslaved Africans] to work in the gardens, and kept them working there for 10 years. For half a mile up the river the bank was terraced; it was half a mile from the house to the entrance gates; the pleasance [enclosed garden] is a mile in circumference, and beyond it, in the old days, the forest on the west and north was open for hundreds of acres, with vistas as in the Forest of Fontainebleau . . .

"At Middleton Place the river curves upon itself, so that, from the terrace before the house, the view is directly down it; and the broad walk which divides the parterre below seems to invite one to go down it and down the river. In the gardener's parlance, not only is the garden on an axis with the house, as all good gardens should be, but by taking advantage of a happy chance, the house seems to have been on an axis with the river as well, and it is a charming effect."

Most significant of all, Duncan drew a garden diagram to accompany her article. As Begg notes, it is the earliest known plan of the celebrated gardens. After much time and study spent at Middleton Place, Duncan "documented existing conditions almost a half-century after the Civil War and about a decade before the extensive restoration undertaken by J.J. Pringle Smith and his wife, Heningham Ellet Smith." Duncan consulted with an unnamed "favorite cousin" of Lillie's (J.J.P. Smith perhaps), along with an "elderly lawyer" (Judge H.A.M. Smith most likely), as well as several Charlestonians who were long familiar with the Middleton gardens. They shared invaluable information about Middleton Place and helped her see what would have been obscured by years of neglect and nature's reclamation. [13]

• • •

Duncan's detailed diagram was featured prominently in the *Century* article. Begg asserts that the illustration "brought Middleton Place to the attention of the nation's cultural elite for both its inherent excellence in design, and its value as an icon of the Colonial Revival." Despite the fact that no earlier drawings of the gardens have been found, there are numerous 18th century verbal references. In 1760, Dr. Alexander Garden noted that Henry Middleton had a "fine garden about 12 or 14 miles up Ashley River." Later in 1791, painter John Trumbull wrote that Middleton Place "is a very handsome house in the style of the old English Country seats on the River side, where much Labour has been employed to distort nature, and to transform a very pleasing variety of Grounds into regular terraces adorned with straight Rows of Trees." [14]

Trumbull's remarks about the effort "to distort Nature," and his references to "regular terraces" and the "straight Rows of Trees" suggest an adherence to the garden philosophy of French landscape architect Andre Le Notre. English gardens at the time reflected the influence of Le Notre's design principles, which had been introduced from France following the 1660 restoration of

King Charles II. Like many 18th century Carolinians, Henry and Mary Middleton copied the fashions and tastes of the mother country. Their English gardener, George Newman, would have been well versed in the Frenchman's landscape doctrine. More than likely, he and the Middletons consulted a popular book of the day called *The Theory and Practice of Gardening*, authored by Le Notre's student Dezalier d'Argenville.

Born in 1613, Le Notre was the third generation of his family to become a royal gardener. As Helen Fox notes in her biography of Le Notre, he "perfected the classical style of gardening, which had grown from Mediterranean roots and developed slowly through the centuries." He remade the park of the Tuileries, remodeled the gardens at Fontainbleau, drew the Champs Elysees, and planned hundreds of estates in France, England and elsewhere in Europe. Most notably, Le Notre designed the palace gardens of Versailles, Chantilly, Saint-Cloud and Vaux-le-Vicomte.

Landscape architecture professor Dr. Reuben Rainey of the University of Virginia highlights the similarities between the formal garden pattern at Vaux-le-Vicomte and that of Middleton Place: "As at Middleton Place, Le Notre's gardens featured a broad terrace, with its main axis flowing outward from the residence, and a geometric series of gardens on either side of its length. Foreshortened perspectives masked exciting visual discoveries, much as the Butterfly Lakes at Middleton Place suddenly come into view from the end of the main axial walk. Le Notre's subtle use of water vistas is replicated in Middleton's incorporation of river, ponds and lakes as 'water mirrors' that reflect the ever-changing light of the sun and the sky. Furthermore, the geometry of Middleton Place suggests that it was deliberately laid out on a triangular grid, just as Le Notre used a grid to plan his own formal designs."

"By Le Notre's time," according to Helen Fox, "house and garden were indivisible and complemented each other. Generally, the garden began with a broad terrace which was part of the house while its main axis flowed out from the principal doorway and often had a series of room-like enclosures on either side of its length. Ponds and fountains were planned to be on axis with windows so as to be seen from certain rooms. Like the house, the outlines of the garden were geometrical and the plan either symmetrical or balanced." Rational order, geometry and balance, combined with vistas, focal points and surprises were the order of the day.

But as garden historian Denise Otis observes, the symmetry at the core of

Garden rooms and geometric shapes provide a sense of order and discovery, inspired by Descartes and Le Nôtre.

Middleton's axis "relaxes at the edges into a balanced composition, adjusted to the topography." She argues in her book, *Grounds for Pleasure: Four Centuries of the American Garden,* that skilled designers in Le Notre's architectural style "took advantage of inequalities in the terrain to create variety; and their designs, while measurably ordered, were not rigidly symmetrical." Furthermore, American aristocrats typically had less money and resources than their European counterparts, according to Middleton Place Foundation CEO Tracey Todd. This increased the need to work with and incorporate the natural landscape.

In adapting Le Notre's concepts to their own gardens, both English and Americans inevitably modified the French style to conform to local conditions, gradually producing what became known as the "landscape garden" (or later replicated by the French as "le Jardin Anglais"). This garden form emphasized working *with* the natural topography and attributes of a site, rather than imposing on it an artificially contrived and rigid design. Planned vistas echoed the scenes of favorite landscape painters of the day. The landscape gardener, working in tones of green, was concerned like the painter with chiaroscuro, the use of light and shade. But living trees and shrubs, not gilt frames, defined his compositions. [15]

The architectural garden reigned well beyond Le Notre's death in 1700 and captivated colonial America. "Cultured people in the 18th century," according to historian Hugh Howard, "regarded the shaping of a landscape as a fine art . . . man's attempt to impose a rigid vision upon the landscape at a time when random forces — such as disease, death and extremes of weather — were regular reminders that nature would not be tamed." And as the Garden Club of America notes in its two-volume reference work *Gardens of Colony and State,* "Middleton Place, with its magnificent terraces and extensive architectural layout, is the only example remaining in this country of an important landscape development of the 18th century."

No doubt Henry Middleton considered himself a product of the Enlightenment, as did Carter Burwell, who began an ambitious landscape plan for his Virginia tobacco plantation, Carter's Grove, in 1751. Both men viewed the practice of landscape architecture as an expression of the perfectibility of man, society and nature. For many planters and statesmen of America's Eastern Seaboard, horticulture especially symbolized the potential of science to advance economic and social progress. It also reflected an increasingly connected world of trade, communication and empire. [16]

• • •

While Mary and Henry Middleton are credited with laying the foundation of the Middleton gardens in the 1740s and 50s — shaping an enduring structure and exacting aesthetic — it is to subsequent generations Middleton Place owes its full flowering. Following Mary and Henry came their son, the revolutionary Arthur (1742-1787), whose own son Henry eventually met Frenchman Andre Michaux, the official botanist to King Louis XVI. Michaux came to the United States in 1785 to collect North American plants and seeds for shipment back to France and the Royal Botanical Gardens.

Michaux landed first in New York, where he set about procuring plant material and creating a specimen garden in New Jersey. As biologist and historian Richard Porcher documents in his *Guide to the Wildflowers of South Carolina*, the French botanist realized he needed a warmer climate and moved to Charleston in the fall of 1786. Thirteen miles outside of town — near the present-day Charleston airport — Michaux purchased 111 acres to establish a garden nursery. For the next decade, it served as Michaux's base of operation, where he grew numerous native plants and exotic species from around the world.

During his 11 years in North America, according to Dr. Porcher, "Michaux named 26 genera, 188 species and 4 varieties [of plants]. He also named 95 species and varieties that botanists have since placed in other genera." While he was collecting and growing American natives, Michaux also shared a number of plants he had brought from Europe and Asia with various Charlestonians, including the Pinckneys, the Draytons and the Middletons. He introduced to Middleton Place, and to the nation, many species from overseas, including the mimosa, crepe myrtle, chinaberry, ginkgo, tea olive and *Camellia japonica* — horticultural glories that have graced the Middleton gardens for more than 200 years. [17]

Mary and Henry Middleton's grandson, Henry the second (1770-1846) — in addition to serving as governor of South Carolina, U.S. congressman and minister to Russia — was an enthusiastic botanist. His friendship with Michaux engendered in the young man a lifelong passion for horticulture. In one plant order to England, Henry purchased 253 different species, including 52 types of flower seeds, 54 sorts of bulbs, 71 hardy herbaceous plants, 41 varieties of greenhouse plants and 35 kinds of vegetable seeds. [18]

With Michaux's encouragement, Henry planted many more camellias at Middleton Place, as well as tea olive and crepe myrtle. His "Tree List" (including shrubs) is one of the earliest documents about the gardens. The list, as described by Elise Pinckney for the *South Carolina Historical Magazine*, records "five varieties of oaks, four of pine, poplar, flowering maple, buckeye, catalpa, umbrella magnolia, dogwood, fringe tree, redbud, holly, as well as mountain laurel, euonymus, trumpet honeysuckle, jessamine, sweet shrub (calycanthus), and century plant." Henry also notes in his diary the blooming of violets, jasmine, arrowhead, andromeda, wild orange, roses and sassafras.

Henry's wife, Mary Helen Hering Middleton, took an interest in gardening too. She wrote her brother in England for advice in 1832 and he responded, giving directions for use of a pump for irrigation, as well as suggesting reed mats "to shade tender young plants." Moreover, during Henry and Mary Helen's ownership, the following description of the Middleton Place garden appeared in the *Charleston Courier* in 1840:

Governor Henry Middleton's plant list.

"The garden is enriched with a great and beautiful variety of indigenous and exotic trees, plants and flowers, both in the open air and in the hot house. We remarked three varieties of the *Camellia japonica*, growing luxuriously and in wasteful bloom in the open air — one of them (a red) being a tree of about 15 feet in height, and of no inconsiderable circumference."

Henry and Mary Helen's son Williams also began as a young man to take a hands-on interest in the plantation he was to inherit. This interest developed into a passion as an adult. When he was 33 years old and still a bachelor, his mother wrote in 1842 to his sister Eliza in Philadelphia: Williams "has been very busy planting out violets . . . the whole length of the Elm Walk on the orchard side. Young camellias are innumerable on that walk." After a decade of ownership and having wed Susan Pringle Smith, Williams describes in an 1855 letter to Eliza his hard work and plans for the future: ". . . only sketched out: The complete clearing (except of course the fine trees) on the bluff and hill on the other side of the creek [future site of the mill pond and azalea hillside] . . ."

Updating the report two years later, he states: "I have confined my labors almost entirely to planting out young camellias, which I have raised from seeds and when I was last here put out about 220, arranging them in clumps chiefly; and I have scarcely got through more than half the number I have to dispose of." Then in 1858, Williams describes "the most gorgeous show of camellias you can well conceive. The garden is anything but wintry to look at . . . I have multiplied the numbers of them so much within the last three or four years that you can scarcely turn your eyes in any direction near the house without seeing a mass of their flowers." As Williams' nephew H.A.M. Smith later writes about his uncle, "His energy was untiring in the extension and care of the garden; and to him is due the magnificent lines of the Indian Azalea [*Azalea indica*], which when in blossom make such a crown of coloring over the terraces."

In expanding the garden, Williams incorporated romantic influences, popular in the latter half of the 19th century. However, he did not remake the formal framework implemented by his great-grandparents 100 years earlier. He simply added to it, by extending the garden at the south end, and damming up a creek to construct a naturally curving mill pond with an undulating azalea hillside above it. Subsequent generations would expand the garden northward, impounding a wild cypress swamp to create a lake of ancient moss-draped trees that attracted statuesque long-legged wading birds — bookending the original classical design with a more modern, less formal landscape interpretation.

Williams' stewardship embodied both the classical order, so venerated by his ancestors, and his own generation's growing understanding of the natural order — especially as revealed through scientific observation and discovery. He carefully blended the two into one garden. Most significantly, he never gave up. Even in the aftermath of war, pleasure could be found where flowers bloom. In January 1869, Williams writes to Eliza following 10 days of mild temperatures: ". . . the garden and Middleton Place is a sight for the masses, I may say, of camellia flowers in every direction and of every hue, literally wasting their beauty on the desert scene — to say nothing of the sweet olives [tea olive] which I was so industrious in setting out during the existence of the Confederacy."

His workers displayed even more resilience, forced to rely on paltry wages and primitive living conditions. Nonetheless, in reports to Williams during the 1870s and 1880s, caretaker Patrick Dolan usually concludes with a reference to the flowers: "Several of the white Camellias are in bloom . . . I send you a few." And in the spring before Williams' death, Eliza writes to Susan from Philadelphia: "These last rains must have brought out the Azaleas in great beauty." The rebirth and flowering of the gardens year after year — made possible by formerly enslaved African Americans working under an Irish supervisor — provided a measure of hope and reassurance during those dismal times. [19]

• • •

On June 17, 1915 — five years after *Century Magazine*'s Frances Duncan reintroduced the nation to the "rare old estate" — its owner, Lillie Middleton, passed on. The obituary notice in the Charleston *News and Courier* was brief: "Died at Greenville, South Carolina on June 15, inst., Elizabeth Middleton Heyward, beloved wife of Julius H. Heyward and only daughter of the late Williams Middleton and Susan Pringle Smith, his wife." [20]

Lillie dedicated her life to saving Middleton Place. In death, she strove to guarantee its future. The first item in her will regards her ward, Elizabeth Viola Williamson. Having had no children of her own, Lillie adopted Elizabeth in Greenville. Musically gifted, the young woman became a professional musician in New York. Lillie bequeathed to Elizabeth an annuity of $1,200 a year for life, along with some property in the upstate, a piano and a Victrola.

The remainder of Lillie's will is all about Middleton Place and its people, as illustrated by the following directives:

"I will and direct that Ansel Horlback [sic] and his wife Molsey, be allowed to occupy the house they now live in at Middleton Place during their natural lives and that Ansel shall be employed as a gardener as long as he is able to work, and to be paid the sum of twenty dollars per month during Ansel's life.

"I give and bequeath to Annette May, my faithful cook at Middleton Place the sum of one hundred dollars.

"I give and bequeath to Mary Dolan and Susie Dolan, the daughters

of Pattrick [sic] Dolan, the sum of one hundred dollars each to be paid within a year after my death. Also fifty dollars each every year during their natural lives.

"I will and bequeath to my husband, Julius Heyward, for the term of his natural life the property on Ashley River, called Middleton Place, and the adjoining tracts, unless he marries again, when it is to become without division the property of my cousin, J.J. Pringle Smith [grandson of her mother's brother of the same name and a Middleton descendant]. Whatever money, or bonds, or mortgages remain after my legacies have been deducted, I desire that the funds shall be divided in two parts: One-half to keep up Middleton Place, house and garden and the other to be given to the Asylum for the blind in Spartanburg."[21]

• • •

Before long, Lillie's remains would be carried from Greenville to Summerville. The estate lists the following expenses for transfer of her casket to Middleton Place for burial: hearse $5; buggy $3; four hands to put casket in vault $1. Some portraits, silver, furniture, china, jewelry and other valued items were distributed among relatives and to what would later become the Gibbes Museum of Art. A portion of the family papers was sold to the South Carolina Historical Society for $50.

The following year Lillie's husband, Julius Heyward, married his cousin Anne Louise Heyward. On March 20, 1916, he relinquished "all my right, title and interest of every kind and description in and to the tracts of land commonly known as Middleton Place" to Lillie's cousin John Julius Pringle Smith for the sum of $4,000. But it appears that Heyward retained numerous Middleton family heirlooms subsequent to relinquishing the estate. After his death, his widow — a descendant of Arthur Middleton herself — returned the majority of objects to the family and sold the remaining papers of Arthur Middleton to the South Carolina Historical Society.[22]

At the time, J.J. Pringle Smith (29), his wife Heningham Ellet Smith (24), and their 3-year-old daughter Josephine were living at 26 Meeting Street with his parents, Judge H.A.M. Smith and Emma Rutledge Smith. Heningham, a native of Richmond, was a first cousin of Charleston author Josephine Pinckney. Her mother had died when she was young and her father was

Pringle and Heningham Smith with their dog on the surviving steps of the main house.

largely absent, leaving Heningham to raise her siblings. Though not wealthy, she possessed education and social standing, and later met Pringle at a debutante party. They subsequently married and moved to Charleston in 1913.

Deprived of a stable home for much of her youth, Heningham was deeply inspired by the prospect of permanence and continuity at Middleton Place, though Pringle warned her that he had inherited "a white elephant: a 6,000-acre estate and nothing to maintain it with" — its buildings run down and the grounds a wasteland. Nevertheless, Heningham understood Middleton's significance and embraced its challenges. In a memoir for her grandchildren, she gives the following account of her first years at the historic plantation:

"One evening Grandpa [Pringle] *returned a little earlier than usual and said he had a piece of news, and in a calm unexcited manner he told me he had inherited Middleton Place from his kinswoman, Cousin Lily* [sic] *Middleton, Mrs. Julius Heyward, who had died a short time previously. I was utterly thrilled, never for a moment anticipating the life ahead of us, but excited over the idea of a home of our own.*

"The house had been in disuse for many years, was in great disrepair,

with no modern conveniences. The garden, before the War Between the States, so perfect and exquisite, now more or less a wilderness overgrown with tangled honeysuckle, southern smilax and bramble, yellow jessamine completely covering the great groups of camellia bushes. First the house must be made livable — and so little to do it with. Brushing and sweeping and painting, then rearranging furniture. For days, Granny [Emma Smith] helping me. We sat under the old oak tree near the house sewing strips of matting together for rugs, cutting them from several rolls found in the house. Blistered fingers and broken finger nails, but wonderful results.

"Excitement of finding chintz, 15 cents a yard, with a pattern of pink azaleas in a shop in Charleston and making the bedrooms gay and fresh. Finding chintz for 25 cents and one at a time covering the living room sofas and chairs — measuring — cutting — pinning and then tacking, fingers hit as often as the tacks; but how beautiful it all looked when finished. Sore knees and a tired back meant nothing.

"Next, light: kerosene lamps must be kept clean, filled, and wicks trimmed . . . the lamp chore was mine, and a real chore because one's hands seemed to smell continually of kerosene. No ice, as no rural electric lines came as far as Middleton Place. No fresh milk . . . as we couldn't afford a cow. No bathrooms and no water in the house. Open fireplaces, making warm rooms impossible. Living 17 miles from any source of supply, over incredibly bad roads, having a T-model Ford which I couldn't drive, no telephone, no mail service. It is difficult now to believe how we carried on and surmounted the obstacles as they came.

"A few years went by and we bought a cow; we could have fresh milk — Klim [powdered milk] served us well the first years. For a refrigerator, we used the 'oldest refrigerating plant,' the spring house. There in the channels where the cool spring water ran, were set the pitchers of milk and the crocks of butter. On tables covered with oil cloth the pans of milk were set out and skimmed. Eggs and other foods could be kept fresh for several days in the even temperature. It was a real journey going to Charleston for fresh supplies. One couldn't think of emergencies that might arise, sickness or accidents . . .

"Old fashioned wash stands were in every bedroom and all water was brought to the house from a spring. When we felt inclined, if at night,

Photograph of Middleton Oak with Heningham Smith in foreground.

a lantern hanging on a nail in the back hall came into use. When bath nights came, screens were put a short distance from the fireplace, a foot tub and pitchers of hot and cold water placed near, and ablutions were performed. Heavens what I couldn't do with a kettle of hot water in those days!" 23

• • •

Heningham and Pringle Smith embraced their new role as pioneers of garden restoration, possessed by a love of the soil and a love of history and place. But neither had more than a novice's experience in gardening. Fortunately, Heningham was endowed with an intuitive sensibility about horticulture. In spite of no formal training, she had grown up in Richmond surrounded by beautiful old homes and accomplished garden matrons. The ladies' handiwork could be seen all over the city, in private gardens large and small. Horticulture study, flower shows and garden club memberships were a source of great pride, and largely the domain of women with leisure time.

The rejuvenation of Middleton Place, however, was no leisurely endeavor. Few private gardens were 65 acres large, as was the case at Middleton. Nevertheless, Pringle and Heningham put their youthful enthusiasm and talents into the challenge, charting the course of the estate for the next 50 years. As one visitor later ruminated, ". . . To be born a Middleton descendant, to inherit these gardens, must be like inheriting the burden of a throne . . . Though he surveys a paradise, he must feel like a prisoner entangled by the very giant roots in the pleasant but costly work of carrying on the tradition of Middleton Place Gardens."

The Smiths' ambition was to restore the gardens — to the best of their ability and financial means — to their 18th and 19th century appearance. To generate revenue and cover expenses, they raised poultry and grew vegetables to sell, along with flowers in season and bunches of evergreens. The Smiths also marketed saw timber and various other wood products, such as fat-lighter (rosin saturated longleaf pine strips) harvested from their extensive woodlands. In addition, sugarcane was grown and pressed for syrup; benne (sesame) was planted and the seeds painstakingly harvested; pigs were raised and slaughtered, and cows milked for cream and butter.

When it came to the garden, clearing out vines, unwanted volunteers and overgrowth was the first order of the day, followed by extensive pruning of camellias, azaleas, and myriad other varieties of shrubs and trees. Fortunately, the bones and structure of the garden were so well established that Heningham, by getting down on her hands and knees, could discern the original "groundwork" — the allees, the brick-lined paths, the outlines of garden rooms, the geometric patterns — finding it miraculously intact.

As Elise Pinckney recounts for *South Carolina Historical Magazine,* "Help and support came from several family members. 'Heningham mentioned that the rose garden was much in need of replenishing,' wrote a cousin in Rhode Island, sending some plants from her own garden." Heningham and Pringle also established a nursery and propagated many famous Middleton Place camellia varieties and specimens. In addition, they filled orders for young azaleas, which were gaining in popularity. Pringle's account records of 1921-1922 indicate that for orders of as many as 25 azalea plants, two to three feet in height, they could charge a sales price of five dollars a plant.

In 1922 Pringle's father, Judge H.A.M. Smith, arranged for sheep from his farm on Edisto Island to be relocated for the benefit of the lawns at Middleton Place. "The sheep were put on a boat at the island dock and floated to Yonges Island," according to Pinckney, "then came by railroad to Middleton Place." Two years later, Judge Smith noted in his diary: "Went to Middleton Place . . . and hunted for the fox that took the lambs — no success."

Judge Smith continued to take an active interest in his son and daughter-in-law's campaign to revive Middleton Place. He also brought several native plants to the gardens, including a variety of aquatic species such as lotus, iris and bladderwort. When Heningham and Pringle could no longer cover their expenses, the judge assumed ownership of the plantation and took control of the finances. To raise revenue — beginning in the 1920s — the Smiths opened the gardens to the paying public for three months each spring, while continuing to beautify the grounds.

Later, when their daughter, Josephine Smith Duell, returned to Charleston with her three children — Anne, Charles and Scottie — Josephine expanded the plant nursery with the help of horticulturalist Bud Ashley of Walterboro and neighbor Norwood Hastie, owner of Magnolia Gardens. The camellia varieties developed at the Middleton Place nursery, formed the nucleus of the New Camellia Garden, created by Josephine at the north end of the gardens — where the 18th century formal landscape gave way to the cypress lake and river beyond.

Those early years spent at Middleton Place are etched in Charles Duell's memory: "As a boy, I remember coming inside the house in the evenings and we'd sit in the living room with my grandfather in his red leather chair and my grandmother on the sofa. They would sometimes play cribbage or read; then my grandmother would go out to a table on the porch of the south flanker and pick up a book that visitors to the gardens were invited to sign. They would write a little note about how much they had enjoyed their visit and so on. If they had left their name and address, she would write each of them a personal note telling them how much she enjoyed their being at Middleton Place and thanking them for their comments. That was part of my grandmother's regular evening routine, every night, sitting there on the sofa writing notes to the visitors, thanking them for coming." [24]

Tracey Todd holding Bancel LaFarge's original 1930s plan for the stableyards.

• • •

It was after Judge Smith's death in 1924 that funds became available for a major renovation of Middleton Place. Within sight of the original 18th century south flanker — where Heningham, Pringle and Josephine lived from November through April — nine 19th century wooden farm buildings stood. Though screened by a long picket fence, they detracted from the aesthetic of the plantation and gardens, and also posed a fire hazard. Yet shelter was necessary for the horses, mules, cows and other animals; and storage space was required for farm and garden equipment, as well as supplies and machinery.

In the midst of the Great Depression and on the recommendation of their new son-in-law — Charles Halliwell Duell — Heningham and Pringle hired young New York architect Bancel LaFarge to design a group of brick structures to replace the wooden buildings. Plans were drawn for a stable, storage sheds, workshop, garage and other enclosures. A guest house was created, with the downstairs serving as an office and later a tea room. All the old buildings were demolished (except for Eliza's House) to make way for what LaFarge termed a new "plantation farm group."

LaFarge based his plan on studies he conducted of 18th century outbuildings in Barbados and the Lowcountry, consciously incorporating the same roof line as the original south flanker, as well as that of the grist mill built by Williams. Today, LaFarge's buildings form the nucleus of the plantation stableyards. Connecting the stableyards and gardens with the house ruins and south flanker is a pierced brick wall, believed to have been designed by Heningham. The wall encircles the greensward — which was expanded southward to focus the entrance view on the south flanker — and unifies the 18th, 19th and 20th century structures in one harmonious whole. 25

The 1926 issue of *National Geographic* that put Middleton Place on the map.

Meanwhile, the Smiths had begun extensively advertising Middleton Place, placing half-page ads in the Charleston *News and Courier* describing the plantation as "a botanical paradise . . . at the height of beauty. . . azaleas, dogwood and wisteria in full bloom," and boasting that "three of the four camellias from Michaux [are] blooming — and a tunnel of camellias not only form a wall on both sides, but also meet overhead." Likewise, the Atlantic Coast Railroad Line launched a promotional campaign in the 1920s, placing ads in numerous Florida newspapers as well as papers in Thomasville and Savanah, Georgia. They touted Charleston as a stopover for snowbirds headed north, who wanted to visit the Ashley River gardens at the height of their spring flowering.

In 1926, *National Geographic Magazine* featured an article by E.T.H. Shaffer entitled, "The Ashley River and Its Gardens," giving wide exposure to Middleton Place and the Herculean efforts of Heningham and Pringle to restore the plantation to its former glory: "The owner resides for a portion of the year in the restored wing of the ancient building, where he has gathered

The National Geographic Magazine.

E.T.H. Shaffer's story in *National Geographic* reflected the "garden fever" of the era.

The music room (or red room) of the south flanker as it looked in the early 1900s.

about him priceless treasures of the past. Many of these were once hidden in remote places in the garden by loyal retainers of the family, and so escaped the flames . . . Happily, the gardens escaped unharmed, and to-day, under the loving care of a direct descendant of that first Henry Middleton who visioned here a river paradise, they are maintained and graciously opened to the public."

Seven years later in April 1933, English author and poet Vita Sackville-West arrived in Charleston on a lecture tour. As a matter of course, her hosts took her to Middleton Place. Sackville-West marveled at how the Carolina estate reminded her of her own beloved Sissinghurst Castle and garden in Kent. "Stand I indeed in England? Do I dream? . . . No England! but a look, an echoing tone . . ." she mused in a poem entitled "Middleton Place, South Carolina." Later she would write to her friend Virginia Woolf: "Charleston is the home of azaleas. They grow wild in all the woods; bushes about twenty feet high in the gardens. They are all out now." 26

The "garden fever" sweeping the country happily coincided with the Smiths' restoration of Middleton Place and Charleston's full-court press to become a tourist destination. New and improved roads were making the Lowcountry more accessible. Mayor Thomas Stoney and the city's leadership believed tourism could lift the distressed region out of its malaise and propel it toward a more prosperous future. Moreover, as Heningham and Pringle developed Middleton into a visitor showcase, they were inadvertently advancing a new literary, artistic and preservation movement known as the Charleston Renaissance. Local preservationists, writers and artists, many of whom had connections to Middleton Place — including H.A.M. Smith, Josephine Pinckney and Alice Smith — all played a role in promoting the beauty and culture of, in Mayor Stoney's words, "America's most historic city." This fusion of history, landscape and art would redefine Charleston for the 20th century, albeit through "a golden haze of memory." 27

• • •

By 1941 the number of visitors to the gardens had risen to 15,000 each winter and spring. Despite the heavy workload, Heningham welcomed the return of "the season," noting in her diary, ". . . Impossible to tell the utter joy of being here once more." That year, First Lady Eleanor Roosevelt came to visit on the occasion of the Middleton Place bicentennial, nine months before the United States entered World War II.

Mrs. Roosevelt, in an interview with the *Richmond News Leader,* described her visit, which took place on Sunday, March 16 as she was heading back to Washington from Florida: "We drove from there [Cypress Gardens] to Middleton, which I think is one of the most beautifully laid out places I have ever seen. The natural setting is charming and as you come up the stairs through the main gate, which was once the main entrance to the house, you see before you the terraces. They were made 200 years ago by 100 men who worked 12 years . . .

"The home of the present owners is the wing of the house which still stands. It is very beautiful and welcoming. Inside, fires burned and flowers everywhere made a perfect picture of finely proportioned rooms." Serving the First Lady that day was Mary Washington Sheppard, who had cooked for five generations of Middleton and Smith descendants. At the age of 16, she began working for Judge H.A.M. and Emma Smith at 26 Meeting Street. After the judge's death, she shifted her employment to Pringle and Heningham at Middleton Place, where she lived, raised her family and worked until her death at age 87. Thanks in large part to Sheppard's culinary expertise, invitations to enjoy the Smiths' hospitality were coveted and prized by relatives, friends, celebrities and dignitaries such as Mrs. Roosevelt.

The Bulkley Medal (front).

Middleton historian Barbara Doyle interviewed Sheppard about the First Lady's visit and recorded her eye witness account: "I had to wear a black dress with white collar and cuffs, and a black band for my head," she recalled. In addition to "a glass of wine [sherry]," tea was served in the "red room." The present music room in the south flanker — or red room — was where the Smiths entertained guests. Today it looks very similar to how Mrs. Roosevelt and Sheppard remembered it in 1941.

Sheppard tells of serving the First Lady and her party cinnamon toast, benne wafers and sugar cookies. "I was introduced to her [Mrs. Roosevelt] and she asked me about the benne wafers — how to make them, because they were so delicious. I tried to tell her, but you just can't tell a person exactly how you make something. I told her I had parched the benne; then I told her I added brown sugar and butter; and then I put enough flour in it to

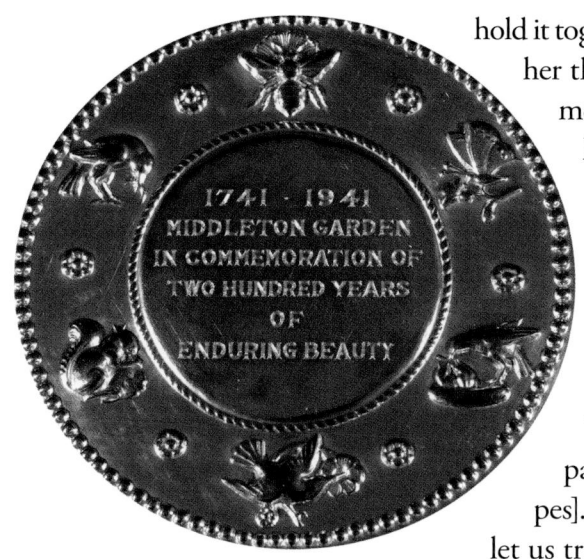

The Bulkley Medal (back).

hold it together. You see I couldn't tell her the amounts because I never measured things . . . [and] it's kind of hard to judge heat when you're cooking on a wood stove."

Sheppard learned cooking basics from her mother, but the fancier dishes she got from Heningham. "Miss Henny would go to parties and get receipts [recipes]. Then she would say, 'Mary, let us try it.' Of course, we'd try it out on the dogs first. Not real dogs — what Miss Henny meant was that we'd try it out at home first. If it was good, then we would serve it at parties. Miss Henny was the one who loved company . . . [she] used to have up to 40 head of people here in the house."

That same spring of 1941, Heningham and Pringle traveled to New York City to attend the annual meeting of the Garden Club of America. There the club awarded the coveted silver Bulkley Medal, its highest honor, to Middleton Place. The award recognized the Smiths' outstanding horticultural achievement and their dedication to garden restoration and preservation, "in commemoration of 200 years of enduring beauty."

Upon accepting the medal on behalf of Heningham and himself, Pringle remarked: "Recognition should be given to those owners who through their work and loving care, often made with personal sacrifice, kept up and added to the beauty of the gardens. It is fitting to pay tribute likewise to those wives and daughters, who through their love, interest, and hard work, have helped to restore and keep the loveliness and charm you admire today — and especially is that true of its present mistress.

"When I look back over the years of too much rain — too little rain — rain at the wrong time — freezes in the spring and the hundred and one things that you as gardeners know will come to disturb the soul and harrow one's peace of mind, I recall those lines by Rudyard Kipling found in another garden in Coastal Carolina that are as follows:

*"Oh, Adam was a gardener, and God who made him sees
That half a proper gardener's work is done upon his knees,
So, when your work is finished, you can wash your hands and pray
For the Glory of the Garden, that it may not pass away!
And the Glory of the Garden it shall never pass away!"* [28]

• • •

Fifty years later on the occasion of Middleton Place's 250th anniversary of the gardens, *South Carolina Historical Magazine* editor Elise Pinckney looked back on that auspicious year: ". . . Favorable weather that spring of 1941 attracted throngs to Charleston's famous gardens. Middleton Place was applauded by a spread in *The New York Times Magazine*. National magazines ran features. Even the movie industry brought Paulette Goddard for scenes in "Reap the Wild Wind." And the great terraces absorbed it all with comely dignity.

"That year's celebration was a milestone in a continuum. Gardens won't wait. Pringle and Heningham annually ordered new supplies of azaleas, spirea, and camellias. They cut the forest back; they created the New Camellia Garden, propagating new varieties. Within a decade the nursery was a flourishing business, including on its plant list sixteen *Camellias Middletonii*, 'the finest of the Middleton strain.' And, extending the boundaries, they planted the bamboo grove and defined the Cypress Lake.

"But the contribution of that generation was drawing to an end. In 1957 [shortly before Heningham's death] a young student at Yale, looking forward to the June recess, wrote his grandparents: 'My intense thought is of the happiness of returning home to Middleton Place.' " In little more than a decade, grandson Charles Halliwell Pringle Duell would become the man in charge — the next Middleton to bring renewed energy and commitment to the venerable plantation. [29]

Costumed interpreters at Middleton Place.

Five

HERITAGE TOURISM

When Judge Henry Augustus Middleton (H.A.M.) Smith died in 1924, his estate consisted of about 60,000 acres. In addition to Middleton Place (which comprised a little more than 10 percent of his holdings), he owned Seabrook Plantation on Edisto Island; lands in Berkeley, Dorchester and Charleston counties, and various plantations across the Lowcountry. These landholdings represented slightly less than the total amount of acreage owned by the Middleton family prior to the Civil War. It was a remarkable legacy to have held on to for so long, especially considering how many properties were deeded out of local family hands after the war.

Nonetheless, the judge's executor sold everything except for Middleton Place and the 6,500 acres associated with it. The plantation was saved because of its historical importance and because Judge Smith had granted a life tenancy to his only surviving son, Pringle. The land sale in 1924 averaged a value of between three and four dollars an acre, amounting to total proceeds of approximately $200,000. When the estate settled a year later, half the money was invested in the stock market and the other half in government bonds. While both investments suffered during the Great Depression, gradually the stock values rebounded.

Desperate for cash, Heningham and Pringle eventually opened the gardens year-round; however, summer visitations were low and ticket sales did not substantially increase. "The visiting public still demonstrated an interest during the off-season," recalls Charles. "People would enter the gate and drive up the circle toward the house. They would park in the greensward, stop at a little booth to pay a couple of dollars, and walk into the gardens."

But when Heningham died in 1957, Pringle had to carry the load alone. His ill health and advancing years made stewarding Middleton Place difficult. By the time of his death in 1969, the family was struggling to break even with a budget of plus or minus $30,000 a year. Since Pringle's wife and daughter had both predeceased him (Josephine Smith Duell succumbed

Charles Duell and Carol Wood Duell with their four children at Middleton Place.

to cancer in 1954), it was his grandchildren — Anne, Charles and Scottie Duell — who inherited Middleton Place and all the contents. Fortunately, Judge Smith's estate had paid the inheritance taxes in 1924. With the historic house, gardens and timberlands valued at $17,000, the estate taxes amounted to just several thousand dollars.

Judge Smith established what today is tantamount to a generation skipping trust. Charles and his elder sister Anne were charged with sorting it out. The two agreed that Charles would receive all the family property and Anne all the stocks and securities, worth approximately $1 million. Younger sister Scottie, who suffered from a mental disability, benefitted from a trust fund set up earlier by the Duells. In addition, she would receive support from her brother and sister for the remainder of her life.

Also among the Smith properties was the Edmondston-Alston House at 21 East Battery. The downtown, harborside mansion had served as Pringle and Heningham's summer home when they were not in residence at Middleton Place. The former owner, Susan Alston, was a cousin of Judge Smith. When she died in 1921, the prominent judge was appointed executor of her will. Susan's father, Charles Alston, had purchased the home in 1838 from its builder Charles Edmondston. Susan outlived her siblings and in her will left the Edmondston-Alston House to the Medical College of South Carolina and Judge Smith — in a 50-50 split. The college didn't want the mansion and sold its share to Judge Smith, who became the sole owner.

In 1969 the Edmondston-Alston House appraised at $110,000. "So we had to pay taxes on that," Charles explains. "But in his enormous wisdom and foresight, my great-grandfather [Judge Smith] made it possible for my generation to hold onto Middleton Place and undertake its restoration, despite little cash on hand. With only the real estate and a few financial assets, I was able to borrow a half-million dollars to begin the process of slowly advancing Middleton toward becoming self-sustaining. No longer could rice do it, but hopefully heritage tourism would." [1]

...

"When I inherited Middleton Place," recalls Charles, "Carol and I had already moved from New York City to Charleston four years earlier [in 1965], where I had taken a job in the trust department at South Carolina National Bank. At the same time, I was working to try and achieve solvency for the plantation. This experience deepened my understanding of the financial status of Middleton Place and its potential for the future. I concluded that in order for Middleton to succeed, it needed every aspect of the place to come into play — all of the assets must complement and support each other."

During the winter of 1969, Charles, wife Carol and their two young daughters, Josephine (named for Charles' mother) and June (named for Carol's mother), moved into the south flanker at Middleton Place. Though fully furnished, the house had not been lived in for some time — Charles' grandfather had moved permanently to the Edmondston-Alston House, living out his final days on the third floor there. Establishing a residence at the plantation fulfilled Carol and Charles' dream of raising their family in a rural setting. Soon a third child was born: son Holland, named for Charles' uncle, grandfather and great-grandfather.

Meanwhile, Charles wasted no time in launching Middleton Pace's transition to sustainability. In addition to the gardens, he had an agricultural operation to deal with. "My grandfather refused to buy his morning cream and sausage from the grocery store," Charles relates, "so he raised his own

Milby Burton.

dairy cows and hogs." To feed the livestock, Pringle grew corn and hay, which required a bailer and other equipment for cultivating and harvesting. "We figured the bales of hay being produced and the corn being grown probably cost somewhere in the neighborhood of 10 times what they would at the local market. Ironically, we got rid of the old farming operation, only to bring a new one back — in the form of an 18th and 19th century demonstration stableyard.

"With the $500,000 loan we began building an interactive, interpretative historic site," Charles continues. "I knew we had to have more going on to give Middleton Place enough viability, mass and economic activity to survive. We thought the stableyards were a natural extension of the gardens and that they would appeal to families with children. We also believed they were an important part of history and would give a more complete plantation experience — especially since African Americans had lived and worked on this particular site for generations."

But the stableyards were now a de facto maintenance area for the gardens. Buildings overflowed with mowers, tractors and other machinery. Visitors would peek through a tall wooden fence and see the modern tools and equipment. They yearned to experience something of the old plantation. Charles took a long look at the existing facilities and their potential. He noted that the stableyards' masonry structures, built in the 1930s, were both well designed — conforming to the older architecture of the house — and in good condition.

"So we constructed a metal Butler Building, hidden out of view on the opposite end of the gardens, to house all the maintenance equipment. This freed up the brick carriage house, barn and sheds for demonstration and interpretation." He envisioned an assemblage of animals, artifacts and implements, curated to illuminate economic activities and day-to-day life on an 18th and 19th century plantation. [2]

• • •

Charles soon traveled to Williamsburg, Virginia — flagship of the Colonial Revival — to meet with Colonial Williamsburg Foundation president Carl Humelsine, who would become a mentor. "Carl often came and stayed at Middleton Place with Carol and me. He invited us to send our craftspeople to Williamsburg as we were developing our exhibits, to find out what they were doing in carpentry and coopering, in pottery, and in spinning and weaving." Colonial Williamsburg was the gold standard of historic restoration and interpretation in America. Its revival in the 1920s and 30s was conceived of by College of William and Mary professor, the Reverend William Goodwin, and funded by Standard Oil heir John D. Rockefeller, Jr. By 1970 Williamsburg was attracting one million visitors a year.

Charles also consulted with leaders of Charleston's historic preservation and arts community, including Milby Burton, director of the Charleston Museum. Burton was a well traveled, sophisticated man with extensive knowledge of Lowcountry history and culture. He was also Charles' neighbor, having rented 25 East Battery next door to the Edmondston-Alston House. "He had access to a lot of objects demonstrative of the agricultural era that had been turned over to the museum from area plantations — plows, rakes and carpentry equipment, even a loom — all of which the museum agreed to let us borrow to tell the story of the stableyards." Burton's generous expertise and friendship were invaluable to Charles.

They pulled out old farm equipment from barn lofts and attic space, and searched ads in the *Market Bulletin,* a publication of the state agricultural department. "We found more implements and even a couple of mule wagons among the things advertised. We drove a large truck to Denmark, Bamberg and other rural communities in South Carolina. We explained to the farmers what we were doing and negotiated to buy their stuff. Eventually we acquired enough artifacts to tell the story of a self-sustaining plantation." [3]

How to display the artifacts and present the narrative fell to Emmett Robinson, director of the Footlight Players, Charleston's community theater group. Robinson had worked under poet and playwright Dubose Heyward, author of the novel *Porgy* published in 1925. *Porgy* was one of the first works to afford Black characters dignity and humanity, according to Charleston Renaissance historians Harlan Greene and James Hutchisson. Heyward's wife, Dorothy, transformed *Porgy* into a play, which became the basis for the Gershwin brothers' opera *Porgy and Bess.* The Heywards' successful dramatizations of their writings elevated African American characters and later provided Black actors with professional opportunities to play the roles.

Robinson brought all his many talents and perspectives to the stableyards project. "Emmett being Emmett, was a dramatic showman," remembers Charles. "He believed that you could meet curtain time whatever day the play was scheduled to be performed; that you could be ready, regardless. Emmett taught us the meaning of 'the show must go on.' "

Robinson was born in Ocala, Florida, graduated from the College of Charleston and became the first director of the Footlight Players. Later he earned a master's degree from Yale and went on to produce 182 plays, including 22 original productions. Robinson was expert in every aspect of theatrical production — as an actor, stage designer, writer, artist and director. Greene and Hutchisson assert that he carried on the spirit of the Charleston Renaissance well into the second half of the 20th century, becoming "a prime cultural force in town, mentoring many."

"We knew the spring of 1970 was going to bust open with all the celebrations around Charleston's Tricentennial," Charles continues. "In fast order, Emmett was able to design and produce multiple working displays of various agricultural and domestic enterprises — including candle and soap making, corn milling for grits and cornmeal, spinning and weaving, blacksmithing, and pottery." Robinson also produced large black and white illustrations to accompany each demonstration, similar to theater sketches for the scenes of a play. His drawings still hang on the walls of the stableyards today.

The year 1970 was also when *Porgy and Bess* was first performed in Charleston. Robinson designed and built the sets for that production, which was held in the city's new municipal auditorium (the Gaillard) before an integrated audience. A hospital workers strike had just been resolved, following a month-long curfew and the arrest of 1,000 people. Protesting unfair treatment and pay of Black employees at two Charleston hospitals, the strikers were assisted by the Southern Christian Leadership Conference. Eventually hospital leaders agreed to some of the workers' demands, but refused to accept unionization.

Emmett Robinson.

Jennet and Jack Alterman

Consequently, the Charleston production of *Porgy and Bess* became a pivotal event for the community. As Greene and Hutchisson note in their book *Renaissance in Charleston: Art and Life in the Carolina Low Country*, "The show was highlighted for all America to see on the CBS television program 'Sixty Minutes.' Here was the city that had begun the Civil War, showing to all that it had integrated successfully, was preserving its past while paying attention to black cultural heritage, and was simultaneously celebrating its legacy of 20th century accomplishments." [4]

• • •

Reporting from Middleton Place in 1970, writer Jean May submitted the following account to *Sandlapper* magazine: "On a crisp, clear March day the stableyards were opened to 2,000 invited guests. Their excited response was a good omen. The spring brought a record visitation, including more than 6,000 school children in May. Holding its collective breath, Middleton Place waited to see if summer doldrums would set in. But records continued to be broken, and by summer's end more than twice as many people had visited Middleton than during the previous year." In fact, annual visitation rose from 28,710 in 1969 to 76,444 in 1970. Increased revenues enabled Charles to hire more staff and make additional improvements, including burial of overhead power lines that stretched from building to building. Arthur Middleton Williams happened to be chairman of South Carolina Electric and Gas at the time, which expedited the work.

"During the months of preparation," May reported, "the noise of hammering and sawing was intensified by the rising pitch of the barnyard babble outside. The livestock population now includes Jersey and Red Devon cows and calves, quarter horses and their foals, mules, sheep, deer, pigs, guinea fowl, peafowl, ducks, geese, chickens and turkeys. But the agrarian show wouldn't be a show without people. A staff was acquired to serve as costumed guides on the walk back through South Carolina's early history."

While not completely devoid of stereotypes, the historic pageant that Charles Duell, Milby Burton and Emmett Robinson created at Middleton Place was uniquely descriptive and compelling. Among the interpreters were Mary Sheppard and Anna Perry, African Americans whose memories of Middleton Place spanned more than half a century. As May describes, "Taking up their posts in the household sections, surrounded by the apparatus of candle and soap making, leather tanning and spinning, they give modern homemakers a glimpse of the expertise and muscle power necessary for basic survival in another century. After a few turns of the hand-operated millstone used to grind corn into grits, guests are convinced."

Anna Perry mastered the loom on loan from the Charleston Museum and became a demonstration weaver, in addition to her other roles. Born Anna Millhouse of Dorchester County in 1897, she married Richard Perry at age 19. Not long after their wedding, the couple came to work for Pringle and Heningham Smith — Anna served as a housekeeper and cook; Richard cared for the animals in the stableyards. The Perrys resided in a wooden cabin not far from the south flanker; then moved into one of the small brick residences built by the Smiths in the 1930s. Anna Perry worked for more than 60 years at Middleton Place. Today her house is used as an office for

Mary Sheppard and Anna Perry.

the garden volunteer coordinator and stableyards staff. Her name and dates are engraved in the masonry beside the front door.

Mary Sheppard famously served tea to Eleanor Roosevelt when the First Lady visited Middleton Place in 1941. Born Mary Leas Washington of Charleston in 1906, she started working in the household of Pringle's father, Judge H.A.M. Smith, at the age of 16. In 1925, she moved permanently to Middleton Place to work for Pringle and Heningham as their cook. There she met and married fellow employee Thomas Sheppard, who served as the Smiths' butler and chauffeur. The Sheppards resided next door to the Perrys in another brick house in the stableyards — now the accounting office — where Mary Sheppard's name and dates are also engraved.

During her 70 years at Middleton Place, Mary Sheppard cared for five generations of her own family, as well as five generations of Smiths. In addition to witnessing the 20th century revitalization of the gardens, Sheppard was an indispensable resource in the development of the plantation stableyards and restoration of the house museum, where she continued to welcome visitors until her retirement in the mid-1980s. Her reminiscences inspired research that resulted in the 1991 debut of Eliza's House — the clapboard freedman's cottage built by Williams Middleton — ushering in a new era of African American interpretation at the plantation. When Sheppard died in 1994, Charles Duell referred to her as "our institutional memory" and "our guiding light and star."

Anna Perry and Mary Sheppard, along with other Black interpreters at Middleton Place — namely Martha DeWeese, Eliza Leach and Mary Smalls — were pioneers in the interpretation of African American plantation life. At the time, historic interpretation in America had created a homogenous national identity that favored the White and the wealthy. In 1970, Colonial Williamsburg — the nation's expert authority on colonial history and restoration — had yet to incorporate significant historical diversity and inequality into its definition of the early American. While the common White man or ordinary White woman, as distinguished from the planter elite, was often depicted as a striving laborer or skilled craftsman or savvy tavern keeper, rarely was the Black protagonist given much attention. That changed as social historians and academic researchers set new standards, challenging the status quo and constructing a more accurate and inclusive American identity.

Middleton Place was no exception in its initial focus on the Middleton family, their English roots and culture, their rice empire, and their role in establishing the Carolina colony and new nation. It would be another two decades before the story of slavery and the enslaved would begin to be fully fleshed out. Nevertheless in 1970, the voices of slave descendants were being heard at Middleton. While these African American interpreters were delivering a sanitized portrayal in service to the White aristocracy, many crucial elements of their heritage and culture were conveyed. Visitors noted a distinct element of authenticity, along with a tangible connection to the past — thanks to the extensive knowledge and experience of the Black interpreters, and the progressive outlook of the stableyards' creators. [5]

• • •

In 1971, Middleton Place was listed on the National Register of Historic Places by the National Park Service. The following year, the house and 110 acres — comprising the heart of the original Middleton estate — were designated a National Historic Landmark. While all National Historic

Landmarks are automatically included in the National Register, only a fraction of Register properties are named as Landmarks. Landmark designation, transcending regionalism, is a unique status given to a limited number of sites based on their exceptional value to the nation. Roughly one half of one percent of National Register listings become national landmarks. Middleton Place made the cut.

The next step was to open the south flanker to the public as a house museum, which would expand the plantation's offerings and visitor experience, while increasing revenues. "Carol and I had lived there for five years, during which time the first three of our eventual four children were added to the family," relates Charles. "The south flanker served as a comfortable residence, but was a little like living in a fishbowl. Most importantly, the plantation's portfolio of interpretive assets needed the house in order to complete the Middleton Place story and experience."

"I had set up a corporation called the Middleton Place National Landmark, Inc., governing the house and landmark acreage," Charles continues. "Now it was time to establish a foundation to serve as a vehicle for the operation and educational interpretation of a house museum, enabling it to receive donations as a nonprofit — especially gifts from members of the Middleton family who might want to send back furniture, silver, china, paintings and so on to help us tell the story. A descendant who owned a family painting, for example, could be persuaded to loan it to the foundation; or better yet convert the loan into a gift and receive a tax benefit."

"I determined that the house and 110 acres included in the landmark and family corporation were sacrosanct, a sacred area that should be preserved in perpetuity and ultimately belong to the American people. The intention was that upon my death, I would leave the house and landmark designated property to the foundation" — including the gardens, stableyards and greensward."

Meanwhile during the winter and spring of 1974, Charles engaged attorney Irvin Slotchiver to finalize documents to create a 501(c)(3) nonprofit called the Middleton Place Foundation — to administer the house museum, educate the public, receive monetary contributions, and serve as a repository for donated items important to the plantation's history and interpretation. The response was generous and immediate. Objects began returning to Middleton Place from across the globe.

In June the foundation received a $25,000 grant-in-aid from the Department of the Interior, awarded under the 1966 Preservation Act. With matching funds and in kind services from Middleton Place, the value of the grant was leveraged to formulate a master plan for the orderly development of the historic site and to implement its first phase: the rehabilitation of the south flanker as a house museum. Charles was determined to open the house to the public on February 22, 1975 — 110 years after Union soldiers set fire to the property. With only eight months to go, there was much to do. The estimated cost of the project was $185,000.

The first order of business was to answer such questions as "How should the house be restored?" "What facts are known about the family's history?" "How should the story be told, and by whom?" While the south flanker had undergone numerous changes between 1865 and 1974, it was decided that the exterior should be presented as Williams Middleton designed it immediately following the Civil War. But certain alterations were required to accommodate paying visitors and the growing collection of historic objects — electrical fixtures needed to be replaced; attic stairs closed; doors rehung or removed to facilitate traffic flow; ceilings recanvased; floors refinished, and climate control installed.

Design questions also had to be answered, such as the choice of moldings and cornices, re-plastering, appropriate paint colors, upholstery, bed hangings, window treatments and placement of furniture. To help with these decisions, Charles called upon local preservationists and experts, including Charleston architect Jimmy Small and Middleton Place Foundation trustees Milby Burton and Charles Waters. Waters owned a design firm in Florence, South Carolina and was an authority on historic interiors.

Researcher and educator Cheves Leland was hired to coordinate the project. A descendant of Thomas Middleton and Charles' cousin, Leland had grown up in Charleston and visited Middleton Place frequently as a child. She began researching her ancestors while in college and was adept at combing through archives — having acquired superb investigative skills from her parents, journalist Jack Leland and historian Isabella Gaud Leland. Leland, Charles and the founding trustees were adamant that information disseminated at Middleton Place adhere to rigorous factual documentation.

Leland set up home base in the south flanker and immersed herself in the enormous task ahead. The Duell family had moved out by that time, so she occupied an upstairs bedroom at the far south end of the house (now the research and archives office) and used the kitchen below. "Eliza Leach was living in a freedman's dwelling nearby, and Mary Sheppard, Anna Perry and another lady were living in the brick dependencies in the stableyards," Leland elaborates. "Groundskeepers and gardeners Jim Woodle and Bill Green also stayed on the place, working under property manager Ben Chapman. The nights echoed with the cries of peacocks roosting in the trees and owls on the hunt. Returning from town in my VW Beetle, I would turn off the headlights once through the gate and roll down the windows, soaking up the sounds in the darkness."

The papers, letters and artifacts that Leland unearthed in the old house were breathtaking. "Shoeboxes and trunks full of letters, bottles of brandy in the attic, even a hidden door in the floor," she recalls. Leland enlisted research assistant Alan Powell and her own mother to help review and catalogue materials dating back centuries. "Reading the letters and documents gave us a great deal of detail about the house and family life, which would guide both the restoration and the interpretation." Because the Middleton story was being told through the lives of four generations, no particular era was emphasized. The family furniture and items of historic significance remaining in the house served as the foundation for the exhibit rooms. At the same time, a call went out to descendants far and wide to loan or donate additional objects from their personal collections.

"We went to Colonial Williamsburg and I took copious notes," Leland relates, "particularly on Williamburg's volunteer guide program, which I used as a model for Middleton Place." In January 1975, thirty-nine women began a six-week orientation program to become interpreters at the house museum. "They received foundation memberships and came from all over the Charleston area, including Summerville and the Charleston Navy Yard." Among the inaugural class, many stayed on for two decades or more. They included Kathy Caffrey, Annette Mole, Priscilla Clement and Jan LaFave. Leland (who was later succeeded by Sarah Lytle) and this first group of guides set the standard for future generations of interpreters. Today the Middleton Place Foundation's volunteer guide program boasts some 300 participants. [6]

• • •

On February 22, 1975 at 6p.m., all was ready for the Middleton Place House Museum to welcome its first visitors. "We held an evening reception for invited guests and it rained cats and dogs," recalls Charles, "but that did not diminish the celebration. The next day we opened the house to the general public. It was an emotional and historic event for all of us. By virtue of a series of miracles, Middleton Place had survived, never having been deeded out of the family. I had come to understand it as something of a microcosm, a prototype of American history and culture. I believed its story belonged to all people, not just to me. I did not want it to come to a screeching halt on my watch."

Soon after the opening, Roger Williams wrote the following for a cover story in *Americana* magazine: "Middleton Place is a family trust in the broadest sense of the word, and Duell is the incumbent trustee. He has spearheaded the movement to revive its glories and to herald the greatest of them, the 65 acres of formal gardens that are the oldest surviving landscaped gardens in the United States. His aim is simply to preserve what he calls the 'special sensibility' of Middleton Place, and to that end he has forged an unusual accommodation between private ownership and public interest . . .

"To ensure 'a degree of ownership that's *supra* human mortality,' Duell created the Middleton Place Foundation. It oversees the house, garden, and adjacent lands that constitute the National Historic Landmark portion of the plantation; it also conducts research into the plantation's historic lifestyle and surroundings, both natural and manmade. Much of this effort has gone into locating and cataloguing antique furniture, accessories, and works of art that belonged to various branches of the family. All of these are eligible for inclusion in the Middleton Place collection, and Duell has proved skillful in persuading distant relatives to donate objects. Pieces have come from as far away as Arizona and England."

Indeed six weeks before the south flanker opened to the public, two ancestral portraits arrived from England. Lord De Saumarez and his sister, the Honorable Mrs. Llewellyen Palmer — descended from Henry Middleton's brother William — agreed to loan Middleton Place two family portraits painted by Benjamin West: one of Henry Middleton, president of the First Continental Congress; and another of his son Arthur, signer of the Declaration of Independence. The *Charleston Evening Post* featured their arrival in an article accompanied by a photograph of Charles and two staff members carefully uncrating the valuable paintings. Eventually they would become part of Middleton Place's permanent collection.

Less than a week later, the *News and Courier* announced that another Benjamin West painting would be returning on loan to Middleton Place — the 1772 portrait (nicknamed "The Holy Family") of Arthur Middleton, his wife Mary, and their firstborn child, Henry. The large family portrait was owned by Dr. Henry Middleton Drinker of Flourtown, Pennsylvania, a cousin of Charles and descendant of Eliza Middleton Fisher of Philadelphia. Forty years later, in cooperation with the Drinker family, the Middleton Place Foundation acquired the painting in perpetuity.

Williams Middleton, with the help of Moro Brewer, had successfully concealed the West family portrait during the torching of Middleton Place in February 1865. With the destruction and confusion surrounding the end of the Civil War, Brewer's constancy and shrewdness proved invaluable to the Middleton family and to the survival of Middleton Place and its contents.

Charles Duell, Ben Chapman and Edward Smith unpack portraits of Henry Middleton and his son Arthur.

It was nearly a year before Williams and the rest of the family learned the fate of the painting. They first thought that Dr. Henry Marcy, the Union medical officer who visited Middleton the day after it burned, had carried the painting to Boston. (Dr. Marcy did take three Italian paintings, which he returned to Williams after the war.) However on February 15, 1866, Williams wrote to his brother-in-law Francis Fisher in Philadelphia: "West's picture was brought down to me two days ago minus the frame & plus several holes in it: none luckily in very important parts."

Fisher wrote back immediately that he would pay to have the portrait repaired in New York. Though Williams appreciated the offer, he refused Fisher's generosity: "[Y]ou have already taxed yourself too much to relieve my necessities to allow me to increase this burden by expenditure on luxury." Williams then added:

The main room of the south flanker featuring the Middleton family portrait painted by Benjamin West.

"The holes in the canvas do not injure, or indeed, even disfigure it very much; and it is only in unison with . . . all my thoughts at present. It seems more in sympathy in its tattered condition with the crushed and shattered hearts & hopes of all those who are, or indeed comes under, my roof and possesses more suggestive power in many respects than I have supposed possible in an inanimate object of that kind. I cannot have it smartened up now."

Eliza Fisher and husband Francis repeatedly offered to have the painting cleaned and repaired. Sometime after October 1870, Williams relented and sent it to them in Philadelphia. On February 17, 1871, Francis wrote that the portrait was cleaned and repaired, and was hanging in their back parlor. He told Williams, "I wait for the accumulation of a little spare cash to have it copied & framed anew then shall return it to you, unless you desire to have it returned at once."

Williams replied, "I think that you had better keep it as long as it is your pleasure to look at it for I have no place to hang it." Thus, the painting remained with the Fishers and their descendants for the next 100 years. In 2015, the family portrait was officially acquired by the Middleton Place Foundation and returned permanently to the plantation — having spent its first century at Middleton Place (1772-1870); its second in Philadelphia (1870-1975); and now, halfway through its third century, back at Middleton Place. [7]

• • •

"A curatorial point of pride," says long-time Middleton Place curator Mary Edna Sullivan, "is that an overwhelming percentage of our house furnishings were actually owned and used by family members" — whether originally at Middleton Place or in other Middleton households. One of the best vehicles for retrieving Middleton heirlooms are family reunions, regularly held at the site and attended by hundreds of relatives from across the country and abroad. Charles invariably urges his cousins to loan or donate items to the collection.

At one such reunion, Middleton descendant Edward Murray of Green Spring Valley, Maryland approached Charles about loaning the foundation a set of four "architectural," 18th century English silver candlesticks — much in vogue when Arthur and Mary were on their Grand Tour from 1768 to 1771. Middleton curators and archivists had studied the 1793 inventories filed by the widowed Mary in which she listed a number of fashionable silver household items at Middleton Place, among them: a fish strainer, a silver cross and lamp "for setting a dish on," two rummers [large drinking glasses], and four pairs of candlesticks.

Murray's candlesticks, shaped in the form of ornate Corinthian columns, were made in 1771 and bore the hallmark of London silversmith John Carter. Each 14-inch tall candlestick boasted an oval cartouche that contained the Middleton coat of arms (meticulously engraved) and another cartouche marked with the monogram "A.M.," surmounted by a finely detailed Middleton crest. Three candlesticks still had their original drip guards, marked with a smaller Middleton crest and monogram. No doubt, these were part of the ensemble of English silver goods purchased by Mary and Arthur before returning to the United States. "You can visualize the young couple posing

The dining room table in the south flanker set with eight silver candlesticks encircling a silver epergne, all purchased in London by Mary and Arthur Middleton in 1771. The portrait at right is of their daughter Septima.

with their infant son in Benjamin West's London studio in 1771, then going for a stroll on Aldersgate Street and engaging with their silver agent to buy some fine sterling before sailing home," comments Charles.

Some two decades after Edward Murray loaned the first four candlesticks to Middleton Place, a third pair was donated by another Middleton descendant, Clementina Rutledge Edwards. Curator Sullivan recounts the story of their return:

"Charlestonian Tina Edwards first lent her pair of candlesticks at my request for a reunion exhibit, after which she was persuaded to allow us to continue exhibiting them. We agreed that whenever she needed them for a dinner party, etc., I would deliver them to her, polished and ready for use. After several years, Tina noticed she was not using them and with the consent of her family decided to donate them to the foundation."

That left one pair to complete the original matched set. Shortly before the 2006 family reunion, Sullivan learned that the two were owned by Harriet

Pullen Phillips, another Middleton descendant. She and her daughter Eleanor Phillips Brackville agreed to lend them for a reunion display, as well as for a "Rice to Riches" exhibit in 2010. Shortly afterwards, Charles negotiated with the family to sell the candlesticks to the foundation at a much-reduced price.

Thus for the first time in more than 200 years, the full set of eight Arthur Middleton candlesticks graced the dining room table in the south flanker. They had all been owned by descendants of Oliver Hering Middleton — the cousins having received the candlesticks from their aunt Anne Louise Heyward, who was a descendant of Arthur Middleton and the widow and second wife of Julius Heyward. Julius Heyward was the widower and heir of Elizabeth Middleton Heyward (his first wife), the owner of Middleton Place until her death in 1915. [8]

One of four pairs of silver candlesticks made by John Carter of London and engraved with the Middleton coat of arms and Arthur's monogram.

"All these pieces as they come in from various family members not only enhance the overall collection," Charles explains, "they also expand the connections and significance of objects through their associations and relationships, filling out a larger, more complex narrative. This is how things come together, working to complete the pieces of a grand puzzle of objects and people. It's so gratifying to me to see how this large, extended family — numbering more than 2,000 living descendants — is so interested and excited to tell the story of their ancestral home."

"The reason that the family connection is important is two-fold," Charles adds. "One is that it becomes more credible and understandable by visitors if they can associate human life with the property. If it becomes antiseptic and has no connection, it's really hard to identify with it. The other is the almost subconscious memory of family members and the way their values and perspectives influence the property. When combined with our ongoing research, this is a very healthy way to keep the continuum going." [9]

• • •

During the five years that the Duell family lived in the south flanker at Middleton Place, another historic house underwent a transformation. Following his grandfather's death, Charles began an extensive renovation of the Edmondston-Alston House at 21 East Battery in Charleston — the other residence he inherited. The main part of the house had settled, but the side piazzas had not, creating a reverse slope that carried rainwater toward the house. Under the direction of architect Jimmy Small, 27 columns were removed from the side of the house, the piazzas readjusted and the columns reinstalled to recreate a proper outward slope. Next, the Duells renovated the third floor, turning it into a comfortable living space for their growing family. The children were about to enter school in downtown Charleston, and Carol and Charles wanted to be close by.

At the same time, Frances Edmunds, director of the Historic Charleston Foundation, encouraged Charles to consider turning the first two floors of 21 East Battery into a house museum to compliment the foundation's Nathaniel Russell House. Fortunately, a great quantity of Alston furniture, silver, portraits and other heirlooms had survived *in situ*. While a number of Historic Charleston Foundation trustees were skeptical of taking on management of a second house museum, Frances Edmunds and Charles were confident that the Edmondston-Alston House would succeed.

Entering into a contract with Historic Charleston in 1974, Charles guaranteed that the operating budget for the house museum would be profitable. If there was a shortfall, he would cover it. The two parties agreed to share net income after expenses, with two-thirds going to Historic Charleston and the remaining one-third placed in a special "house fund" to cover taxes, insurance and exterior maintenance. During the 15 years that Historic Charleston operated the Edmondston-Alston House, it garnered an estimated $300,000 in net revenue. Following Hurricane Hugo in 1989, Historic Charleston transferred management of 21 East Battery to the Middleton Place Foundation, which by then had developed a professional and volunteer staff capable of operating the house.

Charles' collaboration with Frances Edmunds proved transformative for the Edmondston-Alston House and for him. Born in Charleston in 1916, Frances Ravenel Smythe came from a distinguished family of lawyers and historians. After graduating from the College of Charleston, she married attorney Henry Edmunds and worked as a newspaper reporter and real estate agent while raising three daughters. She was savvy and indefatigable in defending her city — persuasive about why it was worth saving, and insightful about how to do it.

Edmunds became her generation's most consequential preservationist and Charleston's most influential woman. She received numerous accolades, including the Louise du Pont Crowninshield Award — the National Trust for Historic Preservation's highest honor. She was also named a trustee of Monticello and appointed by Jimmy Carter to the President's Advisory Council on Historic Preservation.

Edmunds cared deeply about the Ashley River corridor and led the charge that prevented an interchange of the Mark Clark Expressway (Interstate 526) from being built on the historic Ashley River Road. What began as a mentorship evolved into a partnership, with Charles becoming treasurer of the Historic Charleston Foundation during Edmunds' tenure and eventually succeeding her on the President's Advisory Council. [10]

"As Charles came of age," comments George McDaniel, former director of Drayton Hall, "he sought out guidance from the foremost historic preservationists of the time . . . and became completely invested. He imbibed the historic preservation ethos represented by Frances Edmunds and other mentors. That polestar was there and Charles measured his success and failure against it." [11]

• • •

Charleston was no longer America's best kept secret. Bernard Collier of *The New York Times* came down in 1971 to research an article he was work-

The east drawing room of the Edmondston-Alston House, one of the first dwellings built on Charleston's High Battery.

ing on entitled "South Carolina: A Yankee View." The stableyards had been open a little more than a year when Collier drove out to Middleton Place to meet the Duells. "To my surprise, Middleton Place Gardens . . . is charming, educational and refreshingly relaxed," he wrote.

"The Duell family consists of Charles, 32; his wife Carol (a Wyoming girl he met in Paris), and their two daughters," Collier continued. "They live in the restored south wing of the once immense (300-feet long) mansion . . . Charles is a direct descendant of the Middletons, and he gave up a Wall Street career in investment trusts to turn Middleton Place Gardens (etc.) from a family charity into a paying project . . .

"We tour part of the old Middleton house before sitting down for a late

(l-r) Peter Manigault, Frances Edmunds, George Rogers and Peter McGee speak at a 1970 National Trust for Historic Preservation conference in Charleston.

afternoon drink. A silk Signer's Copy of the Declaration of Independence is inconspicuously exhibited on a side wall. An oil portrait of Czar Nicholas, a gift to Minister Arthur [Henry, actually], hangs in the library. A portrait of Williams Middleton, his features and the look in his eyes strikingly like those of Charles Duell, hangs over the living room fireplace."

Collier approached his assignment with a combination of empathy and skepticism, finding himself both charmed and puzzled by the subjects of his story. What is it about these South Carolinians, living so closely with their past and at the same time going about their modern lives? How do they reconcile the grandeur with the tragedy of slavery and civil war? Why are they seemingly unfazed by the exquisite beauty all around, when decay and rot await, and bulldozers chomp at the bit? What is the source of their gentle calm and patient good humor as they confront the dilemma of being cash poor and land rich?

Collier got a partial answer when he later caught up with Frances Edmunds in downtown Charleston. She told him, "The house I live in has been in our family for more than 100 years. Nobody came along one day and decided, 'Let's spend $50,000 and restore the place.' No. Things just got [accustomed] to it; it got painted, and screens and indoor plumbing and heating — all slowly. It never went down. It was never a slum. It's like a lot of houses down here. Gently lived in houses."

Celebrated gardener Emily Whaley — in her book *Mrs. Whaley and Her Charleston Garden*— perhaps more closely captured the basis of Charleston's tenacious hold on the past, and its embodiment in the person of Frances Edmunds: "When Ben and I came to Charleston in 1937 . . . the Historic Charleston Foundation was not yet in full force. [Incorporated in 1947, the foundation trustees elected her husband, Ben Scott Whaley, as its second president.] Ideas of preserving the city were in the backs of the minds of Albert Simons, Harriet Smythe, Josephine Pinckney and a lot of others. Frances Smythe Edmunds had been brought up in a house where this discussion was going on. All her parents' friends had talked about it — how to stop the destruction of these priceless old houses.

"Frances came from a family that was confident about dealing with anything, so she didn't hesitate when she was asked to be the executive director of a new preservation organization. The old preservationists were beginning to die off, but Frances was young and had her dander up. She would take on anybody. Charleston wouldn't begin to look the way it does today if it hadn't been for her willingness to make enemies anywhere. Practically speaking, she saved the city and put it back on the map."

Whaley's description hit at the core of this formidable lady and at the heart of Charleston's preservation movement — including the heritage tourism industry that it spawned. In 1948, Edmunds volunteered as a hostess for the inaugural season of a new fundraising effort — the annual spring house tours — which later grew into the celebrated and lucrative Festival of Houses and Gardens. At the conclusion of the season, Edmunds was hired to run the tour program and eventually run the Historic Charleston Foundation as its first paid director.

Edmunds was particularly innovative when it came to selling and financing preservation, something Charles embraced in his vision for Middleton Place. Patrons were buying into an educational experience in support of a worthy cause, one that would help preserve the beauty and integrity of the historic places they were visiting. As author Robert Weyeneth notes in his history of Charleston's preservation movement, "In both the content of the advertising campaign and its national distribution, Frances Edmunds and Historic Charleston Foundation were promoting what would come to be called 'heritage tourism' in a later decade." [12]

Charles Duell pages through a 1731 first edition of Mark Catesby's *Natural History of Carolina, Florida and the Bahama Islands*, part of the family library.

∙ ∙ ∙

Another mentor and friend to Charles who understood how to finance and sell historic preservation, was Dick Jenrette — co-founder of Donaldson, Lufkin and Jenrette investment firm and later described by *The New York Times* as "the last gentleman on Wall Street." Jenrette's firm was managing some of Charles' money and in 1968 he came to Charleston as a guest of the Duells at 21 East Battery. On a moonlit walk along the harbor one evening, Jenrette noticed the Roper House, a Greek Revival mansion several houses down from the Edmondston-Alston House.

"I remarked — rather tastelessly, since I was a guest in the Duells' house, one of the handsomest in town — that my favorite house in Charleston was Nine East Battery (the Roper House)," Jenrette recounts in his book, *Adventures with Old Houses*. "Instead of being offended, Charlie remarked, 'It just might be for sale.'"

"The next day he introduced me to Drayton Hastie [brother of Norwood], the owner," continues Jenrette, "and I learned that the house of my *Gone With The Wind*-influenced dreams was indeed for sale." Thus began Jenrette's lifelong commitment to historic preservation and lifelong friendship with Charles, whom he calls "heroic" and "an inspiration." Roper House was the first of a dozen historic houses that Jenrette would eventually own and restore, six of which are National Historic Landmarks.

Jenrette's enthusiasm for Charleston would inspire him to join Charles as a trustee of the Historic Charleston Foundation, whose director, Frances Edmunds, he knew from his service on the board of the National Trust. It was Edmunds who convinced Jenrette to spearhead the revival of the Mills House Hotel, where Robert E. Lee was staying on the night of the 1861 fire. (When the inferno spread to Meeting Street, Lee retreated to the Edmondston-Alston House.) Edmunds recognized that a full-service, luxury hotel in the heart of the historic district would augment the rise of heritage tourism and lend even greater support to Charleston's preservation movement.

As lead investor, Jenrette formed the Charleston Associates partnership with Charles Duell and Charles "Pug" Ravenel. They joined with Historic Charleston Foundation to purchase the dilapidated antebellum building at auction. The new owners carefully dismantled the old hotel under the guidance of architects Curtis and Davis of New York, in consultation with local

architects Simons, Lapham, Mitchell and Small. They replaced it with a close replica — adding two stories, reusing the old iron balcony, and casting reproductions of the original terra cotta window pediments. On October 9, 1970, the resurrected hotel registered its first guests.

"Rebuilding the Mills House Hotel was the first major investment by anyone (other than the U.S. government) in downtown Charleston in the post-World War II period," asserts Jenrette. "While we struggled with cost overruns and low occupancy in the early years, the hotel's subsequent success turned the tide of apathy about the economics of downtown Charleston." Charles notes that, "Before we rebuilt the Mills House, rooms were going for $19 a night. After renovation, the price rose to $120 a night. When we sold the hotel in 1979, everyone recouped their investment and more."

"Due to my partnership with Dick on the Mills House," Charles adds, "I became a director of several Donaldson, Lufkin & Jenrette/ Alliance Capital funds, as well as a director of GRC International. I was also invited to serve on the board of the Grand Teton Lodge Company under the chairmanship of Laurance Rockefeller. Fellow trustees included Mel Grosvenor (former president of the National Geographic Society), Carl Humelsine (former president of Colonial Williamsburg), Ladybird Johnson (former First Lady) and Cliff Hansen (former governor and U.S. senator from Wyoming). Sustaining the Rockefeller family legacy of Grand Teton National Park by means of these for-profit lodges provided me with inspiration for the mission of Middleton Place."

Soon enough, Middleton Place began generating revenue and gaining stature. By the mid-1970s, the plantation was operating in the black with an annual budget of approximately $150,000. In 1977 visitation exceeded the 100,000 mark, and that June, the newly formed international Spoleto Arts Festival staged its finale at the foot of the Butterfly Lakes. By the end of the decade, Middleton Place would be featured in *Architectural Digest, Americana, The New York Times, Better Homes and Gardens* and on the cover of *Antiques* magazine. Charles had transformed what family members once called "the dear old wreck" into one of Charleston's top tourist attractions. [13]

Rick Rhodes

The early 18th century house that would become Middleton Place was built on a high bluff and aligned with a natural straightaway in the Ashley River. This alignment still serves as the main axis for the gardens.

Six

MARSHALING the ASSETS

"We want our artifacts and habitats, like those of the civilizations we admire, to form an allegiance with the land so strong that our existence is seen as an act of adoration, not an act of ruin."
– W.G. Clark

Early on, the Garden Club of America had determined that Middleton Place possessed not only the oldest surviving landscaped garden in the nation, but also the "most important and interesting." Still Charles needed to marshal all of the plantation's assets to sustain the national landmark for the future. He believed that every possible part of the whole should contribute toward generating sufficient income to cover expenses.

In 1970 Charles opened the plantation stableyards to the public, the same year as the 300th anniversary of the settlement of "Charles Town" downriver on Albemarle Point. For the first time, life in back of the Middleton Place main house was on display to the public. Others including school groups could finally see behind the scenes, and it was obvious that most of the tasks of the past were carried out by enslaved Africans and African Americans. This awakening would later launch a pioneering study of enslaved culture, coupled with enhanced interpretation of the lives of the Middleton Place workforce.

While the garden and stableyards attracted increasing numbers of guests to the property, there still remained untapped opportunities for broadening the visitor experience. With an educational mission in mind, Charles established the Middleton Place Foundation in 1974, not long after the Department of the Interior had declared Middleton Place a National Historic Landmark. The nonprofit entity provided tax benefits for descendants who gave money to the new house museum, or desired to donate in kind contributions to the collection.

The refurbished plantation stableyards.

In the late 1970s, Charles prepared to give the historic landmark and its assets to the foundation: the land, the structures and the collection. New tax laws no longer incentivized lessening the taxable part of one's estate at death. A gift or bequest in a will would simply shrink the estate, without the additional income tax benefits. "This meant that it was better to make gifts during your lifetime," explains Charles, "gifts constituting charitable deductions that you could write off on your income taxes."

"But my primary motivation," he continues, "was to have Middleton Place go into the foundation while I was still alive, believing that I could help guide and affect its destiny as an educational institution more than if I waited to make the gift when I died. I wanted to play a part in the future of Middleton Place beyond me and my family.

"I was also becoming more aware of what circumstances and conditions were necessary to guarantee Middleton Place's perpetuity. The foundation was originally set up to take care of the house and collection. All the while it was getting its legs as a nonprofit. The change in tax law emerged as a catalyst for a more urgent mission — the preservation and ongoing survival of the property as a whole." [1]

By the winter of 1983, Charles had completed the gift of the national landmark to the Middleton Place Foundation. As a result, the value of the foundation's assets increased tenfold to more than $11 million. As it took on the added responsibility for maintenance of the gardens and stableyards (all 110 landmark acres), the foundation's annual operating budget rose to over $2 million. Today the annual budget is $7 million and the value of the national landmark acreage and assets is approximately $25 million. [2]

At the time of his gift, Charles expressed the following sentiment: "It is not as though the historic core of Middleton Place has been transferred to an outside party. Rather, it is in effect a transfer of the ownership of Middleton Place to itself, in order to perpetuate a continuity of stewardship beyond the limits of a lifetime, or of several lifetimes." [3]

Heyward Carter, a former trustee of the Middleton Place Foundation whose family owns neighboring Millbrook Plantation, elaborates on Charles' gift: "There would be no Middleton Place Foundation, no 501(c)(3) charitable organization, if it weren't for Charles. His realization of what had been bestowed upon him by his grandparents and forebears, and his willingness to take on the burden — not for personal benefit, but rather for the benefit of the state and country — speaks volumes. Middleton became his principal focus in life. The plantation could have been lost to development. Charles took it in the total right direction and saved it." [4]

• • •

With the stableyards, the house museum and the foundation up and running, Charles began projects to further enhance and fine-tune the guest experience at Middleton Place. Since his grandparents' time, visitors would drive straight through the entrance gate to the house and park cars on the greensward. "When the house museum opened to the public in 1975," remembers Charles, "you would look out the second-floor windows and see all the cars and buses. It was really jarring. We desperately needed to separate the 20th century from the 18th and 19th.

"My mother and grandparents had established a plant nursery just beyond the reflection pool, on the northwest boundary of the gardens. They planted pine trees in rows roughly 12 feet apart to give shade to the azalea and camellia seedlings. Fortuitously, the spacing of these pine trees [which were 30 years old by then] lent themselves perfectly for parking cars."

Robert Marvin, South Carolina's preeminent landscape architect at the time, quickly grasped the efficacy and aesthetic of using the former nursery for parking. Charles hired Marvin to draw up a plan whereby visitors would enter the main gate from Ashley River Road, glimpse the house across the 12-acre greensward (with the suggestion of the gardens beyond), turn left, and follow the outer perimeter of the pierced brick wall to park beneath and between the pines.

Later, Charles relocated the museum shop from what is now the restaurant's private dining room to a new building bordering the parking area, designed by Charleston architect and Drayton descendant Sandy Logan. Instead of an imposing visitors center, Logan devised wooden kiosks to house ticket sales and visitor orientation, at much less cost and intrusion. All the structures were painted a dark "Charleston green."

"The ticketing and orientation kiosks," Charles says, "face each other and are balanced on an axis that visually crosses the reflection pool out to the sun dial in the rose garden. People get out of their cars and put their feet on the ground. They get a feel for the place before they have to decide what they want to do and what tickets to buy. When first meeting our staff, they are asked if they would like to learn something about Middleton Place. They review a menu of opportunities for exploring the plantation before paying for anything. This has worked well for visitor engagement and as a business model."

Knitting them together is a tall, elegant wooden portal — designed by architect W.G. Clark — which ticket holders walk through to enter the gardens. It acts like a time machine, in which visitors gently transition from a high-tech 21st century world into an agrarian 18th and 19th century world. *Post and Courier* architecture columnist Robert Behre likens Clark's portal to what he terms a "spare riff" on *torii*: the traditional Japanese gate built at the entrance to a Shinto shrine, demarcating the boundary between a secular space and a sacred space.

Such fine-tuning and adjustments continue at Middleton Place. Each week as Charles walks the grounds — just as he walked hand in hand with his grandmother some 75 years ago — he makes a mental list to discuss with his successor, Tracey Todd, various improvements: a gatepost in need of paint; a camellia bush in need of pruning; a new volume to enhance the museum shop bookshelves; a compelling speaker to add to the spring lecture series; a work of art to bid on at auction. In addition to his sophisticated taste and keen eye for detail — honed over decades of study, travel and collecting — Charles possesses a heightened aesthetic and appreciation for authenticity.

"Charles has sought authenticity all his life," says former Yale classmate Chris Seger. "Authenticity, especially at Middleton Place, has been a driving force for him — nearly a total focus — since taking over the reins in 1969. When you are with him at Middleton, you can tell that he is a perfectionist and very hands-on. For the plantation to become what it is today, required a singleness of vision and purpose. It is an outstanding achievement."

Indeed, visitors enter the plantation through the same narrow gates that carriages and other vehicles have used for more than a century. There is no pavement, only dirt roads and paths. Modern facilities and offices are scattered about the plantation in discreet outbuildings, most of which are old and repurposed. While automobiles and machinery are hidden behind trees and fences, electric golf carts can be seen occasionally ferrying workers and visitors with limited mobility from point A to point B.

There are no trams, no videos, no interactive displays. One must discover Middleton Place on foot, quietly and slowly. Expert guides and interpreters deliver history and stories at various points, as do attractive signs and passive exhibits. There are no bells and whistles to spoil the satisfaction of absorbing and discerning Middleton at your own pace, in your own time. Yet Middleton Place is not pure in a historical sense; it is a subtle blend of various historic eras and periods. [5]

• • •

A key ingredient to guest satisfaction is food. Middleton Place has offered food and refreshments to visitors since the first tea room opened on the ground floor of the mill house in the 1930s. A fundraiser for the Junior League's community projects, the tea room not only afforded people a chance to linger and enjoy the plantation, it also provided many of them with their first taste of authentic Lowcountry cookery.

Before the term "foodways" was invented, the Junior League ladies were serving up Lowcountry standards such as she-crab soup and shrimp paste sandwiches, benne wafers and Huguenot Torte. The tea room menu cel-

A cooking demonstration — part of the "Living History" program.

ebrated the natural bounty of the region and the closely woven culinary heritage of both the White aristocracy and the Black men and women who served them — not unlike the relationship between Charles' grandmother Heningham Smith and her cook Mary Sheppard.

Known as Gullah people, descendants of enslaved Africans who had lived and worked on the rice coast of South Carolina preserved culinary customs of their ancestors and blended them with the European styles of their employers — who, more often than not, were descendants of slave owners. The result was a unique mingling and adaptation of different Old World cooking traditions converging in the New.

In the 1950s, Charles' grandparents took over the tea room from the Junior League and moved it from the mill house into the brick guest house that Heningham and Pringle had built 20 years earlier. "It expanded a little bit beyond just soup and sandwiches," says Charles, "but essentially it was a place for lunch." It has had many growth cycles since then, becoming the Middleton Place Restaurant in the 1970s and later opening for dinner in the evenings. "Seating doubled when we pushed out the southeast corner of the dining room and added a tiered sunroom designed by local architect

The expanded Middleton Place Restaurant.

Randolph Martz," Charles notes. Martz's addition melded seamlessly into one, enhanced by the extra light and expanded views of the mill pond and azalea hillside in the distance. The kitchen underwent a commensurate expansion. [6]

Charles enlarged not only the physical footprint of the restaurant, but eventually its menu and mission. One day in the mid-1980s, Eric Brooks (former manager of the Mills House Hotel in Charleston) drove to North Carolina to have lunch at Fearrington House Restaurant near Chapel Hill. Its celebrated African American chef, Edna Lewis, was about to quit. As Patricia Lynden wrote in a profile of Lewis, "Edna was not happy when such fashionable but un-southern foods as kiwi fruit arrived for the compote, or when pasta crept into the menu to accompany Virginia ham without her permission."

Brooks was coordinating several hospitality projects around Charleston, including advising Charles on guest services at Middleton Place. He had also been following Edna Lewis' career. After finishing his lunch at Fearrington House, Brooks called Charles to tell him he had found someone he thought they should recruit for the restaurant. "She was farm-to-table before the term became popular," he related to *Post and Courier* food critic Hannah Raskin years later. "It was really Alice Waters on the West Coast, and Edna Lewis on the East."

In 1985 Lewis accepted Charles' offer to come to Middleton Place and serve as the restaurant's chef-in-residence. "I think it clicked with her when she saw what Middleton was all about," explained Brooks. "The setting and the aspiration struck a chord with her, and the Lowcountry and the tradition of Gullah cuisine . . . Charleston then was just beginning to develop its culinary flair."

Edna Lewis.

Lewis was charged with developing a menu based on historical records of early Carolina plantation cooking. She stayed for nearly three years. Walking a few hundred yards each day from her residence on the second floor of the mill house to the restaurant, Lewis drew on her time spent with Middleton cook Mary Sheppard, as well as from recipes found in *The Carolina Housewife* — written in 1847 by Arthur Middleton's niece Sarah Rutledge. Combining these essential sources with her rural Virginia roots and a culinary career in New York City, Lewis connected diners to the past with a distinctive flair and refinement.

Her menu included rabbit pate, watercress soup, tomato aspic, broiled oysters on the half-shell, panned quail with julienne of country ham, spoon bread, suckling pig, fried flounder, shrimp and grits, caramel layer cake and chocolate soufflé — the same soufflé that made the cover of *Gourmet* magazine in 1984. Eager patrons began lining up at Lewis' door. In 1986, she was named to Cook's Magazine "Who's Who in American Cooking" and later received a James Beard Living Legend Award.

Lewis died in 2006 but her legacy continues to inspire chefs and foodways across America. Many of her recipes still grace the Middleton Place Restaurant menu. Lewis' influence positioned Middleton Place as a sought-after location for learning about food history and culture. Since her time there, the plantation has hosted the annual Southern Food Symposium (co-founded by Lewis with Atlanta chef Scott Peacock), as well as a television episode of "Top Chef" and a culminating session of the Lowcountry Rice Forum. As Raskin declared, "Her installation at Middleton was a big deal," and as for Charleston's nascent food scene, "her stay was extraordinarily significant." [7]

• • •

Meanwhile, tourism and resort development were surging on the coast of South Carolina in the 1970s and 80s, threatening to overwhelm the unique landscape and culture. Ever since the Civil War, the region's real estate values had remained low, and economic opportunity marginal. Suddenly, landowners on the coastal plain saw a chance to cash in on the lure of the Lowcountry.

Adjacent to the northern and southern borders of the Middleton Place national landmark, Charles owned hundreds of acres of prime riverfront property. He also held title to 5,700 acres of pine forest and bottomland on the other side of Ashley River Road — including the old Middleton tract known as Horse Savanna. A broken network of earthen dikes crisscrossed the tupelo-cypress swamp: remnants of inland rice impoundments, dug out and banked by enslaved Africans nearly three centuries ago.

Charles' challenge was to figure out how to marshal the plantation's large land base to create a steady revenue stream, and at the same time maintain the authenticity and context of the surrounding Ashley River historic corridor. What enterprises, both traditional and novel, might be pursued on the property to achieve financial and environmental sustainability?

Like generations of Middletons before him, Charles continued to selectively harvest saw timber from the upland pine woods across the Ashley River Road. Although the phosphate industry was no more, mining of sand and fill dirt for construction was another extractive venture that he and his Ashley River neighbors pursued. Because the shallow water table meant that excavated areas would fill with freshwater, Charles hired wetlands and land planning experts to determine how best to locate and execute the digs. Care was taken

Charles Duell (center) fox hunting with the Middleton Place Hounds.

to preserve trees around the perimeter of each excavation. Over time the resulting 11 lakes afforded genuine scenic and wildlife benefits.

But Charles needed to do more than just cut timber and mine dirt to help make his landholdings sustainable. One of the traditional uses he turned to was horses. "The whole equestrian life of the plantation is very appropriate, considering its long history at Middleton," Charles notes. Since the early 18th century, members of the Middleton and Alston families had been actively engaged in raising and racing thoroughbred horses. The first formal competition in Charleston was held in 1734, the same year a group of planters organized the South Carolina Jockey Club.

Henry Middleton and sons Arthur and Thomas were well known horse breeders and racers. Frequent advertisements from 1772 to 1784 note that Middleton Place and the Oaks were used as stud farms for prize-winning thoroughbreds. Middleton and Alston relatives were also among those who funded the Washington Race Course, built in 1792 where Charleston's Hampton Park is today. The one-mile, park loop road traces the original path of the oval course. The track boasted a stately "Grand Stand" and four stone pillars at its entrance. Today the pillars serve as the entrance gates to

Charles Duell established an equestrian center and conservation development on his lands adjacent to Middleton Place.

New York's Belmont Park.

Back on the plantation, what began as the "Horse Farm" eventually became the Middleton Place Equestrian Center. Instead of breeding and racing, the equestrian program focused on high quality boarding and training facilities, as well as miles and miles of some of the best trail riding in the Southeast. The plantation began hosting horse shows and competitions, and most significantly, the Middleton Place Hounds — established in 1973 by Charles and other fox hunting enthusiasts. Each year the opening and closing meets begin on the Middleton Place greensward — a colorful pageant of men and women on horseback dressed in formal hunting attire: red jackets ("pinks"), white breeches, vests, ties, gloves, black leather riding boots and black velvet helmets. At the sound of the horn, riders and hounds cross Ashley River Road *en masse* and set off into the woods in search of a fox (or the scent of a fox in the event of a drag hunt).

An even more elaborate equestrian spectacle of the 1970s and 80s was Coaching Day. Antique, four-in-hand carriages from along the Eastern Seaboard — drawn by matched teams of horses and driven by "whips" in top hats — descended on Middleton Place with armies of grooms and equip-

The Inn at Middleton Place, just south of the national landmark.

ment, ready to demonstrate agility and elegance. *Town and Country* magazine sent renowned photographer Toni Frissell to chronicle the inaugural event on a spring weekend in 1975, two months after the Middleton Place house museum opened. Charles called on artist and equestrian Frolic Weymouth to organize the affair. Weymouth, founder of the Brandywine Conservancy and Museum of Art, was one of two Americans who were members of England's Coaching Club. The stunning promenade of impeccably restored carriages in full regalia accompanied by beautifully appointed horses, drivers and footmen, drew several hundred spectators daily.

Adjacent to the equestrian center, Charles launched another new, land-based venture — a conservation development called Middleton Oaks — on 150 acres Charles purchased along Middleton Place's southern border. Under the guidance of landscape architect Robert Marvin and Sea Pines Company president Phil Lader, approximately 30 house sites were laid out. Marvin carefully oriented the 1 ½-acre sites so that sylvan buffers surrounded them and none were visible from the river or the historic landmark. The remainder of the acreage stayed wooded and undeveloped. Lader, an attorney who later became U.S. Ambassador to the Court of St. James, wrote the covenants. Each house site averaged $200,000 in value at the time and included access to the common woodlands and waterfront, as well as to Middleton Place next door.

"Middleton Oaks has given residents the opportunity to live in a low density, rural setting and to become co-stewards of Middleton Place and the Ashley River corridor," says Charles. "We believe this type of conservation development is appropriate and compatible with the traditional landscape and activities of the historic corridor. At the same time, sales of these house sites have provided much needed liquidity over the years to help pay off debt and support the educational and preservation programs of Middleton Place." [8]

• • •

Charles made his most daring and visible mark on Middleton Place with the completion of the Middleton Inn in the late 1980s. A decade earlier, in consultation with hotelier Eric Brooks, he began formulating a plan for a riverfront inn situated on a wooded bluff along the southeast boundary of the gardens between the national landmark acreage and that of Middleton Oaks. He envisioned the inn as a complementary asset to the historic landmark — one that would generate revenue. According to Charles, "The purpose of the Middleton Inn from day one was to support the programs and operations of the Middleton Place Foundation." But the big question was, what would it look like?

Beginning with his studies at Yale under architectural historian Vincent Scully — followed by his postgrad travels across Asia and the Middle East, and later as a resident of the Le Corbusier building at the Cite Universitaire of Paris — Charles had become knowledgeable and passionate about architecture, particularly its influence on landscape and culture. "My love for architecture was inspired by the lectures of Vince Scully," Charles reflects. "He taught us not just to look, but to see."

Scully believed that art history must be simultaneously "conservative, experimental and ethical." He once told the *Yale Bulletin*, "God is in the landscape, and God is in the building. And in that relationship is the typical Greek balance between what nature wills and what man wants." In the same interview, Scully went on to say, "We expect our buildings to outlive us. It's very important."

New Yorker critic Paul Goldberger (also a student of Scully's at Yale) summarized Scully's credo: "For him the very point of honoring the past is to allow it to unleash the highest and best new ideas in the present; and he is

W.G. Clark used concrete, stucco and wood to create, over time, "a ruin in the woods."

profoundly ethical, for he believes that the noblest mission of architectural history is to encourage the building of community, and hence, of civilization."

Charles drew upon these principles in his search for someone to design the inn. He first approached Robert "Bob" Venturi, a post-modernist Philadelphia architect who had also taught at Yale and, like Scully, believed in using history and the particulars of place and cultural context in the design of contemporary buildings. Early in his career, Venturi worked for Louis Kahn, the great modernist and a hero to Charles. "Bob was interested in the inn, but was not available at the time," Charles explains. "So he recommended a student of Louis Kahn's who had been associated with the Venturi and Rauch firm for several years named W.G. Clark."

In 1974 at age 32, Clark moved to Charleston and set up his own practice. It was risky for any modern architect to try and succeed in South Carolina, especially one so relatively young. Architect Charles Menefee — a Charlestonian — later joined him to form the partnership of Clark and Menefee. The two would collaborate on the final design and execution of the Middleton Inn, and several more projects in succeeding years.

From the outset, Clark approached the inn with a variety of factors in mind. First, he wanted the structures to reference the buildings of Charleston. More specifically, he aimed to evoke architectural ruins that could be found across the Lowcountry — ruins that seemed to emerge out of the native soils and primeval forests, such as Old Sheldon Church near Yemassee, 50 miles southwest of Middleton Place. Clark wanted the inn to look like it had always been there, as if it had risen organically.

Secondly, Clark wanted the buildings to blend into the natural landscape. He strove to incorporate the surrounding woods to appear as though they would reclaim the inn at any moment, siting the compound amidst century-old oaks and pines — the trees naturally shrouded in Spanish moss; the structures anchored with sprigs of climbing fig vine.

Clark chose concrete, stucco and wood as primary construction materials, reflecting historic Charleston while at the same time eschewing reproduction architecture. Spare, subtle and contemplative were the watchwords of the tall masonry cubes with their simple wooden shutter walls and window grids. Plantation nostalgia was scrupulously avoided; but at the same time, modern references to the plantation infused every room — including louvered window shutters, braided rugs, and working fireplaces.

His philosophy of architecture posited that all building should be atonement for the disturbance of the land. "At the necessary juncture of culture and place, architecture seeks not only the minimal ruin of landscape, but something more difficult: a replacement of what was lost with something that atones for that loss," Clark wrote in a 1991 essay. "In the best architecture," he continued, "this replacement is through an intensification of the place, where it emerges no worse for human intervention, where culture's shaping of the place to specific use results in a heightening of the beauty of the landscape. In these places, we seem worthy of existence."

The architect soon became aware that the wooded site chosen for the inn contained two rectangular "terraces" leftover from a phosphate mining operation owned by Williams Middleton. According to Clark's biographer Robert McCarter, "The terraces, the longer sides of which ran parallel to the river, were to be transformed during construction from raw, overgrown mining scars to grass-covered lawns, not dissimilar to the landscaped terraces of Middleton Place. Clark wrapped the main building along the L-shaped embankment of the uppermost terrace . . .

" 'It is stretched the length of the terrace so as to become a boundary rather than an object,' as Clark notes. The main building is both boundary and space-shaper, separating and joining the dense forest to the south and the sunken lawn overlooking the river to the north. Clark said, 'It became immediately clear that the inn would not be a box, but a distended, occupied wall along the embankment, an inscribed mark of the long past occupation. It was satisfying to find a reason for shaping a building derived from the physical place and its history.' "

Complementing the main hotel building, which paralleled the river, Clark and Menefee designed three smaller L-shaped buildings of guest rooms to the east and west. Each of the multi-story, masonry structures is punctuated with wooden towers of floor-to-ceiling windows painted "Charleston green," a color that is nearly black. While boasting a total of 55 rooms with all the modern conveniences, the complex of gray stucco walls and green wooden towers appears to originate from the ancient marl of the Ashley River, while simultaneously being subsumed by the forest behind it. Clark christened their creation "a ruin in the woods."

Not long after its opening in June 1987, the Middleton Inn received a National Honor Award from the American Institute of Architects, the profession's highest accolade for individual buildings by American designers. Managed for several years by Charles' brother Rod Duell — a graduate of Yale with an MBA from the University of North Carolina at Chapel Hill, and a veteran of the corporate world — the inn was featured in *Architectural Digest, Vogue, Time* and *New York* magazines.

Clark credited contractor Stier Kent and Canady for their "great care in construction." He also paid tribute to Charles, stating, "During the course of one's work there are people who make a huge difference. Charles Duell, owner of Middleton Place, is one of those. He had the courage to entrust me with the design of Middleton Inn in the very beginning. He had studied with Vincent Scully at Yale, and was a truly enlightened patron of architecture."

Today the inn serves as a powerful expression of its contemporary era, just as Middleton Place is an enduring expression of the past. As Charles says, "I feel confident that 100 years from now, those who visit Middleton Place will not only have great architecture of the 18th and 19th centuries to admire but also a great architectural achievement of the 20th century as well." 9

• • •

Aesthetics aside, the Middleton Inn got off to a rocky start monetarily.

Thirty partners financed its construction — each contributing $150,000 to a limited partnership known as the Middleton Inn Associates. While Charles was the only Class A limited partner, an assortment of family members and friends, a handful of TV and movie stars, and a group of Morgan Stanley investors from Chicago contributed funding to Middleton Inn Associates as Class B partners. Because the inn was to support the Middleton Place Foundation, the limited liability partnership was structured to receive a substantial tax deduction.

Middleton Inn Associates raised $4.5 million, but before construction was completed, another $2 million was needed to finish paying for the buildings. Charles borrowed part of the amount from a bank and called on the partners to make up the rest. The Chicago group balked, then sued Charles and general partner Pug Ravenel in federal court in Chicago, claiming misrepresentation and fraud. Charles sued those partners who did not contribute to the negative capital call in state court in South Carolina. The Chicago partners then filed a counterclaim.

Halfway through the court case, the bank initiated foreclosure proceedings and listed the inn for sale. Eventually 20 of the 30 limited partners anted up, enabling Charles to pay off part of the loan and forestall foreclosure. The remaining partners, including the Chicago investors, pressed on with their lawsuit.

The case in Chicago had its venue changed to federal court in Charleston. Meanwhile the state case was adjudicated first, in February of 1990, in a temporary courtroom in North Charleston — across the Ashley River from Middleton Place. Identifying himself as a historic preservationist, Charles reminded the court that the sole purpose of the Middleton Inn was to sustain the Middleton Place National Historic Landmark. The judge listened and dismissed the counterclaim filed by the Chicago investors, who had failed to show up. A sympathetic jury awarded Charles $1.65 million in damages. The damage award allowed him to pay off the bank loan, put $1 million into the Middleton Inn Associates operating capital and save the inn.

Charles and Pug Ravenel then used the win in state court to get the federal case dismissed, ending a five-year, multifaceted legal battle. Attorney J. Rutledge Young, Jr., a Middleton descendant and former trustee of the Middleton Place Foundation, represented Charles, as did New York tax attorney Marty Major. The cases were complex and expensive. In addition

Hurricane Hugo delivered a powerful blow to Middleton Place.

to saving the inn, "it was one of the biggest tax deductions to survive IRS scrutiny for a limited liability corporation in the history of the United States at the time," Young remembers. "We had to counter sue [for abuse of process and malicious prosecution] to bind everybody in order to save the inn. However, in the end, all the partners still received a large tax deduction." [10]

• • •

Ordinarily, the Middleton Inn case would have been tried in the U.S. Courthouse at the historic "Four Corners of Law" in downtown Charleston. But four months earlier, a much harder blow struck in the form of Hurricane Hugo. The storm made landfall on September 21, 1989 with wind speeds of 137 miles per hour and a circumference measuring 250 miles around a 40-mile-wide eye — nearly as big as the State of South Carolina. The Category 4 storm so severely damaged the 19th century federal courthouse that it was forced to relocate to a metal warehouse in North Charleston, the temporary courtroom where Charles, Rutledge Young and Marty Major later fought to save the Middleton Inn.

The inn's solid masonry structure stood strong and withstood Hugo's furious winds. But 85 percent of the forest surrounding it was lost. As architect W.G. Clark lamented, "One is prepared to lose one's building in such a natural disaster, but not to lose one's entire landscape." [11]

The buildings at Middleton Place also held firm. But more than 450 significant trees were destroyed, as the hurricane came ashore and sped northwest. Loblolly pines, red cedars and magnolias suffered the most. The venerable live oaks and great Middleton Oak — while losing limbs — survived intact. The stableyards' gingko trees also pulled through, as did the garden statuary and Middleton family tomb. However, nearly the entire pierced brick wall surrounding the greensward had to be rebuilt, as did much of the fencing on the property.

"We had no electricity or water for three weeks and the roads were impassable for several days," Charles recounts. "I first saw Middleton Place with house museum director Sarah Lytle. We drove as far as Drayton on the Ashley, then climbed into a canoe and paddled the rest of the way. As we got closer and closer, we saw limbs and branches strewn everywhere, but fortunately no loss of life and very little destruction of buildings."

Lytle recorded her observations in a newsletter published that winter: "We had paddled through an eerie, no-man's land, hearing little sound and seeing few people en route. But noise and activity greeted us as soon as we put in at the Rice Mill: chain saws were buzzing, the back hoe was beeping, the Cushman was backfiring. Middleton Place was at work; and the people who were hurricane bound there, trapped by miles of tangled fallen trees on the river road, were clearing tons of debris from the Middleton roads and paths.

"These same people have been hard at work ever since that first day after. As soon as the highway was opened, the entire staff arrived, augmented by family members and old and new volunteers. Many left battered houses and families behind to come to Middleton to prepare lunch for the workers, to clear and rake, to rig emergency power and plumbing, to care for the collections and animals, and to communicate to the world just how well Middleton Place had survived."

After the storm, the obvious task was to begin clearing the grounds and to reestablish some degree of normalcy, even without electricity, telephone or reliable plumbing. Help came from many sources and in many guises. Hundreds of friends showed up to lend a hand. Within a week, Colonial Williamsburg sent a team of tree surgeons to assist Middleton Place Vice

In 1999, Middleton Place was the setting for a garden party in the movie "The Patriot." The film crew built a fake façade to recreate the main house.

President of Horticulture Sidney Frazier; and brick masons to repair brickwork in the stableyards and along the garden wall. "Unsolicited, a caravan of trucks and experts arrived from Williamsburg," remembers Charles. "They went right to work. Their presence made an enormous impact."

The Center for Historic Plants at Monticello also came. They culled seeds from fallen trees to ensure their propagation and eventual replanting, and donated more than 100 red and yellow Crown Imperial bulbs to provide blooms for the upcoming spring. The Brooklyn Botanic Gardens followed suit, dispatching their director of horticulture, Edmond Moulin, to consult with Frazier and survey garden restoration needs.

On October 9 (three weeks after Hugo), the gates to Middleton Place opened to the public, albeit with no electricity and many parts of the grounds blocked off. One of the most dramatically affected sites was the Cypress Lake. Giant tree trunks lay prone in every direction, crushing the vegetation beneath and cutting off the flow of water, rendering it impenetrable. Miraculously, the camellias and azaleas on the high ground escaped relatively unharmed — bent, but not broken, by the winds.

Across the Ashley River Road, the hurricane and tornados it spawned either snapped the pine trees like matchsticks or twisted their trunks, destroying some $4 million worth of saw timber. It took more than a month for property manager Jim Woodle to clear the debris. The value of the wood quickly plummeted due to the glut of fallen trees on the market.

FEMA provided approximately $800,000 in emergency relief. At the same time, the Middleton Place Foundation established a "Hurricane Fund" that raised more than $700,000. Additional financial support and in kind services came from more than 25 states, the District of Columbia and Paris, France. "If we hadn't had our 501(c)(3) status, I don't know where Middleton Place would be today," reflects Charles. With the support of members and friends, combined with the Lowcountry's long growing season and mild climate, nature quickly began to heal itself. As Sidney Frazier promised, "The gardens *will* recover. It's just a matter of time." Eighteen months later, the plantation was back up and running. [12]

Rick Rhodes

A recent reunion of the descendants of Middleton Place.

Seven

TO BEGIN AGAIN

"There was a time when you could tour an entire plantation and not hear slavery mentioned once."
— Dr. Robert Bellinger

In the spring of 1989 several months before Hurricane Hugo hit, the Middleton Place Foundation announced a new interpretative initiative centered around African Americans associated with the Middleton family and their plantations. A panel of authorities in African American history convened to lend their expertise, including Dr. Myrtle Glascoe, director of the Avery Research Center; Dr. John Rashford, ethnobotanist at the College of Charleston; Gary Stanton from the Historic Preservation Department at Mary Washington College, and Dr. Theodore Rosengarten, noted historian and author.

Eliza Leach's former home — a clapboard duplex built after the Civil War to house Middleton Place workers — was chosen as the focal point for the program. Since Leach's death in 1986, the building had served as the foundation's accounting office. But everyone continued to call it "Eliza's House," in remembrance of the African American who had lived there for nearly half a century. Soon, a team of folk life specialists from the McKissick Museum in Columbia began conducting oral history workshops at Eliza's House to capture accounts and memories of the people connected to it.

In describing the project, Dr. Glascoe remarked, "I think it is a wonderful idea to build these efforts around the restoration and interpretation of the 1870s house [Eliza's House] . . . This initiative will add a much needed dimension to the overall interpretive program of Middleton Place . . . [and] will be a major step toward correcting the interpretation of African American life on South Carolina plantations in the Lowcountry."

Similar to antebellum slave dwellings, Eliza's House was constructed of mill-sawn weatherboard with a central, double (back-to-back) brick fireplace

Circa 1870 freedman's dwelling, now called Eliza's House, at its original location (today the site of the Middleton Place Restaurant).

that heated each two-room unit. The interior and exterior wooden walls were whitewashed with lime and water. There was no connecting access between the units, but each shared a common front porch and storage loft. By the time of Eliza Leach's occupancy, the structure had been converted into a single residence. Leach lived much as her predecessors did, her self-sufficient ways an echo of earlier, harder times: raking the bare "swept yard" clear of leaves and debris (an African custom of both utilitarian and decorative origins), chopping wood for the fire, and carrying water from the spring house (long after plumbing had been installed).

In the fall of 1991 a ceremonial housewarming was held to mark the opening of Eliza's House and the inauguration of a formal African American interpretative program. Blending traditions of the Mende and Yoruba peoples of West Africa with those of Lowcountry African Americans, the afternoon celebration included scriptural readings, prayers, gospel songs, lectures, dancing and drumming. Sparsely furnished, the house displayed a collection of household objects appropriate to post Civil War Black life, objects familiar to Eliza Leach — herbs hanging up to dry, iron cook pots hung over the fire, and homemade brooms made of marsh grasses, corn

Eliza's House at its new location after restoration.

husks and dogwood twigs.

Dr. Rosengarten articulated the significance of launching the initiative at Eliza's House — a nexus of endings and beginnings and continuity for the inhabitants of Middleton Place: "History, which is what people did with their time in the past, takes place here, in Eliza's House, just as it does up there in the Big House ... The tenant house itself is no less a document that can be read, than is the Big House. The tenant house expresses a conception of life; it embodies hopes and meets needs. It shows off the builder's skills and knowledge. It is built in a style that has roots, a history. It belongs to traditions of house building and architecture that go back to Europe and Africa and meet here on the Ashley River." [1]

• • •

When Charles Duell called Ted Rosengarten to assist Middleton Place with its African American history initiative, Rosengarten had just been named a McArthur Fellow. His Ph.D. research at Harvard in the late 1960s and early 70s resulted in the book *All God's Dangers: The Life of Nate Shaw,* an oral history of a Black Alabama sharecropper — published in 1974 by Alfred A. Knopf and winner of the National Book Award. His next book, *Tombee: Portrait of a Cotton Planter*, won a National Book Critics Circle Award after its release in 1986.

Rosengarten became a professor of American Studies and a resident of McClellanville, S.C. His particular focus on the enslaved, the freedmen and the sharecroppers of the Deep South — especially the degree to which he explored his African American characters — was pathbreaking. Rosengarten was following in the footsteps of another Harvard scholar Philip Curtin, who in 1969 published a seminal work titled *The Atlantic Slave Trade: A Census*. Curtin co-founded with his colleague Jan Vansina a department of African languages and literature at the University of Wisconsin — one of the first to establish African Studies as an academic discipline.

In 1974 Knopf published a second trailblazing volume called *Black Majority: Negroes in Colonial South Carolina from 1670 through the Stono Rebellion* by Peter Wood, also educated at Harvard. Wood's research proved that in colonial South Carolina "the role of the black majority was major rather than minor, active rather than passive." As early as 1708, Africans and African Americans began outnumbering settlers of European descent. A Black majority would prevail in the state until 1922, when a White majority emerged for the first time in more than two centuries.

Curtin, Rosengarten and Wood were among a cadre of scholars at the time who were documenting and describing aspects of the American experience rarely revealed. They laid to rest the notion that the African American past was unrecoverable, and made it clear that Blacks played a significant and determinative part in U.S. history. Moreover, they presented new perspectives not only on the institution of slavery and its economic impact, but also on the nature of human interactions and relationships within a slave-based society.

Thus the fields of social science and African American history in the U.S. expanded significantly in the 1970s. Due in no small part to the Civil Rights movement and heightened awareness on college campuses, many Americans were waking up to the fact that the experience and heritage of whole segments of the population were largely absent from the history books.

With more funding and research directed to the study and interpretation of African American history, a more inclusive national identity emerged at numerous universities, museums, libraries and historic sites. In the mid-

Eliza Leach.

1970s, Colonial Williamsburg's Carl Humelsine, who had been an advisor to Middleton Place, formed a committee to examine Williamsburg's interpretation to better meet the new standards emerging in the social sciences. On the eve of the nation's bicentennial (and Charleston's tricentennial), reform in the teaching of U.S. history had begun.

Since the stableyards and house museum were first established, Middleton Place had more or less conformed to the traditional Williamsburg model. While a few African American slave descendants worked as interpreters in the stableyards, their script mostly took its cue from the history and stories of the wealthy White Middletons and their peers: namely family lineage, property, enterprise and culture, and contributions to colony and country. As a 12th generation Middleton, Charles was proud of his ancestors' accomplishments, but also aware of their slave-trading, slave-owning past. Coupled with the legacy of generations of Black workers Charles had known at Middleton Place since childhood, that past was far more complex than what was being conveyed. [2]

• • •

Middleton Place was one of the first historic plantation sites to employ African American interpreters, but their own history was mostly communicated in the context of service to the Middleton family. Charles understood there was a more complete and accurate narrative waiting to be told, especially given the large Black population connected to Middleton Place. Furthermore, an archaeological dig in 1979 had uncovered some 3,000 shards of colonoware: a low-fired, hand built pottery of African origin commonly made and used by enslaved plantation workers. This was a tantalizing indicator of how much there was to discover and learn.

With the help of the Middleton Place Black community, along with experts from the McKissick Museum and members of the 1989 advisory panel, new instructional materials and tours were developed in the early 1990s. Under the direction of Sharon Cooper-Murray, coordinator for African American interpretation, Middleton Place also began highlighting aspects of Black history and culture through special programming and events centered on African American spirituals, work songs, cookery, labor and war service.

Then in the fall of 1995, Charles received a call from Earl Middleton. Born in 1919, Middleton had grown up in Orangeburg, South Carolina and graduated from Clafin College, a predominately Black Methodist university where his grandfather had been a founding trustee. After training as a Tuskegee Airman and serving in the Pacific Theater during World War II, Middleton returned to his hometown in 1946 and founded what would become one of the largest real estate brokerages in the Orangeburg area.

Earl Middleton.

But his success did not come without adversity. As civil rights activists in the 1950s and 60s, Middleton and his wife, Bernice, witnessed firsthand the bravery and suffering of Orangeburg's Black citizens, joining protests and sit-ins and even going to jail. In 1974 Middleton was among the first wave of 20th century African Americans to be elected to the S.C. House of Representatives. He became a founding member of the Legislative Black Caucus and an influential voice on the U.S. Civil Rights Commission.

Middleton had called Charles to invite him and son Holland Duell to attend a celebration at the Koger Center in Columbia to recognize the state's African American leaders. Middleton was among the honorees. BellSouth, sponsor of the event, was presenting a video about each leader and had requested a film clip from Middleton Place. The reason being, as Earl Middleton explained, "that is where my great-grandfather is said to have been enslaved."

Seventy-six years old and retired, Earl had never met Charles. Nevertheless the two men had many mutual acquaintances and quickly became friends. The following spring, Charles drove to Orangeburg to invite Earl to join the Middleton Place Foundation board. "I will never forget his response," reflects Charles. "He said: 'Your ancestors once owned mine. Now I will own you!'"

That fall of 1996, Earl's relatives from around the country gathered at Middleton Place for a family reunion of descendants of Thomas Middleton, a late 18th century enslaved African American. A decade later, Earl would reflect on his association with Middleton Place in an autobiography published shortly after his death:

"Historically black folks and plantations have gone together like prisoners and jailhouses. When prisoners get out of jail, most don't want to return. This is the same feeling many blacks have about plantations; they want nothing to do with them. Black families have passed down to their children the picture of plantations as being places where blacks were kept enslaved, shackled in chains, beaten, and mistreated. Some of this is true for all slaves, and for some slaves all, unfortunately, was true.

"In my own particular case our family had a good sense of who we were from day one. We knew we were descended from Methodist ministers and that Granddaddy Middleton had been well respected when he was living and had set the values by which our family lived . . . my parents never mentioned anything about slavery. Actually we never knew [growing up] whether our ancestors had been enslaved or free. In my cousin Mamie's [Mamie Garvin Fields] memoir 'Lemon Swamp and Other Places,' she cites a servant-master relationship between our ancestors and the white Middletons. Knowing for sure that our family was from Charleston, many assumed, and still do, that our ancestors were from Middleton Place.

"It is within this context that we heard Duell's invitation . . . I was intrigued with the possibility of service on the Middleton Place Foundation's board for several reasons, including the fact that I would become the first black person to be a member of this group, whose duty was primarily oversight . . . While many blacks are put off by the thought of being on a plantation, my mind was working

in another direction. Today's Middleton Place principals were there to preserve a historical property and interpret the lives of those who had lived and worked there. Whether it was positive or negative for my people, it was our history. That history is going to be told whether I or any other black person serves on the board. So if I am interested in having anything to say about it then it seemed to be a no-brainer to accept Charles' invitation and get involved.

"As soon as I accepted membership on the board at Middleton Place I began to educate myself for the task. The timing was perfect as I learned of a symposium, 'The Grand Estate — Yesterday, Today and Tomorrow,' that was to be held in Charlottesville, Virginia, within the next 60 days. Although I had been in real estate for many years, none of my experience touched on multi-acre historic properties. Since this seminar was close to Monticello, it was the opportune time to visit that estate and see how history was being interpreted . . .

"We visited Monticello the first day of the trip. We had contacted Dr. Dan Jordan, president of the [Thomas] Jefferson Foundation, ahead of time, and he and his staff made us feel very welcome. Other than Middleton Place, it was my first visit to a historic property.

"First we took a tour of the Monticello house museum, which by necessity was brief since there are hundreds and hundreds and maybe even thousands going through each day. By this time guides were giving extended tours that emphasized the experiences of African Americans who had been associated with Monticello. This portion was all outdoors. We viewed the sites that had housed plantation buildings used by Jefferson's slaves as they built and maintained the property. We spent most of the day there going over the extensive grounds, which included the well-known cemetery where Thomas Jefferson is buried. In the museum shop we were able to find many books relating to the lives of blacks in the historical period represented by Monticello. And, yes, the tour guides did discuss the controversy about whether or not Jefferson fathered children by his slave Sally Hemmings. It was a day full of education for this black man!"[3]

• • •

Earl Middleton returned from Monticello excited about the possibilities for enhancing African American historic interpretation at Middleton Place. Charles and other trustees shared his desire. Building on the initial exhibits, tours, oral history workshops and programs begun in Eliza's House at the

African American pottery, called colonoware, excavated at Middleton Place.

start of the decade, the Middleton Place Foundation dedicated considerable resources in the 1990s toward expanding research, staff and infrastructure to tell the story of the plantation's Black community.

With a matching grant from the S.C. Department of Archives and History in 1998, and additional funding from Dorchester County, the Joanna Foundation and the John and Kathleen Rivers Foundation, renovation began on another structure of significance to African Americans at Middleton Place — the spring house. Believed to be the oldest surviving building on the plantation and constructed by enslaved labor, it dates from at least the mid-18th century when Mary Williams brought the property with her as part of her dowry when she married Henry Middleton. It may have been built even earlier for Mary's father, John Williams, to shelter the natural spring that flows into it.

A century later, the spring house was being used by Henry Middleton's great-grandson Williams Middleton as a dairy — a cool spot in which to store the milk and butter from his cows — with the second floor (which Williams added) serving as a chapel for the enslaved community. The chapel was part of a host of additions and expansions Williams undertook in the decade before the Civil War. A reference to the structure was found in a letter at the Historical Society of Pennsylvania, written by Williams to his brother-in-law Francis Fisher in 1851. His description aligns with the appearance of the second floor:

"I believe I told you that I had built a pretty good room with a vaulted ceiling over the dairy with the intention of placing a billiard table in it one of these days. This has been converted into a Chapel by particular request & the neighbourhood Parson is at this moment holding forth there in full swing to a large & fashionable congregation of all colors." Whoever made the request for a plantation chapel is unknown. Whether it was Williams' wife Susan, or his enslaved foreman, Luke Maddox, or the Reverend J. Stuart Hanckel of neighboring St. Andrew's Church, no documentation has been found.

Even in bondage, West Africans who survived the Atlantic crossing carried their religious beliefs and rituals with them. In fact, about 20 to 30 percent of Africans brought to America were Muslim. Ethnic groups such as Coromantee, Angola, Mandingo and others would continue the religious observances of their homelands on the Carolina plantations. By the late 18th century, however, a large number of bondsmen were Carolina born and becoming distanced from direct African cultural influences. Many embraced Christianity, frequently merging ancestral religious beliefs and practices with those of the White church.

In the early 19th century, the "Second Great Awakening" — a religious revival — swept across the United States. Black as well as White missionaries were allowed to visit plantations to preach Christianity. Then in 1822 a failed slave rebellion in Charleston, and the ensuing trials of the men involved, virtually eliminated missionary activities. Denmark Vesey, a free Black man and African Methodist lay leader, was tried and executed as the instigator of the planned revolt. Afterwards, plantation owners banned evangelists and lay leaders from the countryside.

Several years later, however, a group of rice planters called on the S.C. Agricultural Society to support a renewed missionary effort directed at the plantation slave community. They raised funds to hire White clergymen to spread the Gospel. Beginning along the Santee River, this new missionary movement quickly spread to plantations on the Ashley River and elsewhere. Many slaveholders used the Bible to justify slavery. They believed that enslaved men and women who practiced Christianity were more easily controlled and less likely to rebel. Some "slave Bibles" even omitted the Exodus story for fear it would inspire revolt.

Planters, clergymen or the enslaved people themselves chose religious leaders from within the Black community to assist with religious instruction, church services and funerals. Archival records show that marriages and family units were recognized at Middleton Place and other plantations, even though they were not sanctioned under South Carolina law. Some planters

The Middleton Place spring house (bottom floor) and plantation chapel (top floor).

encouraged and tacitly recognized such unions to foster a sense of stability, believing marriage and family ties would help forestall unrest and discourage runaways.

Records show that marriages between slaves and freedmen were allowed as well. The Reverend Paul Trapier, minister of Charleston's Calvary Church — organized in 1847 by the Episcopal Diocese to provide religious instruction to African Americans — wrote the following account in his register book: "William Elwig (free colored) and Rachael (servant of Mrs. Williams Middleton) were married December 16, 1852 before several witnesses and with consent of her owner, in Mrs. Dehon's house." [4]

Documents also note that marriages took place among Black men and women enslaved by different owners. In an 1847 letter addressed to Williams Middleton, a Mr. H. Walker writes, "My servant Abraham being desirous of taking a wife at your place has requested a certificate of Character etc. I take pleasure in stating that he is remarkably steady and industrious — and I would recommend him to your favourable consideration." Once married, the couple would continue to live on separate plantations, with the husband allowed to visit his wife at specified intervals. Their children would become the property of the wife's owner.

Church affiliation of slaves was not always the same as their owners. To date, no records have been found to determine the Middleton Place chapel's religious denomination. Sunday services consisted of scriptural readings, a sermon and hymns. Catechism lessons, baptisms, marriages, confirmations and funerals were held in plantation chapels, on porches, in the big house and along the slave street. They might occur on days other than Sunday, subject to work schedules on the plantation and the travel itinerary of the clergyman.

Inside the plantation chapel.

Large numbers of African Americans strongly identified with the suffering of Christ, according to Yolanda Pierce, dean of the divinity school at Howard University. Christianity brought them "this powerful and profound sense of hope that Jesus would return; that there is a life and world after this life; that what is going on with the human body, the mortal realm, is just temporary; that there is eternity; that you will be rewarded, you will experience joy and peace and comfort . . . No wonder it was embraced."

By claiming Christianity as their own, African Americans seized on the language of their oppressors and often transformed it into a vocabulary for the oppressed. As they studied English and mastered the Biblical texts, Black Christians understood the deity of the Old and New Testaments to be a just God. Jesus' radical message convinced them that Christ was on their side — a friend, a champion and a liberator of the downtrodden. Hence, they reinterpreted their enslavers' most sacred text. "They very quickly learned," says Pierce, "that the only way we can be heard is to speak the language of our slaveholders, to speak to them about the text that they love, that they believe in."

In doing so, African Americans also developed insight into the thinking, justifications and workings of a slaveholding society. While the church offered solace and salvation, it also provided a training ground, an educational platform, and an organizational and leadership structure for the enslaved community. Autonomy soon became an important issue for Black Christians and separate Black congregations began to emerge, offering fellowship and solidarity. The church was also where Blacks could experience a sense of freedom — a glimpse of heaven on earth. For those church leaders who survived slavery and the Civil War, many would play key roles in Black political and religious life during Reconstruction and beyond. [5]

• • •

As better understanding of the spring house chapel and its uses developed, a clearer picture of Africans and African Americans associated with the Middleton family came to light. This was the direct result of a comprehensive research initiative begun in 1999 by Middleton Place curators and historians Barbara Doyle, Tracey Todd and Mary Edna Sullivan. With Charles' support, they attended conferences on the latest developments in African American historical interpretation, consulted with experts around the country and set about to make Middleton Place a leader in the field.

For years staff members and volunteers had gone about the difficult task of reading and cataloguing thousands of handwritten 18th and 19th century Middleton family documents — found in assorted shoeboxes and old trunks when the house museum first opened to the public in the 1970s. Reading these letters and papers required exceptional skill to accurately extract information from time-faded words written in pencil or pen by men and women whose "s's" looked like "f's" and whose spelling was irregular. To save paper the correspondents often wrote around and across already filled pages — employing innumerable, hard to decipher abbreviations.

Typically, staff and volunteers reading these missives were searching for references to Middleton family members and their various activities and associates. But archivist Barbara Doyle went further. Every time she encountered a reference to an African American, enslaved or free, she noted the name and particular source citation on a 5x6 index card — one card for every African American mentioned in the Middleton family papers. Eventually hundreds of cards filled up a small plastic box. Here lay the foundation for a new research focus.

"Barbara laid the groundwork," states Tracey Todd. "She recognized early on the importance of the African American story." Having begun her 40-year tenure at Middleton Place as a volunteer tour guide, Doyle became a staff member in 1977. Her skills as a researcher, genealogist and educator were formidable, as was her talent for synthesizing and communicating her findings. She served as chief writer and editor of the Middleton Place Foundation's quarterly newsletter and co-authored and edited numerous other foundation publications. In 1984 Doyle began creating the Middleton Family Tree database, adding to it steadily over the ensuing decades. She was ready to assist anyone who needed help tracing their family history.

This was the basis upon which Doyle, Todd and Sullivan set out to document as far as possible the lives, the families and the contributions of some seven generations of slaves held by the Middleton family. Mary Edna Sullivan, who became curator of museums at Middleton Place in 1998, described their quest: "We sought to learn how these Africans and African Americans adapted, created and forged individual identities, relationships and survival skills; and how they created and preserved social, cultural and economic identities and bonds within and beyond plantation boundaries — down through the generations."

They started with the following questions: Who were these enslaved men and women? What were their names? Where did they come from? Do we know who their families were? Where did they live? Did they ever have any leisure time? What special skills were they known for? What work did slaves do other than plant rice? Did any Middleton slaves ever escape to freedom? What did African Americans from Middleton Place do when freedom came?

It was no easy task. The enslaved population of Middleton Place left few artifacts and generated few personal papers or documents. In the Charleston area, oral histories of former slaves did not exist. The research team "was confronted with the very real challenge of making visible those who were invisible," Sullivan recalls. "We were challenged to extrapolate from the intangibles of their lives to produce a tangible exhibit... to relate clearly and accurately the history of enslaved and free African Americans at Middleton Place."

For several years, Doyle, Todd and Sullivan combed through historic re-

Barbara Doyle with Holland Duell.

cords and papers in the Middleton Place archives and at universities, libraries and museums across the country — piecing together family letters, plantation ledgers, probate records, and other private and public documents. They identified the names of 2,612 (out of a total of approximately 3,500) enslaved Africans and African Americans owned by the Middletons between 1738 and 1865. The team was able to confirm the names of their owners, the plantations where they lived, and their monetary value to individual Middletons and heirs. Moreover, they could list many of the bondsmen by their designated trade — such as carpenter, schooner captain, blacksmith, hairdresser or pastry cook.

Reflecting on the results of their investigation, Sullivan asserts: "By identifying 2,612 slaves once owned by the Middleton family and connecting many of them with their family units, we solidified their history into a tangible reality that should be considered a 21st century extension of the 20th century Civil Rights movement. It is a logical progression — a history that has been long awaiting the attention now given it." [6]

• • •

As Doyle, Todd and Sullivan were conducting their research, Middleton Place received a second matching grant to boost African American interpretation. In 2002, the South Carolina National Heritage Corridor Program awarded $20,000 to the historic landmark to convert half of Eliza's House

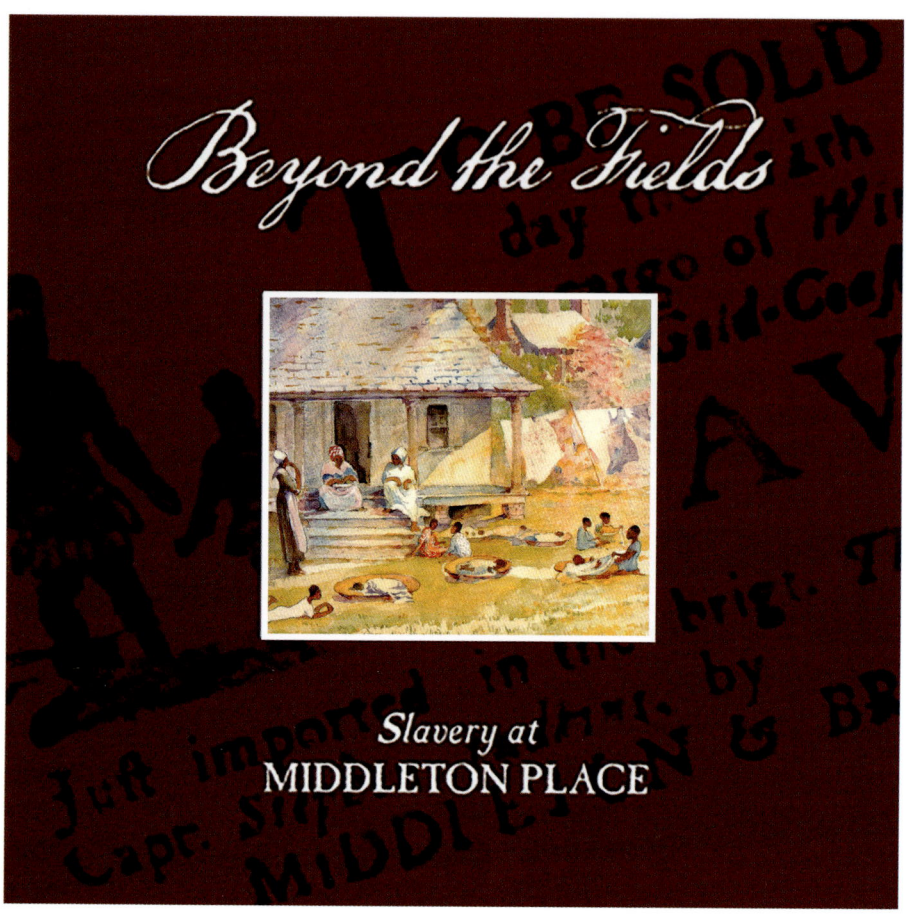

Beyond the Fields

Slavery at MIDDLETON PLACE

into an exhibit area for displaying information panels, archival documents, artifacts and other evidence of the African American community uncovered by the research team. Dorchester County, the 1772 Foundation and several other donors contributed to the project and enabled Middleton Place to meet the match.

The grant monies jumpstarted planning and preparation for a permanent installation that would bring together and highlight the results of Doyle's, Todd's and Sullivan's ongoing scholarship. The first step was to stabilize and adapt half of Eliza's House for public access and viewing of the new exhibit. The existing installation in the other half of the house comprised a re-creation of a freedman's living quarters during the 1870s — a static assemblage of artifacts and objects that visitors viewed through an open door and window, but did not enter. While Eliza's House gave an accurate depiction of postwar Black life on the plantation, the story of the Civil War and the centuries of enslavement that preceded it had not been fully told. For the first time, the origins and history of Middleton Place's African American community were conveyed and correlated with that of the Anglo European community.

That same year Dorchester County donated an additional $8,500 from its accommodations tax fund to augment the interpretation of rice culture at Middleton Place. The funds were used to update images and text panels pertaining to rice cultivation in both the mill house and chapel, as well as new interpretative materials associated with a quarter-acre demonstration rice field underway along the Ashley River.

By the fall of 2004 the new exhibit was ready for installation. Local museum consultant and exhibit designer Peter Coleman, with assistance from graphic designer Lee Helmer, used modern computer technology to create display panels. The panels wove together historic images, primary and secondary source material, contemporary quotes from African Americans and Europeans of the period, and myriad other details the research team had uncovered.

Simultaneously, an African American Focus Tour was developed, conducted by specially trained guides who linked the lives and work of the enslaved to nearly every aspect of the plantation. A donation from Charles Annenberg Weingarten — grandson of philanthropist and publisher Walter Annenberg — funded the publication of a companion book.

"Beyond the Fields: Slavery at Middleton Place" was the title chosen for the book, the tour and the exhibit — a reference to the fact that for too long America's understanding of slavery was frozen in an image of legions of anonymous African Americans toiling endlessly in fields of tobacco, sugarcane, cotton and rice. The plantations could not have existed without the unceasing labor of enslaved Africans who grew and processed the rice that brought enormous wealth to the Lowcountry and to the Middletons. But they also brought with them traditions and skills beyond the fields.

The entry room to "Beyond the Fields" featured a dramatic wall of names — listed under the heading "African Slaves Owned by the Middletons: 1738-1865" — enumerating the name, plantation home, occupation and monetary value of 2,612 enslaved persons associated with the Middleton family and their properties. Mary Edna Sullivan elaborates: "My concept for the panel containing all the slave names was inspired by Maya Lin's Vietnam War Memorial in Washington, D.C., and also from my earlier career in the Navy Nurse Corps. Peter Coleman brought the idea to life." [7]

The accompanying display panels vividly illustrated how slaves helped build the mansion, the cabins and the outbuildings of Middleton Place. Records and drawings showed how they fashioned the tools, sewed the clothes, cooked the food and managed the livestock; how they crafted the furniture and shaped the barrels. Facsimiles of plantation account books referenced the enslaved gardeners, butlers, bricklayers, coachmen, engineers and laundresses. Letters named the midwives and nursemaids who cared for White Middleton children along with their own. Among the bondsmen who lived in Charleston, some were permitted to hire out their services for wages. On occasion a worker might be allowed to keep a portion of the money; and in rare instances, the whole sum.

Away from the big house, the enslaved tended their own gardens and animals, practiced crafts, traded goods and services, played music and danced, cared for their families, ministered to the sick, and conducted weddings and funerals. As they persevered, they laid the foundation for the Gullah culture that survives today. But they were never secure, never safe from the vagaries, whims and capriciousness of a slave-based society. They were chattel — merchandise that could be bought, sold, traded, leased, abused or eliminated at a moment's notice, or no notice.

The death of a slave owner, for example, could be a particularly perilous time for the enslaved. As the owner's property was bequeathed to the heirs, enslaved families could be broken up and their fates uncertain. As Arthur Middleton stated in 1725: "Slaves have been and are always deemed as goods and chattels of their masters." It was a society in which human bondage was embedded in the culture, essential to the economy and codified by law. [8]

• • •

"I had always wanted a demonstration rice field at Middleton Place," says Vice President of Horticulture Sidney Frazier. So when Charles Duell asked the foundation management for their "wish lists" in 2001, a working rice field was at the top of Frazier's requests. Before long, a quarter-acre impoundment at the foot of the garden terraces was chosen for the demonstration site. Fall and winter were spent preparing the field and embankments, and ensuring that water control mechanisms were in good working order.

The following spring, in May 2002, an enthusiastic band of foundation staff and volunteers gathered at the demonstration plot, ready to reestablish an agricultural practice not undertaken at Middleton Place for 130 years. Each person was allocated a small bag of rice seed donated by the Carolina Gold Rice Foundation, a nonprofit dedicated to the restoration and preservation of heirloom rice and grains. The seed, developed by agricultural scientists from around the world, was the closest approximation in existence to Carolina Gold: the prized strain of rice cultivated by West Africans that made South Carolina planters the wealthiest in the world.

Moving slowly over the prepared ground, these latter-day field hands put down the seed in carefully demarcated rows. Someone armed with a rake followed, covering the seed with soil. Water was then pumped in from the nearby mill pond to flood the field and spark germination — called the "sprout flow." A week later the field was drained and in a few days green rice seedlings began to appear. When the plants were several inches tall, the field was again flooded with the "stretch," or "point flow," to keep out weeds and help support the growing stalks.

Throughout the summer, staff and volunteers watched over the flourishing crop. The agricultural operation lent an extra dimension to the self-guided tours of the gardens and the new African American Focus Tour. It also captured the attention of local and national media outlets, including the Food Network, which filmed a segment on Lowcountry rice growing for its "Food Nation" program. In subsequent years, the demonstration plot became the

Demonstration rice field at Middleton Place.

focus of numerous rice culture seminars, as well as a history and outdoor education platform for Title I elementary students.

For Sidney Frazier, the rice crop was an especially important addition to the interpretative program — "to make the telling of the history more authentic and meaningful," he explains. As a Black sea islander, he was attuned to the need to integrate his people's story "on a daily basis, everywhere at Middleton Place . . . to weave it all together and interpret the history more holistically, as it truly was." Frazier regarded Middleton Place as an inspiration in his life and an anchor for the local community. Moreover, he had witnessed its importance and impact far beyond South Carolina: "People come here from all over the world . . . All peoples throughout history have walked these same paths . . . In time, everyone will embrace the full story."

Meanwhile, as the month of August progressed into September, what had been a lush sea of vibrant green stalks gradually receded into small patches of ragged, uncertain growth. The number of precious panicles of grain that had begun to fill out and mature mysteriously dwindled as the days passed. By late September it was obvious to Frazier and others that the rice plot had succumbed to the same perils that often beset 18th and 19th century rice growers: contrary weather and scavenging predators. A lengthy period of heavy wind-driven rain beat down the stalks and rotted the seed clusters. Rapacious crows feasted on the few grains that survived. It was easy to empathize with Williams Middleton, who wrote to his sister Eliza in late 1853: "I shall probably go [to Middleton Place] . . . tomorrow although I expect little satisfaction there as I hear that the season has been most disastrous to my expectations."

Far from being discouraged at the failure of their first crop, rice planting committee co-chairmen Tracey Todd and Clint Noren declared, "Although we have nothing to harvest, we did learn many valuable lessons concerning rice culture and we intend to apply those lessons as we begin preparations for our next crop. Regardless of this year's results, the overall effort has been a huge interpretive success." 9

• • •

With regard to the unsuccessful rice crop of 2002, Sidney Frazier was accustomed to taking the long view. "We are a lot further along than 20 years ago," he says today, regarding both the rice project and the African American experience at Middleton Place. He has managed the world-renowned, 65-acre garden since 1982 (including its restoration after Hurricane Hugo), having begun as an apprentice the summer of 1974 during high school. Frazier lived and worked at Bay View Farm on James Island and had a talent for nurturing soil and plants. He gave up after-school sports to work part-time at Middleton Place during high school. Not long after graduation he became full-time, and within a few years rose to assistant manager.

"I had never set foot here as a young boy, did not even know Middleton Place existed," says Frazier. "But Bill Green was the foreman for the grounds crew at the time and was a James Islander like me and had been employed at Bay View Farm. He knew my family and knew I was a good worker." Green was a well known deer driver for the Middleton Hunting Club and laid the drag (fox scent) for the Middleton Place Hounds for 40 years. He also worked in the Middleton Restaurant kitchen and garden, and went on to found Gullah Grub Restaurant on St. Helena Island.

"In those days, Bill worked under Ben Chapman," Frazier continues. "I followed him and Ben and Charles everywhere asking questions and listening to everything they said. I learned about the garden's national and international significance, about its 'bones' and landscaped 'rooms.' I fell in love with its beauty and structure and layout."

In the late 1970s under Charles' direction, Chapman, Green, Frazier and caretaker Jim Woodle completed major infrastructure improvements to the garden. The men created new paths and garden rooms, and reopened old ones. They refurbished lakes and sculpted new alleys of trees, all the while adhering to the garden's precise geometrics. They installed an underground pump system to manage the natural movement of water through the property: most significantly, the huge west to east flow from Bear Swamp, under Ashley River Road, and across Middleton Place to the river. Frazier remembers building bulkheads for the reflection pool and trimming magnolia limbs along its edge, as well as clearing volunteer camellias that crowded out older specimens. All the work was done in-house. By the time they finished, Frazier knew every inch and aspect of the garden.

Ted Beckett was another mentor on Frazier's journey to becoming a professional horticulturalist and the "King of Camellias" (as *Garden & Gun* magazine dubbed him in 2019). Beckett was a native plant expert and also managed the plant nursery at nearby Magnolia Plantation. "All these men knew I would lead one day, so they invested in me," states Frazier. "In the 1980s, Charles encouraged me to return to school for a degree in horticulture from Trident Technical College. By the time Hugo hit in 1989, I was the garden manager and living at Middleton Place with my wife and five children, including a one-month-old baby. We spent the night in the brick restaurant with three other staff persons. We woke up the next morning and there was not one part of the garden that was not affected."

No doubt his near half-century at Middleton Place and decades of paying close attention to seasons and soil health, ancient trees and shrubs, and the fickleness and volatility of Lowcountry weather have contributed to Frazier's long view. As he told *Garden & Gun*, "A lot of what I do takes time to be realized. If you understand the windows Mother Nature presents to you, you will be rewarded at the right time. If you work against Mother Nature [long pause] . . ." He shakes his head.

But there is something else that prompts Frazier to speak in terms of centuries and millennia. In addition to discharging his duties as one of the vice

Sidney Frazier clipping *Camellia japonica* blooms at Middleton Place.

presidents of the Middleton Place Foundation, he is also a Christian minister. He was ordained at the New Bethlehem Baptist Church on Wadmalaw Island (his wife's church home) and serves as pastor of Full Faith Ministries on John's Island. Whether it's cloning a prize camellia or nurturing his faith and that of his congregation, Frazier is always "envisioning another century or two out."

"My ministry and my spiritual love of plants and wildlife, preserving nature, all come together here at Middleton Place. I manage the Middleton Place garden much like I operate as a minister. This garden and Sidney Frazier . . . I think we work well together. I am always happy to come to work. I like to keep my staff motivated so they feel invested in the whole and enjoy the fruits of their labor," he says.

"The garden is a wonderful marriage of old and new, native and cultivar. It is an inspiration to me and has a calming effect . . . I like to walk down

The Point-Flow, from the series *A Carolina Rice Plantation*, c. 1935, by Alice R.H. Smith.

by the Cypress Lake and meditate. You can hear nature. It is soothing and therapeutic. I do a lot of thinking about shape and color, form and height, light and air, especially as they relate to the whole. I respect this legacy and what I have been charged to maintain. I truly love Middleton Place." [10]

• • •

In February 2005, the exhibit "Beyond the Fields: Slavery at Middleton Place" was officially dedicated in a ceremony at Eliza's House. The display — combined with the African American Focus Tour, demonstration rice field, special lectures and seminars, new re-enactment and musical offerings, and ongoing research — significantly broadened interpretation at Middleton Place. Its African American programming was recognized in several national publications, including *The Wall Street Journal*, which stated, "the plantation's presentation of slave life . . . is the reason to visit."

The research conducted for "Beyond the Fields" (now verifying the identity of more than 2,800 African Americans enslaved by the Middletons) revealed numerous contemporary Black families with Middleton associations — such as the Edwards-Jackson-Prioleau families, as well as the Mayes, Bellinger, Epps, Fields and Middleton families. The White family members who gathered for reunions at Middleton Place every five years expressed a desire to get to know these descendants of African Americans connected to the family and its properties. At the same time, Middleton Place Foundation trustee Earl Middleton, whose relatives also held family reunions at the plantation, suggested an integrated gathering so that everyone — of both African and European descent — might learn more about their family history.

In the spring of 2006 a committee was formed of White and Black members associated with the Middleton family to plan a joint reunion. The group included Joy Barnes, Ty Collins, Charles Duell, Sallie Duell, Marjorie Manigault, Kenneth Middleton (son of Earl, who succeeded his father as a trustee), Mary Frances Middleton, Allston Moore, Al Pearson, Anita Middleton Pearson and Josephine Routh. They adopted the theme of "A Place to Begin" — describing the event as a "mutual voyage of discovery." On March 8, a letter was sent to hundreds of family and friends announcing that a joint reunion of descendants of Middleton Place would take place that fall.

As families began streaming through the gates of the Edmondston-Alston House the afternoon of Friday, November 10, the excitement and anticipation were unmistakable. The reception in the drawing room upstairs went on for hours as more and more relatives arrived, introductions were made and connections renewed. Saturday morning featured a host of tours and demonstrations at Middleton Place. By midday, approximately 300 Black and White Middleton Place descendants were assembled.

After a welcome and blessing, the group "broke bread" on the greensward around a buffet lunch of fried chicken, collards, hoppin' john and biscuits. An afternoon of special programs followed. Charles Duell and foundation staff led with a presentation chronicling the evolution of the interpretative program at Middleton Place. Another session entitled "Geneaology 101" advised participants on tracing one's family tree. Then historian Karen Fields discussed the oral history she conducted with her grandmother Mamie Garvin Fields, culminating in the book *Lemon Swamp and Other Places, A Carolina Memoir*. (Mamie Fields was the great niece of James B. Middleton, a former slave and Methodist minister believed to have been owned by the White Middletons. Mamie Fields went on to become a distinguished educator and civic leader.) That evening, Dr. Joseph Opala of James Madison University delivered a compelling lecture about one Charlestonian's journey to the African country of her slave ancestor's capture.

Throughout the weekend, as Adam Parker reported for the *Post and Courier*, "Guests stood fascinated before the great list of names [on the wall of Eliza's House] — 2,800 people enslaved at various Middleton properties around the state. Violetta Harrigan was there. She has been studying her family history. At the reunion, another piece fell into place: She found her great-grandfather. There was his name among the 2,800: Agrippa, who cost 80 English pounds and worked at Combahee Plantation in the mid-1700s. And there was his offspring, Caesar Carpenter, who worked at Middleton Place beginning in 1793. Caesar. The name appears again and again on the list. 'My grandmother said they kept the name in the family,' Harrigan said. 'I'm just so amazed to see this.' "

On Sunday morning, a non-denominational service of thanksgiving was conducted down by the river by the Reverends Sidney Frazier and Benjamin Smith, a Middleton descendant. Afterwards participants enjoyed brunch in the Lake House at the Middleton Inn. Approximately 100 people lingered to participate in a final "dialogue" session led by author Karen Fields and Middleton descendant Mason Smith. "At first there was a long silence," remembers Tracey Todd. "Finally an elderly lady walked to the microphone and said, 'My ancestors owned some of your ancestors and I am sorry.' Before she could sit down, an African American gentleman from New York stood up and gave the lady a giant bear hug. The ice was broken yet again."

Time spent relaxing and connecting with one another became just as meaningful. Frank Middleton, a foundation trustee and descendant of Declaration signer Arthur Middleton, for the first time met Ruth Saunders Phillips, great-granddaughter of Annette Mayes. Mayes was born a slave at Middleton Place in about 1846, the daughter of Dye and July, who took the surname Wright upon emancipation. Later Mayes worked for Heningham and Pringle Smith as a housekeeper and cook.

Annie Meyers met Ruth Phillips for the first time and discovered they were related. Journalist Adam Parker recorded the encounter: "Meyers' grandmother, Anna Bowens Mayes, was the second wife of Phillips' uncle Bud Mayes. Meyers' other grandmother was Mary Sheppard, a laborer at Middleton Place who learned to be a cook at the plantation from Phillips' great-grandmother, Annette Mayes. 'This is too much,' Meyers said. 'It just brings back too many memories!' " The culinary skills of Meyers' grandmother Mary Sheppard are legendary. Sheppard cooked for Eleanor Roosevelt when the First Lady visited Middleton Place in 1941; she later was featured in *Family Circle* magazine.

The oldest attendee was Julia Middleton Prentiss, descendant of Henry Middleton, president of the First Continental Congress. Five generations of her family were present, ranging from Prentiss, age 100, to her great-great-grandson Cameron Vesel, age 17 months. Foundation trustee Anne Gaud Tinker and her family were there too. Tinker's mother and father were both Middleton descendants: her mother via Arthur and her father through Arthur's brother Thomas. Tinker said of the 2006 reunion: "It created a forum, a common ground with a real, common connection. There was the feeling of relief on both sides, relief from guilt and relief from anger." Most significant for Tinker was the "shared love of place and belonging to place."

Charles Duell agreed: "It was overwhelmingly successful and healing to have more than 300 people, about half of whom were African American and half European American come together and go through the process of seeing what had evolved at Middleton Place in its interpretation — seeing how the whole Middleton Place community works today in its interpretation efforts with the synergy that brings all these efforts together. Digesting all that, listening to lectures from people from both sides of this history and then reflecting on the last day about what the group's experience had been and how they felt about it was really healing. It was remarkable to see the people that came, both Black and White — a little timorously at first, perhaps not knowing what they were getting into . . . As much as we deplore slavery and the history of it, putting that right in front of us on the table and seeing what has happened since then . . . was a very rewarding experience."

Middleton Place descendant and retired professor Ty Collins, who served

The first joint reunion of African and European descendants of Middleton Place, held in 2006.

Rick Rhodes

(l-r) Frank Middleton, Ruth Saunders Phillips and Barbara Doyle greet one another at the first joint reunion in 2006.

on the reunion planning committee, offered this succinct conclusion: "The first joint reunion in 2006 was a microcosm of America." [11]

• • •

The second joint reunion took place in 2011 and the third followed five years later. Attending in 2016 for the first time was Dr. Robert Bellinger, director of Black Studies and the Clark Collection of African American Literature at Suffolk University in Boston. Dr. Bellinger is a descendant of James C. Middleton, an enslaved African American ancestor whom he shares with former foundation trustee, the late Earl Middleton. Dr. Bellinger also descends from the White family who enslaved James C. Middleton — he is the great-great-great grandson of Edmund C. Bellinger, former owner of White House on the Ashepoo River.

In 1868 the White Bellingers sold a parcel of land to their freed slave Abram Middleton, son of James C. and grandfather to Earl. A master carpenter and builder, Abram soon built a home for his family on the property. That same year, he was among 67 Black delegates elected to the 1868 South Carolina Constitutional Convention — the first election in South Carolina where African Americans were allowed to participate. The convention produced a document, albeit short-lived, that was the most democratic and equitable of the seven constitutions in the history of the state. Abram Middleton later became a prominent Methodist minister and a founding trustee of Claflin University.

Dr. Robert Bellinger.

Earl Middleton explained his and Dr. Bellinger's connection to the White Middletons in his 2008 autobiography (written with his colleague Joy Barnes, who served on the first joint reunion planning committee) entitled *Knowing Who I Am*. "E.C. Bellinger became the owner of [my] great-grandfather James C. Middleton [father of Abram] sometime between 1830 and 1848," writes Middleton. "Lowcountry planter families such as the Bellingers and the Middletons had many interactions, including marriages. Thus James C. may have belonged to a Middleton before he came into Bellinger's possession."

As a descendant of both the enslaved and the enslaver, Dr. Bellinger is no stranger to complexity and conflict. He explains: "When you look at the backlash to the *New York Times*' 1619 Project [a series of articles and educational materials published in 2019 on the 400th anniversary of the first arrival of enslaved Africans] — which examines the many ways the legacy of slavery continues to shape and define life in the United States — and [the] clashes over Civil War monuments and other statues in recent years, you can see how contentious this history is and how we're still struggling to tell the story of the United States."

Following the 2016 reunion, Dr. Bellinger began working with then

Martha DeWeese.

Middleton Place Chief Operating Officer Tracey Todd, Director of Preservation and Interpretation Jeff Neale, and Engagement Director Carin Bloom to create a visiting scholar and student internship program with Suffolk University. "[The reunion] was my first visit," recounts Bellinger, "and the beginning of learning about the plantation's history and culture. Middleton Place is very different from what we have in New England, and I wanted to give my students the opportunity to see American history from another vantage point."

Middleton Place was no stranger to internships. For years, it had welcomed students from the National School of Landscape Architecture at Versailles, France, as well as from the historic preservation program of the University of West Indies at Cave Hill, Barbados. Likewise, scholars from universities across South Carolina and the Southeast had conducted research there.

By summer of 2019, planning and fundraising for the Suffolk University program were complete. Dr. Bellinger invited one of his top students, history and biology major Nick Nunez, to be the first intern. Nunez's instructions were to reimagine the rice cultivation exhibit at the mill house. Todd, Bloom and the interpretive staff led by Neale had undertaken incorporating more diverse histories and perspectives in nearly every aspect of the Middleton Place experience — blending the narratives rather than separating them — to convey a truer, fuller story. The rice exhibit was a key target.

The result of Nunez's work was a presentation outlining suggested revisions to the exhibit that more fully acknowledge the enterprise and agricultural skill of Africans and African Americans in the production of rice. He also suggested a new text panel devoted to the Black watermen who ran the Middleton schooner, sailing from Middleton Place to Charleston and south to the Middleton properties along the Combahee River. The enslaved captain and crew enjoyed a greater degree of independence and privilege, with the ability to travel and communicate outside of Middleton Place and conduct their own trade on the side. Bloom embraced Nunez's recommendations, stating, "Nick succeeded in reimagining the entire exhibit. He gave us real things we can implement to offer a better, more inclusive picture of life at Middleton Place." [12]

Nunez's mentor, visiting scholar Dr. Bellinger, provided his own recommendations for Middleton Place's interpretation of African American history: "Weave stories of the enslaved people into the narrative of all the tours and exhibits. If it is weaved throughout, they [visitors] get it whether they want it or not . . . Even with the power differential, their lives [Black and White] were intertwined in a lot of ways — good, bad and ugly. So, if we don't weave these stories together, people miss that importance . . . even though there is this domination, there are also moments when humanity rears its head. You have to re-examine history fully; not sugarcoat it, not close your eyes. You have to really delve into it and you have to talk about how it is part and parcel of our landscape pretty much, and raise questions about inequality." [13]

• • •

The summer of 2019 also brought Martha DeWeese's descendants to Middleton Place. It was June 19th or Juneteenth, the day in 1865 when federal troops led by Major General Gordon Granger landed at Galveston, Texas to enforce cessation of hostilities and guarantee freedom for the enslaved — two-and-a-half years after President Lincoln's Emancipation Proclamation and two months after the Confederate surrender at Appomattox Courthouse. The annual holiday commemorating the end of slavery in the U.S. has been celebrated by Black Americans since the late 1800s.

In recognition of Juneteenth, Middleton Place offered half-price admission to all residents of Berkeley, Charleston and Dorchester counties "to come and join us as we remember and honor those African Americans — both enslaved and free — who lived and worked at Middleton Place." Special tours, presentations and re-enactments centered around slavery and the Black experience were offered throughout the day. Screenings of the award-winning documentary *Beyond the Fields: Slavery at Middleton Place*, based on the book and exhibit at Eliza's House, showed on the hour in the pavilion.

That morning one of many African American families arrived at the plantation for a visit. They approached interpreter Linda Neale at the ticketing kiosk to inquire about Juneteenth programming for the day. The family of six comprised three generations: including a toddler boy in a stroller, his uncle clutching a framed photograph of an elderly lady, and the toddler's grandfather.

The photograph held by the uncle was of Martha DeWeese, dressed in a crisp white apron and bonnet. DeWeese worked at Middleton Place from the 1930s until the 1980s. She was the great-great-grandmother of the toddler in the stroller. After the family introduced themselves, Neale telephoned Middleton Place curator Mary Edna Sullivan, who asked the family if they would come to the south flanker to meet and talk.

Reaching the main house ruins first, they walked up the steps through the iron gate to stand at the site of the Middleton family seat and take in the panorama of terraces, Butterfly Lakes and the Ashley River. It was a beautiful summer day. The family posed for two photographs: one with the river view in the background, and another with the greensward behind them. The uncle held up his picture of Martha DeWeese in each of the snapshots.

Upon arrival to the south flanker, where tours were in progress, they took a seat on the sun porch. Mary Edna Sullivan came down from her office on the second floor and welcomed the family to Middleton Place. She learned that Justin Eady (the toddler in the stroller) and Jalye Eady (Justin's sister) were the children of Brittney Eady, a daughter of Melvin and Viola Wilson. Breanna Wilson (who looked to be about 12) was the daughter of Troy Wilson, brother to Brittney Eady and son of Melvin and Viola Wilson.

The elder Melvin Wilson was the family's oldest living link to Martha DeWeese. Father of Brittney and Troy and grandfather to Justin, Jalye and Breanna (the group of six visiting that day), Melvin was the grandson of Martha and Solomon DeWeese. He was also the great nephew of Anna Perry, sister of Martha DeWeese. Anna Perry had lived and worked at Middleton Place for more than 60 years.

Wilson remembered being young and spending summers at Middleton Place with his grandmother and great aunt. He had been adopted by the DeWeeses — whom he called "Mama" and "Papa" — and roamed and played all over the plantation. He recalled helping his grandmother's brother-in-law,

Martha DeWeese's descendants (l-r): Justin Eady, Jr. (in stroller), Jalye Eady, Brittney Eady, Breanna Wilson, Melvin Wilson and Troy Wilson.

great uncle Richard Perry, milk the cows in the dairy. Later, Melvin Wilson worked for Ben Chapman in the garden. And every Friday, he drove Mary Sheppard and Eliza Leach into Charleston for shopping.

Melvin's son Troy Wilson shared memories of his great-grandmother Martha DeWeese showing tourists and visitors how to grind grain between the two heavy millstones in the plantation stableyards. He also remembered her sewing "all kinds of clothes, dolls and baskets . . . and she would carry a basket on her head. I don't know how she did it, but she did."

Troy and his sister Brittney Eady's most vivid recollection of their great-grandmother was her singing. Eady said, "She sang all the time. If not singing, she would be humming. And she always wore that apron and bonnet, even when she wasn't working." Eady recalled that Martha DeWeese was featured in the documentary "The Story of English." She sang and spoke Gullah in the film.

On hearing this, Sullivan suggested that the family visit the spring house chapel next door. A continuous recording plays inside that features Martha and Solomon DeWeese, among other African Americans, singing spirituals. There are also displays and panels describing Black religious life at Middleton Place and elsewhere in the Lowcountry.

Sullivan described how the DeWeeses were recorded singing in downtown Charleston during the 1986 Piccolo Spoleto arts festival. Other voices on the chapel tapes include those of the Morning Star Hall Singers of John's Island, S.C. and The Plantation Singers of Charleston — all singing spirituals known to have existed prior to the end of the Civil War, yet each group producing a different style and sound. As sociologist and author W.E.B. Du Bois wrote, "the African American spiritual is the most original and beautiful expression of human life and longing yet born on American soil." [14]

It turned out that Melvin and Troy Wilson were familiar with the spring house but not the chapel, which was restored and re-opened after their time at Middleton Place. Before they departed the south flanker, Sullivan gave each family member her business card and a Middleton Place lineage form to fill out. She also offered to hold on to the framed photograph of Martha DeWeese for safekeeping while they were touring, but Troy politely declined.

As they entered the chapel, Brittney Eady and Troy Wilson immediately recognized their great-grandparents' voices singing on the recording — just the two of them, Martha and Solomon DeWeese, singing one of their favorite hymns "I'm Goin' Up." The brother and sister began to cry. Eady explained through her tears, "It's been since 1992 that we've heard their voices. They would sing 'Goin' Up' all the time!"

Then Sullivan arrived with copies of the book and DVD *Beyond the Fields* to give to the family. She said she would also mail them copies of the chapel recordings. As Martha DeWeese's descendants bid goodbye before proceeding on their tour, they expressed appreciation and promised to stay in touch. Sullivan encouraged them to come to the next Middleton family reunion. They said they would. [15]

Interpreter, blacksmith, musician and actor Jamal Hall at the Middleton Place forge.

Eight

A NEW CENTURY

The year 2020 ushered in Middleton Place's most challenging period of the modern era. The decade began as the plantation wedding business — a growing component of Middleton's operating revenue — was targeted by an online racial justice group called Color of Change. It distributed letters to wedding planning platforms including The Knot and Pinterest exhorting them to limit content about plantation venues. Their reasoning:

"Because these plantations are the sites of former forced labor camps that brutalized and murdered millions of Black people in this country, framing them as wedding venue inspiration is inappropriate and disrespectful to their descendants and to their communities, many of whom use your website[s]."

In response, the wedding platform Zola removed all plantations from its venue listings. Wedding Wire and The Knot stopped accepting advertising from plantations and placed restrictions on content promoting them. Dotdash, the parent company of the website Brides, claimed that "glorifying plantations" was "not in line" with the company's values and that it was working to "remove these references." Nevertheless, images and information on plantations continued to populate the websites.

"In the South, there are few historic places that do not have enslavement in their histories," Middleton Place CEO Tracey Todd told the *Post and Courier*. In reference to the interpretation of slavery he added, "Most of the sites here in Charleston are ahead of the curve. But this group put us all into the same category, and we're all going to be hurt if we're not careful."

Todd views special events as opportunities to bring more people to Middleton Place and show them accurate history. Those wishing to marry at the national landmark are required to become benefactors of the foundation, with a portion of their contribution going toward an endowed scholarship program for descendants of the Middleton Place enslaved community and children of African American employees. They are also required to take a tour that includes exhibits and programs focused on slavery.

Forty weddings a year occur at Middleton Place and as Todd says, "We do everything possible to encourage couples to buy into our mission. The money that comes in from these events — though not a main source of revenue — helps fund research, preservation and educational programming. We need every penny of it and more." [1]

Todd's former history professor Dr. Bernard Powers, founding director of the Center for the Study of Slavery at the College of Charleston, gave his assessment of plantation weddings in a subsequent *New York Times* story: "If we cut ourselves off from these things, particularly if African Americans cut themselves off, then I think you are really saying that there is no chance of repair and social repair because they are beyond redemption; and the people who are associated with them, and probably their descendants, are beyond repair, and I don't buy that argument." [2]

• • •

A few months later, the pandemic hit. The first confirmed cases of Covid-19 in South Carolina occurred in early March: one in Charleston and the other in the small town of Camden. By April the coronavirus was sweeping across the state, shutting down the tourism and hospitality industries during their most productive time. As Todd told *Post and Courier* journalist Adam Parker, "[April] is hands down, the most important month of the year for all the outdoor sites. We've lost it. This is unprecedented."

At Middleton Place the operating budget depends primarily on earned income, namely admissions and revenues from its food and beverage services, retail outlets and special events. Fundraising for the nonprofit is used for capital improvements, museum acquisitions and a reserve fund that provides a financial cushion during hard times. "This is such a time," comments Todd. "The reserve has become vitally important right now. Because of the pandemic, most of our income from admissions, tours and special events has evaporated. Yet the gardens and buildings must be maintained, animals cared for, repairs made. This has to happen whether we are fully open or not."

Todd and his staff wasted no time in applying for an emergency grant from the Paycheck Protection Program. The *Post and Courier* reported that the federal $350-million rescue package ran out of money after two weeks,

The Ashley River Road, a National Scenic Byway.

but not before Middleton Place, nearby Drayton Hall and other institutions managed to secure forgivable loans. "Crisis is not too strong a word for what our museums and historic sites are going through," declared Todd, who deemed the aid a life raft. Weeks later, Middleton Place was also awarded a small state grant, along with 99 other cultural institutions in South Carolina.[3]

Marshaling every resource to stay engaged with the public, Middleton Place set out to test novel digital platforms and reach beyond conventional markets. They devised an array of virtual experiences: online tours, public talks, student programming, one on one discussions with thought leaders and more. As Director of Engagement Carin Bloom stated, "We closed the gates on March 23 and started digital programming on March 24. We really wanted to be as nimble and flexible as we could be, and we knew as soon as we closed the gates, we would not see guests for quite a while."

Working with Director of Preservation and Interpretation Jeff Neale, Bloom launched the virtual program "Plugged into History," featuring near-daily online broadcasts from Middleton Place. A more conversational format followed called "Let's Talk Tuesday." Then came Wednesday's "On the Farm" featuring the stableyards, followed by Thursday's "Hands-On-History" focusing on crafts and cuisine. On Fridays, Tracey Todd and various colleagues led a weekly exchange of views centered on historical interpretation and current events. Bloom posted all content at middletonplace.org, on Facebook, and on the Middleton Place YouTube channel.

When the gates reopened and limited visitation resumed, Bloom and Neale continued to develop digital options for experiencing Middleton Place. Their goal was to enhance both in-person and virtual visits for guests, while cultivating online patrons and reaching new constituencies. In addition, extra signage and text panels were added to the house museum and stableyards to augment self-guided tours. Moreover, America's most historic landscaped garden was demonstrating its added value as a public health asset. By midsummer, memberships in the Middleton Place Foundation were increasing across South Carolina and the nation. Nevertheless, revenues hovered at between 35 and 40 percent of what they were in 2019. [4]

• • •

The long hot summer brought another shock: racial unrest in the wake of the killing of George Floyd by a Minneapolis policeman. Floyd was an unarmed Black man alleged to have been trying to use a counterfeit $20 bill to buy cigarettes. (Five years earlier, the City of North Charleston experienced a similar tragedy when Walter Scott, a Black motorist, was gunned down by a policeman after running away from a traffic stop.) Five days following Floyd's death, a mix of mostly young Black and White marchers gathered in Charleston on a Saturday afternoon to protest. As night fell a portion of Charleston's prime downtown shopping and dining district was ransacked, causing millions of dollars in property damage. The community was shaken.

The next day citizens gathered to help businesses clean up and reopen. Peaceful marches and rallies continued through the summer, resulting in Charleston City Council's unanimous decision to remove a towering statue of South Carolina's famous pro-slavery politician John C. Calhoun from Marion Square — a focal point of the protests. Representatives of Black Lives Matter, National Action Network, the NAACP and other social justice organizations met with city officials and community leaders to forge a way forward. The mayor and police chief pledged to ensure fair policing and build a culture of trust, but tensions remained high.

Middleton Place CEO Tracey Todd was invited to join one of the discussions titled "Reconciling the Past with the Present." The group met at Fort Moultrie on Sullivan's Island at the entrance to Charleston Harbor. Eighteenth century enslaved Africans were quarantined on Sullivan's at what was called a "pesthouse" before being sold in Charleston. According to county historian Nic Butler, records indicate that between five and 20 percent of slaves imported into South Carolina passed through the island. Later in the first decade of the 19th century, slaves were quarantined on the other side of the harbor at a pesthouse on James Island. In 1808, the importation of enslaved Africans into the U.S. was outlawed.

Todd was the only White person asked to speak at the meeting and Middleton Place was the only historic site represented. The group praised Todd and his staff for what they had accomplished in researching and describing African American life on the plantation. As Todd readily acknowledged, for too long Middleton Place had conveyed a segregated history, where a White version of the story was told in the house museum and a Black version was delivered in the stableyards. The challenge now was to integrate the two stories by intertwining the lives and activities of Blacks and Whites with all the inherent interdependence and conflict. [5]

Around the same time, Adam Parker wrote in *The Post and Courier* an account of Cairy Lester's visit to Middleton Place. Lester was a 55-year-old African American resident of Charlotte who had posted a comment on the Middleton Place website expressing the following concern: "If it's not appropriate to have a wedding at a former Nazi concentration camp, it's really not appropriate to have a wedding at a plantation. There's a lot of pain associated with this place." What he wanted, he told Parker, "was, in a word, transparency."

Middleton Place's Jeff Neale responded immediately to Lester and they had a long telephone conversation. Neale invited Lester to attend Middleton Place's annual Juneteenth program, at which several public figures were scheduled to recite the names of 2,800 persons enslaved by the Middleton family. However, the community at large was still reeling from the events in Charleston. Soon Middleton Place and other plantation sites were caught up in a social media firestorm — a "hurricane of emotion," as Todd put it. "We were receiving threats to the property and to our staff." After someone hurled a Molotov cocktail at the Magnolia Gardens gate, Middleton Place hired round-the-clock security. On June 17, two days before Juneteenth, Todd canceled the event out of concern for the safety of patrons and his colleagues.

Lester and his wife came anyway and spent the day touring Middleton Place with Neale. As Lester told Parker, "I have to admit I was impressed... Could they do more? Probably. But are they sweeping that under the rug? By no means, and I saw that."

According to Lester, the docents and interpreters didn't avoid the subject of slavery. They explained freely what life was like for Black people at Middleton Place. "I wasn't getting a skewed version," he said. But Lester added a caveat. Though much progress has been made improving the presentation of history at former plantation sites, there's still a little "Gone with the Wind" nostalgia that permeates these places. It's past time to extinguish the nostalgia, he argued.

Another improvement Lester suggested was to make bifurcated tours obsolete. Visitors should not be able to choose between, say, the house tour and the slavery tour. Every tour should include a full discussion of slavery. Generally, though, these sites are striving to do better, according to Lester. Their importance, in his mind, was unquestionable. "There is, I think, a place for them," he concluded. "If for some reason they didn't exist, there's a lot of history that African Americans want to know that would disappear." [6]

• • •

Artist Jonathan Green agrees with Cairy Lester on the significance of historic sites such as Middleton Place to African Americans. Green is a trustee of the Middleton Place Foundation and believes in its mission of preservation, research and education: "Middleton Place is one of the most important places in America in terms of the history and culture of Black people, and the history and culture of early American people." [7]

An acclaimed painter of African American life, Green grew up in Beaufort County at Gardens Corner, South Carolina and studied at the Art Institute of Chicago. He is considered as much a preserver of Lowcountry Black culture as an interpreter. He returned to South Carolina to devote his life and art to building up his native Gullah community — to celebrate its history and culture — which today enjoys overdue national recognition.

(l-r) Sallie Duell, Tracey Todd, Charles Duell, Jonathan Green and Lee Pringle at the unveiling of Green's portrait of Edna Lewis.

Green has focused on South Carolina's rice culture. In 2014 he completed his rice portfolio, a collection of paintings depicting the cultivation of rice as though "African people came here like everyone else — unchained, unenslaved." That fall the Gibbes Museum of Art paired 11 of Green's bold, exuberant acrylics with 10 exquisite watercolors from White Middleton descendant Alice Smith's *A Carolina Rice Plantation* series. The juxtaposition of the two bodies of work — produced nearly a century apart — was stunning. [8]

Simultaneously, Green launched the Lowcountry Rice Culture Project and began collaborating with Middleton Place on lectures, exhibits and events. Soon Charles Duell asked Green to join the Middleton Place Foundation board. "What Charles has facilitated at Middleton Place transcends history books," Green explains. "His vision and work have helped people have deeper, more meaningful conversations and dialogues about our history honestly, rather than having dialogues about myths." [9]

Charles shares Green's vision of bringing to fruition an exploration of Middleton's Black community that delves as deeply into their identity as

West Africans and New World immigrants, as their history of being enslaved. "Plantations should personalize enslaved West Africans and recognize them as human beings," says Green. [10]

The imperative to disclose slavery's truths while at the same time commemorating the strength and achievement of the enslaved and their descendants, is shared by fellow Middleton Place trustee and South Carolina native Lee Pringle. Pringle was born in Moncks Corner and raised in the Pringletown community. He graduated from Cross High School, then entered Baptist College (now Charleston Southern University) and went on to graduate from Strayer College in Washington, D.C. He spent the next eight years in the navy, after which he pursued a 25-year career in the insurance and pension fund sectors in New York City and Charlotte. All the while Pringle stayed deeply connected to the Lowcountry, building a house there and eventually returning to live full-time. He joined the Middleton Place Foundation board in 2017.

Pringle knew his family had a connection to the Middletons. In 2008 he was among the Black Pringle descendants who organized the first-ever Pringles of Pringletown Family Reunion. The reunion was held on land obtained by Isom Pringle, who was the genealogical connection to the Middleton family. During a chance encounter at an event at the Edmondston-Alston House, Lee Pringle shared the results of his research with Tracey Todd. Todd immediately informed Middleton Place historian Dr. Dottie Stone of the findings, which Pringle had substantiated with 19th century census data.

With Dr. Stone's assistance in further exploring the genealogy records, Pringle confirmed he is the great-great-grandson of Scipio, an enslaved African American purchased by John Middleton (Williams Middleton's brother) in 1831. Scipio's son, Middleton Pringle, great-grandfather of Lee Pringle, lived through Reconstruction and settled in Pringletown, where Lee grew up. The area around Pringletown was once part of St. James Goose Creek Parish, the site of the Middleton family's first foothold in North America. [11]

Dr. Stone, who received her doctorate in Holocaust history, stands ready to assist anyone who is connected to the Middleton family or Middleton Place with tracing their ancestry. The joint reunions over the last decade have spawned more communication between Black and White descendants. In the future, these connections may help in documenting Middleton descendants of mixed ancestry. While the written record is scarce for African

State of South-Carolina.

KNOW ALL MEN by these Presents, That *We Elizabeth B Lowndes Widow and Rawlins Lowndes of Charleston State aforesaid* for and in consideration of the sum of *Two Thousand Dollars* to *us* in hand paid, at and before the sealing and delivery of these Presents, *by John Izard Middleton of the state aforesaid* (the receipt whereof *we* do hereby acknowledge) have bargained and sold, and by these Presents, do bargain, sell and deliver to the said *John Izard Middleton the following Seven Slaves to wit Mingo Maria and Deana Scipio Judy Will and Sunday with the future issue and increase of the females*

TO HAVE AND TO HOLD, THE SAID *Seven Slaves*

unto the said *John Izard Middleton his*

Executors, Administrators and Assigns, to *his* and *their* own proper use and behoof forever, **And** *We* the said *Elizabeth B Lowndes and Rawlins Lowndes our*

Executors and Administrators, the said bargained premises, unto the said *John Izard Middleton his*

Executors, Administrators and Assigns, from and against all persons shall and will warrant, and forever defend, by these Presents.

In Witness Whereof, *we* have hereunto set *our* Hand and Seal. Dated at *Charleston* on the *twenty first* day of *January* in the year of our Lord, one thousand eight hundred and *thirty One* and in the *fifty fifth* year of the Independence of the United States of America.

SIGNED, SEALED, AND DELIVERED IN THE PRESENCE OF

C C Pinckney

Elizabeth B Lowndes (Seal)
Rawlins Lowndes (Seal)

C C Pinckney made oath that he was Present and saw Elizabeth B Lowndes and Rawlins Lowndes Sign and Seal the with in Sale for the uses and Purposes therein mentioned and that he Witnessed the same Sworn to before me this 21 Jany 1831

John Hand N P

Recorded Jany 21 1831

Bill of sale for Middleton Place Foundation trustee Lee Pringle's great great-grandfather, Scipio, who was purchased in 1831 by John Middleton, Williams Middleton's brother.

descendants, oral history is a key source of evidence and corroboration when combined with calendar records, account books and the like. "Memories were much sharper back then," says Tracey Todd, "since so many things were not written down. Think of those who memorized the Bible and could quote it freely, or those who could sing hundreds of hymns from memory, or recite long, detailed stories."

Two years after the first joint reunion of Black and White descendants, Lee Pringle's extended family held a reunion at Middleton Place. Pringle spoke with Charles Duell and became acquainted with what was happening at the historic landmark, especially with regard to research and interpretation of African American history. "I was very interested in helping expose the reality that there is no American history without Black history; no Black history without White history. It is America's story."

Pringle — a singer and musician — is a lover of history and music. Like Jonathan Green, he uses his art to inspire a fuller, truer understanding of the American story. While a board member of the Charleston Symphony Orchestra, Pringle launched the Charleston Gospel Choir. His goal: to honor the pioneers of gospel music and stretch the genre's boundaries, all the while educating audiences about how the African American spiritual laid the foundation for numerous musical forms. The 75-member, multi-racial chorus debuted with the symphony orchestra in December 2000 and continues to this day.

A decade later Pringle established the Colour of Music Festival, a performance program that nurtures and showcases Black classical musicians and composers. The Middleton Place Foundation is a sponsor and Pringle stages concerts at Middleton Place and at the Edmondston-Alston House, in addition to venues around the country. "I use spiritual and classical music to enlighten audiences how musicians of African descent have helped shape venerated art forms around the world for centuries." One of his favorite examples is Chevalier de Saint-Georges, an 18th century African French composer whose opera and classical masterpieces were enjoyed throughout Europe, including by John Adams when he served as U.S. commissioner to France. [12]

The name Pringle chose for the festival was partly inspired by another founding father, James Madison. During the Constitutional Convention of 1787, Madison stated, "We have seen the mere distinction of colour made

"Living History" at Middleton Place.

in the most enlightened period of time, a ground of the most oppressive dominion ever exercised by man over man." Indeed, this is America's great contradiction, one that Pringle and the Middleton Place Foundation board and staff are dedicated to unveiling and understanding.

To that end, Pringle traveled with Tracey Todd in the fall of 2018 to Madison's Virginia home, Montpelier, to participate in the inaugural National Summit on Teaching Slavery. The year prior, Montpelier opened a permanent exhibition entitled "The Mere Distinction of Colour." The exhibit, funded by philanthropist David Rubenstein, occupies the entire ground floor of the historic house. It examines slavery and its many ramifications for the founding era. The Rubenstein grant also enabled Montpelier to reconstruct its south yard, where enslaved domestic and field workers lived and worked.

Joined by more than 50 historic site administrators, academics and descendants, Pringle and Todd spent a rainy February weekend at the Virginia landmark discussing how to better engage descendant communities when teaching slavery. Together they developed guidelines to create richer more inclusive narratives and to reimagine historic sites as community resources

Greg Smith, Director of Education at Middleton Place, leads a school group.

for today's world.

"I absorbed new ideas and strategies. I also learned that Middleton Place is considered a leader among its peers in African American interpretation," says Pringle. "This is a credit to Charles Duell and his family, and the foundation Charles created, which continues to reevaluate and reinterpret the shared history we have as Black and White Americans."

Christian Cotz, director of education and visitor engagement at Montpelier concurs: "Middleton Place has done a good job. It was one of the earliest historic sites to engage the descendant community. And it has greatly enhanced our understanding of South Carolina's plantation system." [13]

• • •

Another visitor came to Middleton Place in summer 2020 — Moro Brewer's great-great-grandson. Moro Brewer was enslaved under Williams Middleton before the Civil War and continued working for Williams after emancipation. The Brewer descendant and his wife and two children had traveled to South Carolina from New Jersey. When he mentioned his ancestry on a garden tour, the guide immediately connected him with preservation and interpretation director Neale, who gave the man lineage forms to fill out and materials about Middleton Place and its enslaved community. They have stayed in touch and hope to meet again at the next reunion.

Middleton Place strives to respond and engage with world events, in the midst of a tense social and political climate. Despite having to cancel Juneteenth and Fourth of July programming during 2020, as well as the annual naturalization ceremony — where dozens of aspiring Americans take their oath of citizenship every June 26 (Arthur Middleton's birthday) — staff and trustees are determined to reach larger, more diverse audiences.

In a normal year, Director of Education Greg Smith welcomes more than 3,500 students annually, ranging from kindergarteners to high schoolers, from scouts to university scholars. His department's broad program offerings align with state education standards, yet can be customized to meet a variety of needs and specific criteria.

"Living History" experiences — with access to 65 acres of landscaped gardens, the house museum, Eliza's House, working stableyards and a demonstration rice field — have been reworked to explore an array of themes at Middleton Place in more integrated and concrete ways. Topics include the American Revolution, slavery and the Civil War, plantation life, indigo and rice cultivation, botany and animal husbandry.

"Making connections is the best part of our job," states Neale, a retired marine with a master's degree in public history. "I consider myself a public historian and am constantly asking what Middleton Place can mean to people in the 21st century, especially given that today's visitors are more aware and more inquisitive."

One of the first new interpreters Neale hired was Jamal Hall, a history graduate of Temple University. Hall's previous job was as a Civil War interpreter at Fort Delaware State Park, where he learned blacksmithing and performed first-person interpretations of historic characters based on documented primary sources. "It's one of the coolest — maybe even the best — ways to teach history," says Hall.

An early figure whom Hall portrayed at Middleton Place was Charles Middleton, an 18th century enslaved person planning to escape. Guests would encounter Hall hiding in the garden in character as Charles Middleton and attempting to meet his parents to say goodbye. "The biggest thing I tried to convey was his sense of fear . . . Anything can happen at that moment . . . He thinks, he hopes, he is on his way to freedom, and he doesn't want to mess that up. My own personal belief," Hall explains, "is that one of the best lessons we get from history is empathy, and being able to put yourself in the person's shoes as best you can." [14]

Jeff Neale doesn't hesitate to "go off the page" either. He frequently says, "I like my history messy and dirty," and demonstrates this in a variety of ways. Neale strives to deepen his colleagues' and volunteers' understanding of history, whether through monthly "Artifact Spotlight" emails — for Women's History Month he focused on documents about the working relationship between Heningham Smith and cook Mary Sheppard — or his Brown Bag Book Club, where they read and discuss works such as *Black Majority, The Hanging of Thomas Jeremiah* and *Confederates in the Attic.*

During Black History Month a few years ago, Neale converted the second-floor summer bedroom of the house museum into a permanent new exhibit called "Moment in Time." Working with curator Mary Edna Sullivan and museum manager Racena Bowen, Neale restaged the room as it might have looked during the early morning hours — bed unmade, clothing scattered about, toiletries laid out, and letters or books strewn open — as if Henry Middleton had just awakened.

"Moment in Time" set the stage for a fuller interpretation of the complex relationship between enslaver and enslaved. It emphasized the role that house servants played in maintaining their owner's lifestyle, especially the daily routines of enslaved people within the Middleton household. Neale instructed tour guides to recite the names of those who would assist Henry on any given morning. Mary might come in and light the fire, followed by Jenny bringing breakfast. Caesar, the valet, would shave and dress him.

In fact, Caesar attended to most of Henry's everyday needs and was eventually freed. Upon manumission, Henry allocated 1,000 pounds sterling to be invested for Caesar's use for the remainder of his life. Caesar is the only enslaved person Henry or any other Middleton is known to have freed, of the thousands of men, women and children they owned. "In those days, manumission was rarer than hens' teeth," notes Middleton Place's CEO Todd. [15]

"The number one question that visitors ask these days," Todd adds, "is whether the Middletons were good to their slaves. This is my favorite ques-

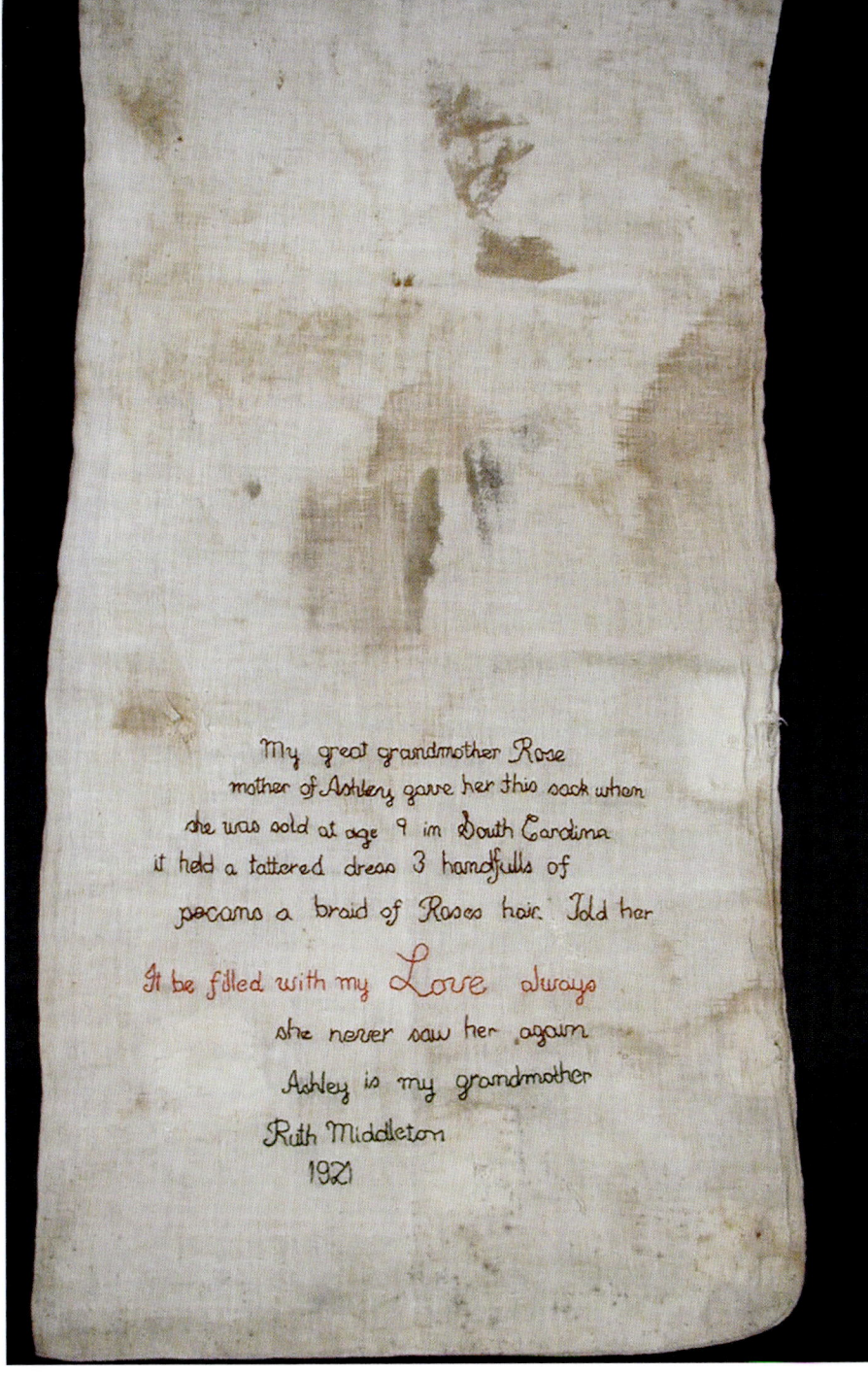

Ashley's Sack is a coarse linen bag dating to the mid-1800s. In 1921, Ruth Middleton embroidered her enslaved grandmother's story on the sack. Donated to the Middleton Place Foundation, Ashley's Sack was on loan to the National Museum of African American History from 2016 to 2021. In 2022, it begins another long-term loan with the International African American Museum in Charleston.

Charles Duell, George McDaniel and Sallie Duell.

tion." Ever patient and measured, Todd takes the time to explain that "good" and "bad" are irrelevant when you are talking about a system — even under a benevolent slave owner — that created a class of people who were denied their most basic human rights.

Therefore, as Todd describes, many African Americans could not accrue the education and property necessary to build wealth and other assets to pass on to their children. "Here we are in the 21st century," he says, "with a large segment of the population that has been held back for so long — beginning with slavery, the dismantling of Reconstruction reforms, the institutionalization of segregation, Jim Crow, redlining, systemic racism and more." [16]

As past Drayton Hall director George McDaniel notes, "There is a natural and necessary tension at former plantation sites like Drayton Hall and Middleton Place between the subconscious and the conscious — the beauty of the place and the horrors of slavery. Charles and Tracey have willingly disrupted the affective message of the lovely landscape with the truth about slavery. Their focus on the complete history has been a critical and unifying framework." [17]

∙ ∙ ∙

While the events of 2020 refocused the Middleton Place Foundation on the dual quest of continuity and relevance, the critical component of land protection looms ever large. Visitors to the Ashley River corridor encounter not just individual historic sites, but an iconic landscape found nowhere else in America. The corridor includes some 20,000 acres of permanently protected lands: a physical backdrop surrounding Middleton Place, Drayton Hall, Magnolia Plantation and other historic properties that is critical to understanding their social and economic histories. The preservation of the rice landscape — the river, the bottomlands, the upland forests, the roadways and railways — provides a context that no virtual platform or textbook can match.

Middleton Place — with its two miles of riverfront, two miles of road frontage and more than 6,500 acres — is central to the decades-old protection effort. In 1992 Charles worked with the Lowcountry Land Trust to obtain a conservation easement from property owner Donna Brantley to protect the view of land across the river from Middleton Place. Brantley agreed to permanently protect 905 feet of river frontage and 20 acres of high ground directly in the sightline of Middleton Place at the terminus of the central axis upon which the gardens were designed 280 years ago. Her easement donation guaranteed a 100-foot-deep, undisturbed natural buffer along the riverbank and restricted development behind it to levels less than the law allowed — preventing construction from intruding above or in front of the vegetation along the river.

In 1994 George McDaniel negotiated the sale of two parcels totaling 46 acres in the viewshed of Drayton Hall, downriver from Middleton Place. Zoning allowed 22 apartments or condos per acre, with no ordinance requiring a vegetative buffer across from the National Trust property. Preservationist Marion Kennedy of Cincinnati gave the money to buy the first parcel. Bolstered by Kennedy's generosity, McDaniel launched a campaign to raise the remaining $300,000 to secure the second tract. In less than a year, donors from nearly every state and six foreign countries met the challenge. Together they preserved yet another "remote forest view" prized for centuries by landscape architects and visitors.

Nevertheless, the next decade saw explosive development along North Charleston's Dorchester Road. Directly across the Ashley River from Middleton Place, construction plans called for a condominium complex, three huge housing projects, a school and a sewage treatment plant. Charles and the foundation sprang into action, working with Centex Homes and other development interests to secure permanent vegetative buffers and height restrictions on the river. Seven individual conservation easements were donated in the Middleton Place viewshed. In return, the developers received substantial tax credits.

At the same time, neighbor Heyward Carter of Millbrook Plantation was spearheading a campaign to protect the Ashley River Road (Highway 61). This scenic and historic highway was officially authorized in 1690-1691 and runs essentially the same course that is shown on maps as early as 1771. Carter and his extended family committed to placing voluntary, vegetative buffer easements (held by the Lowcountry Land Trust) along the roadsides to prevent cutting of trees and to perpetuate the canopy overhead. The Duell family joined the effort, donating a conservation easement on 2,178 feet of road frontage. More landowners followed suit.

However, safeguarding road and river buffers, while important, was not enough to save a landscape. Notwithstanding 11½ miles of road designated a scenic highway — also listed with 26 associated properties on the National Register — and despite 22 miles of river declared scenic and the subject of a special area management plan, the Ashley River corridor was named one of the 11 most endangered historic places in America by the National Trust in 1995. Aside from protected road edges and river vistas, there was only one other substantive conservation easement in the area: donated by Ross Hanahan on 141 acres at Millbrook. Without a more concerted effort — in the midst of lax zoning and mounting development pressures — the future of the Ashley River looked bleak.

In spring of 1996, the Middleton Place Foundation joined forces with Historic Charleston Foundation to sponsor a seminar called "Historic Landscapes in a 21st Century Context." Over a two-day period, lectures, tours and discussions by experts from around the country focused on the challenges of preserving historic landscapes. That fall, Charles enlisted the National Trust and Drayton Hall, the Palmetto Conservation Foundation, the Lowcountry Land Trust, and various planning and regulatory agencies to participate in a follow-up conference at Middleton Place entitled, "Envisioning a Future for the Ashley River Corridor." After the conference, a group formed to

The Ashley River corridor.

identify specific threats to the corridor and practical solutions for its future.

But it wasn't until nearly a decade later that the corridor was catalyzed to act. In 2003, two noteworthy parcels came on the market — 4,500-acre Poplar Grove and 6,600-acre Watson Hill. The threat of 3,500 homes being built at Poplar Grove, which abutted Middleton Place and Millbrook Plantation on their western boundaries, was enough to galvanize local residents to hire an attorney to demand that Dorchester County abide by its comprehensive plan, which designated the area as "conservation/preservation." But until that designation became an actual zoning ordinance, it had no power of regulatory enforcement. The development scenario would have been the largest in the county's history, bringing 10,000 more people into the area — almost one-half the current population of Summerville.

Meanwhile on Middleton's northern border, the owners of Watson Hill were drafting plans for up to 5,000 houses and condominiums, a golf course, two schools, a fire station and 245 acres of commercial and office space. They hatched a scheme to annex Watson Hill into the City of North Charleston to take advantage of weaker zoning rules. To do so, they needed contiguity to

Charles Duell receiving the President's Award from the National Trust for Historic Preservation, presented by trustee Marilyn Hill.

the city and convinced a neighbor to sign a contract to sell his 68-acre parcel to provide the necessary connection. Word got out and the conservation and historic preservation communities sprang into action. They persuaded the landowner to repudiate the contract on grounds of misrepresentation. They also pledged to indemnify him for up to $1 million in case the buyer sued for breach of contract.

An annexation war ensued between the cities of Summerville, North Charleston and Charleston entailing years of litigation and delay, and buying time for the conservation community to craft a campaign to save the Ashley River corridor. The coalition combined the land protection expertise of the conservation community with the knowledge and connections of the historic preservationists — tapping a deep reservoir of relationships and funding sources.

Over the course of many years, Ducks Unlimited, the Donnelley Foundation, the Coastal Conservation League, Historic Charleston Foundation, The Nature Conservancy, Lowcountry Land Trust, the S.C. Conservation

Bank and The Conservation Fund worked with corporate and individual property owners — including the Duell family — to achieve a landmark accord, permanently protecting more than 13,000 acres in the Ashley River plantation district.

Using a variety of tools, funding strategies and partnerships, the coalition raised $10 million to buy a conservation easement at Poplar Grove, which significantly limited development rights to a level in keeping with the traditional landscape. They raised an additional $4 million to purchase an easement adjacent to Poplar Grove on the Middleton Place woodlands owned by Charles' children. The family restricted development to 500 homes on 5,600 acres and deeply discounted the price for its protection, the value of which had been appraised at many times more.

Holland Duell points to the conservation ethic with which he and his three sisters — Josephine, June and Caroline — were raised. All have served, or currently serve, on the Middleton Place Foundation Board of Trustees. "Both my father's and mother's families were large landowners, in the Lowcountry and out West, respectively," he explains. "The goal of sustainability has been a primary focus for us. How can we generate income from the land in an environmentally sensitive way? How can business have a positive environmental impact?" To this end, the four siblings have implemented a sustainable forestry management plan and are harnessing the land's parklike tableau of old growth trees and naturalized lakes as a venue for outdoor recreation, music, and visual and performing arts.

Another key leveraging factor in the Ashley River corridor agreement was the gift of easements from the Carter and Hanahan families on neighboring Uxbridge and Millbrook plantations. The release of foundation grants and public monies hinged on the commitment and personal sacrifice of these resident landowners, who were forgoing tens of millions of dollars in real estate value. Given the complexity of family dynamics and shared assets, the accord could have easily fallen apart. In the end, it was consummated and lauded as one of the most innovative conservation and historic preservation agreements in the history of the United States.

Finally in 2017, Watson Hill was permanently protected with a conservation easement donated by its new owner, WestRock (formerly MeadWestvaco, the timber company that first listed the property for sale in 2003). The easement increased the total amount of land preserved to 19,600 acres, which was a tremendous victory. But it remains an ongoing battle — evidenced by the fact the National Trust put the Ashley River corridor back on its most endangered list later that same year. [18]

• • •

Meanwhile in 2014, Charles announced his intention to retire as president and CEO of the Middleton Place Foundation. He planned to step down on his 80th birthday — more than four decades after establishing the foundation and nearly 50 years after inheriting Middleton Place. With his blessing, the board created a new position of chief operating officer to begin the leadership transition. Tracey Todd, vice president of museums at the time, competed with candidates from around the country to become the foundation's first COO. For the next four years, he would work closely with Charles in preparation to succeed him.

When Todd officially replaced Charles on July 1, 2018, almost every news outlet in the state covered the story. It also made headlines around the nation. As the *Post and Courier*'s Adam Parker wrote, "For the first time in 300 years, Middleton Place will be led by someone who is not part of the family."

Assuming responsibility for a National Historic Landmark with assets approximating $25 million in value, an annual budget of $7 million, 175 employees, 300 volunteers and 120,000 visitors a year, Todd seemed unfazed by all the attention. He told reporters he would stay focused on the mission to educate and entertain, strengthening Middleton Place as a community resource. "It's about teaching history; but it's about having fun at the same time," he said.

Yet Todd remains keenly aware of the legacy with which he has been entrusted. He freely expresses his appreciation and admiration for founder and president emeritus Charles Duell: "We've had a long and close relationship. His continued involvement is welcomed. I cherish all of our time together. I would not look forward to the day when he is not at Middleton Place . . . We want to codify the vision that Charles has laid out."

A South Carolina native, Todd graduated in 1991 from the College of Charleston with a degree in history. His most important mentor was Dr. Bernard Powers, who arrived at the college as a professor of southern studies while Todd was as an undergraduate. Dr. Powers taught courses there in American, African American and African diasporic history for 26 years before founding the Center for the Study of Slavery. He also serves on the board of Charleston's International African American Museum.

"I treasure my relationship with Dr. Powers," says Todd. Powers inspired Todd to pursue a master's in history and education at The Citadel while working full-time as the assistant manager and curator of the Edmondston-Alston House. Completing his graduate degree proved a turning point for Todd. Should he teach or go into the museum field? He had risen to manager of the Edmondston-Alston House and was enjoying the administrative and educational aspects of preserving and interpreting a historic house site. He decided to stay.

Todd soon took on management of the house museum at Middleton Place, becoming director of programs and interpretation for the two properties and moving into an office at the foundation's headquarters. By the early 2000s, Charles had elevated Todd to vice president of museums.

Todd's training as a historian, his long association with the foundation and its properties, and his commitment to the community at large propelled him to the top of the national search for Charles' successor. "It's his enlightened perspective and deep engagement," says Charles, "that make Tracey the logical and ideal 21st century leader of the Middleton Place Foundation. We, the trustees, chose exceedingly well." [19]

• • •

On Todd's office wall hang various commendations and awards that the foundation and its founder have received through the years. There is the President's Award, signed by Stephanie Meeks, President of the National Trust for Historic Preservation. There is Charleston Mayor Joe Riley's signed proclamation, declaring a Charles H.P. Duell Day. There is the American flag that flew over the U.S. Capitol and a South Carolina flag that flew over the State House — both in Charles' honor. And finally, there is the Order of the Palmetto, South Carolina's highest civilian award, presented to Charles by Governor Nikki Haley in 2015.

"These tributes belong as much to Tracey and the rest of the staff as they do to me," observes Charles, "which is why they hang in Tracey's office and not mine. I did not earn them by myself. They belong to the Middleton

Place Foundation as a whole. I have worked with excellent people and am only one of many catalysts that have propelled the rising tide that Middleton Place has enjoyed over the years." [20]

Many Middleton Place staff who were hired by Charles in the foundation's early years are still there — including Sidney Frazier, Mary Edna Sullivan, Tracey Todd and Vice President of Accounting Ileen Grange. Their loyalty and affection for Charles are as strong as their loyalty and affection for Middleton Place. The same goes for donors and members of the foundation, many of whom view the national landmark as a beloved community resource.

Ileen Grange, whose South Carolina ancestors go back eight generations, began her career at Middleton Place as a house museum volunteer in 1980. Museum manager Sarah Lytle made her a staff member in 1982 and before long Grange knew the house, the archives and the collection inside out. She assumed the duties of membership secretary from Middleton archivist Barbara Doyle along the way. In 1991 Charles hired her to keep the books for the private partnerships that oversaw the Equestrian Center, the Middleton Inn and the Middleton Oaks development.

Grange was a quick study and learned everything about the operations. "This was Charles' creative period," Grange explains, "and the land and timber deals [orchestrated to sustain Middleton Place] were fascinating. Every day was different." Eventually Grange rejoined the foundation administration. Over the last four decades, she has witnessed its evolution from a family run enterprise to a fully professional organization.

"A lot of stars had to line up," remarks Grange, "but through sheer will and determination Charles succeeded in making Middleton Place sustainable. As a result, people from all walks of life come here to learn about decorative arts, landscape gardening, the nation's founding and the history of slavery. Middleton also provides a sense of place, especially for modern families seeking a sense of belonging and stability."

Charles himself is fond of saying, "It's been a series of miracles that has allowed Middleton Place to survive" — whether through revolution, civil war, hurricanes, a major earthquake, economic depression or the recent pandemic. Grange agrees, as does Todd, who is quick to add Charles to that list of miracles. [21]

• • •

Charles and Sallie Duell.

Another "miracle" is Sallie McPherson Duell, who currently serves as chairman of the Middleton Place Foundation. She and Charles were married in the chapel at Middleton Place in February 2006 and have lived on the third floor of the Edmondston-Alston House ever since. Their light-filled, spacious apartment with its adjoining piazza overlooks Charleston Harbor.

It also sits above the first two floors of one of Charleston's most historic antebellum mansions, where paying visitors come and go nearly every day of the year. In the carriage house and dependencies to the rear, the Duells operate a bed and breakfast that Trip Advisor consistently ranks as one of the Holy City's finest.

Living "above the shop" is not for everyone. But for a person as engaged in the community and as committed to Charles as Sallie, it is a perfect fit. The feeling is mutual. Their paths in Charleston crisscrossed for many years until, both divorced with grown children, the time seemed right. Their combined family now includes seven children and 14 grandchildren. As Charles admits, his intense focus on Middleton Place and his legacy has often proved difficult for those closest to him. But in Sallie, he has found a partner equally dedicated to the foundation and its mission.

Ever engaged and energetic, Sallie comes naturally to her commitment to public service. A native of Greenville, S.C., she graduated from St. Catherine's in Richmond, which was also Heningham Smith's alma mater. The school's motto — "What we keep we lose; only what we give remains our own"— is Sallie's credo. Later in the 1980s, she earned a degree in urban studies at the College of Charleston, enhancing her appreciation and understanding of the city she would call home for the rest of her life.

Not long after volunteering for the Junior League of Charleston, Sallie joined its board of directors and was elected president. While raising three sons, she assumed leadership roles in nearly every endeavor she undertook — serving on the boards of Horizon House (now Carolina Youth Development Center), the Charleston Symphony Orchestra, the S.C. Nature Conservancy, the Coastal Community Foundation, the Charleston Parks Conservancy and Spoleto Festival USA.

Sallie shared Charles' love of historic gardens and gardening, chairing the Charleston Garden Festival and later co-founding the Charleston Horticultural Society, serving as its president. She also worked on behalf of historic preservation, joining the boards of the Preservation Society of Charleston and Historic Charleston Foundation. From 2000 to 2009, Mayor Riley appointed her to Charleston's Board of Architectural Review, which Sallie chaired for two years, as Charles had done earlier.

Sallie has also worked with the African American community, co-chairing the Martin Luther King, Jr. Day celebration for the YWCA and producing the 1990 performance of *Porgy and Bess,* which marked the reopening of the Gaillard Auditorium following the devastation of Hurricane Hugo. Years later, as mass shootings escalated around the country — including the 2015 massacre at Charleston's Emanuel AME Church — she became a founding board member of Arm-in-Arm, a nonprofit dedicated to reducing gun violence.

One of Sallie's many dreams for Middleton Place is expanding the garden to include what she describes as "sustainable landscape design for the 21st century." Consulting with garden historians and landscape architects from around the world, including Andrea Wulf and Thomas Woltz, she envisions adding a new native garden on the national landmark's southern boundary — where visitors can enjoy beauty in the context of ecological regeneration, where nature is healed rather than tamed. Such an addition, Sallie believes, will magnify the restorative power of Middleton Place for a new generation. [22]

• • •

"It's a fruitful partnership," remarks June Bradham, friend and nonprofit consultant who is assisting the foundation in developing a strategic plan. "Charles is really the history and bearer of the family flag and historic interpretation. Sallie has a lot of strategic ideas about funding and building relationships." Bradham expresses amazement and admiration for how Charles has "bootstrapped Middleton Place to where it is."

Bradham sees Middleton Place as both a sanctuary and a place for changing people's minds. Like George McDaniel, Bradham recognizes the tension between past and present — not altogether an unhealthy one — that exists in the foundation's mission and within its board of trustees. For Middleton Place to thrive in the future, according to Bradham, visionary leadership combined with vigorous fundraising and revenue generation are essential. [23]

To that end, several community leaders with business expertise have joined the foundation board. They include former investment banker Hank Holliday, who launched a successful second career as a hotelier and restauranteur. Former Wall Street financier Michael Laughlin chairs the strategic planning initiative. Rich Leadem, a founding partner of Peninsula Capital and a major donor with his wife to their alma mater of Wake Forest University, is also a trustee.

Several past and present trustees of the Middleton Place Foundation gather for a photo: (bottom row, l-r) Zoe Stephens, Anne Tinker, Sallie Duell, June Waterman, Elizabeth McMillen; (top row, l-r) Rich Leadem, Kenneth Middleton, Charles Duell, Mason Smith, Rod Duell, Michael Laughlin.

"I am committed to helping elevate the stature of Middleton Place," says Leadem, whose family foundation has supported numerous schools and organizations in the area, including the College of Charleston, Meeting Street Schools and the Charleston Parks Conservancy. "While Middleton Place does not have the advantage of being associated with a U.S. president, it is home to two founding fathers and America's oldest landscape gardens. It is a national landmark of immense beauty and history, and is now distinguished by its exceptional interpretation of the African American story." [24]

Middleton descendant Caroline Palmer, a communications and marketing consultant, recently moved with her family to Charleston after a career with American Express in New York. She sits on the board with her mother, Anne Gaud Tinker, a retired executive with Save the Children. Charles' daughter Caroline Middleton Duell, founder and president of Elemental Herbs (a multinational skincare company based in California) also serves as a trustee.

Pierre Manigault, chairman of Evening Post Industries and a cousin, succeeds his father, the late Peter Manigault, on the foundation board. Peter Manigault was a leader in historic preservation and land conservation, promoting and elevating the causes in his family-owned newspapers, thereby focusing the community on these important issues. "For my generation," remarks Charles, "Peter Manigault was a force and an inspiration. Son Pierre carries on his legacy." [25]

• • •

A key strategic issue for the Middleton Place Foundation board is absorbing and planning for Charles' final gifts to the foundation: namely the Middleton Inn, the Edmondston-Alston House and the Equestrian Center. Moreover, the next major capital campaign will fund the construction of the Barbara Doyle History and Archives Center, with an anticipated completion date of 2027.

Named for archivist and historian Barbara Doyle (1922-2015) — who worked at Middleton Place for more than 40 years — the future history and archives center is the culmination of a long-held dream of Charles, Tracey Todd and the foundation staff. It will serve as headquarters for researchers and archivists. It will also house a theater, archaeology lab, archival and collections storage, visitor services and space for rotating exhibits — all augmenting, as Charles says, "the intellectual and scholarly focus of Middleton Place." [26]

This focus has been ongoing for the last half-century. Under Charles' and Todd's leadership, foundation staff use historic preservation, documented research, and interpretation as a force for education, understanding and positive change. This mission has generated important and pioneering scholarship — and will continue to do so — in such areas as the study of slavery, the economic history of antebellum and post-Civil War South Carolina, archaeology, Native American history, and the development of modern conservation and historic preservation practices.

Today a 21st century transformation is occurring at Middleton Place. What has been a laboratory for the study of South Carolina life and history is expanding into a center for southern studies. The foundation's commitment to the establishment of the Barbara Doyle History and Archives Center underscores this evolution. The center will continue the groundbreaking work that Doyle performed and inspired in her long tenure at MiddletonPlace.

Charles Duell escorts British Prime Minister Margaret Thatcher on a tour of Middleton Place, followed by Jenny Sanford McKay and Congressman Mark Sanford.

But it also has the potential to become what historian Alex Moore calls "a scholarly clearing house for the next wave — and there will be one — of southern studies."

"There is a revolution and revival of humanities scholarship and humanities preservation going on right now," Moore explains. "And we all know that as long as there is a southern geography and the opportunity for conversation, the Middleton family and Middleton Place will do much to shape our region's and nation's fates." [27]

• • •

The rebirth of Middleton Place is a prototypical American story, and the work continues in this never-ending saga. During the last century, many grand estates and family lands have been lost — rendered obsolete either by altered economics, fractured families and finances, development pressures, taxes, or changing tastes and mores. The properties that survive tend to be held together by individuals passionate about history and thoroughly engaged with the present, not by persons steeped in the past.

These individuals are risk-takers, willing to try and fail. They are also opportunists, facing the realities of the present with enthusiasm and imagination. Every now and then, something succeeds and they build on that success.

Such has been Charles' trajectory and that of his ancestors during 10 generations of stewardship at Middleton Place. Winston Churchill's famous phrase "Never give in" are his watchwords. "All for the cause" is another favorite maxim. To lead, one must be an optimist and an idealist. Without optimism, there is no solution, no path forward. Without idealism, there is no inspiration for people to aim beyond themselves.

All along, Charles' task has been to get others to care about Middleton Place as much as he does. To get them to visit, to come to know it, and then to love it. To feel like they belong to the place, ultimately wanting to become its guardians.

In the days of his grandparents, the gardens were marketed to visitors who were similar to themselves: White and well-heeled, Eastern Seaboard establishment types. The stories they heard were familiar and comfortable. They fell easily in love with the plantation. But Middleton Place was always about more than that, even if overshadowed by past narratives of the Lost Cause, garden fever or Colonial Revival. Charles sensed this from the beginning: on boyhood visits with Ha Ha and Gramps, in his relationships with the African Americans who served them, and as a young man traveling the world and seeking his fortune on Wall Street — one foot in the Old South and the other in the modern age.

Circumstances forced Charles to come to terms with his heritage more directly than he ever dreamed when his grandfather died in 1969. Middleton Place, the Edmondston-Alston House and 6,500 acres were suddenly his at the age of 31. The estate was ailing and its future uncertain. Could he make a way forward, revive it, maybe even reinvent it? Could he convince others to join him?

As the new man in charge, he grew and evolved, as did Middleton Place. For nearly five decades, Charles worked tirelessly to ensure that this essential American place — with all its triumphs and tragedies — stayed intact and relevant. While never forswearing its foundations, the national landmark fearlessly plumbed the historical record under his leadership. The result: a

Charles Duell with his grandchildren on his 80th birthday.

more complex, broad and truthful rendition. As he observes, "The power of place can and does, I believe, impact all who encounter Middleton Place, regardless of their status or ethnicity."

Now in his 80s, Charles still maintains an office at Middleton Place, but he has moved to the second floor of the mill house down by the river, a few hundred yards away from the foundation headquarters. Alligators and herons linger on the edges of the pond outside his door. Tourists stop to ask him questions, sensing this man knows something.

Charles' knowledge is staggering. His grasp and reach extend far beyond Middleton Place. More recently, he has served on the President's Advisory Council for Historic Preservation. And as president emeritus of Middleton Place and a trustee emeritus of the National Trust, he continues to mentor and inspire future preservationists.

"Dum Spiro Spero [While I breathe, I hope] is the motto chosen by Arthur Middleton for the great seal of the State of South Carolina," remarks Charles. "It is my fervent hope that after I stop breathing, my children and those who work to preserve and enrich this national landmark — whether they be trustees of the foundation, thoughtful owners of the woodlands, dedicated staff, loyal supporters or volunteers — will ensure that the whole of Middleton Place remains intact: more valuable united than as separately divided parts."

On this particular July day, Charles walks up the path to the restaurant to meet Tracey Todd for lunch. They sit down at a table on the terrace. Covid-19 still rages, yet the air outside under the moss laden oaks is clean and fresh. Heningham's pierced brick wall envelopes them like an old friend.

Before the food arrives, Charles congratulates Todd on getting the speed limit lowered on a portion of Ashley River Road. They discuss how the staff are pitching in during the pandemic. They talk about the travel industry turning into an education industry. They note the imminent return of "Ashley's Sack" — an embroidered 19th century cotton bag once owned by an enslaved family — on loan from Middleton Place to the National Museum of African American History and Culture.

Today Todd sits at the helm of an institution fast becoming as much about people and place as it is about objects. But objects are the tangible traces of history, he is quick to point out, and vital to telling accurate stories of people and place. As Todd and his staff continue to unpack and unravel the historical record in its myriad forms, they remind us that history is never simple.

Middleton Place is living proof of that reminder as it evolves into a 21st century center for research and learning — a meeting ground and community resource for people of all colors and backgrounds seeking a sanctuary for truth. Middleton Place can also be a springboard for physical and cultural renewal, as society grapples with such critical issues as racial reconciliation, civic participation, environmental sustainability and public health. Its endurance and beauty can even provide solace for the soul. For three centuries, all of this belonged to one family. Now it belongs to the world.

After finishing lunch, Todd stands and notices a shingle missing from the restaurant roof. He takes out his phone and types a memo to himself to have it repaired. Charles recalls a stash of unused shingles in the stableyards, left over from the 1930s. Todd thanks him and says goodbye. Charles then turns and walks back down to his office toward the river — on the same path he followed as a young boy years ago, hand in hand with his grandmother.

Rick Rhodes

ACKNOWLEDGMENTS

At an early age, Charles Duell dedicated himself to preserving his ancestral home of Middleton Place. That alignment would subsequently define his life and open a window into the legacy of what is one of our nation's most important foundational sites. It has been my privilege to chronicle Middleton Place's story of stewardship, restoration and reinterpretation, especially at this seminal moment in American history.

Charles' lifelong friend Steve Snyder proposed the idea for a book and provided the impetus and support to make it a reality. The strength of that friendship sustained the project over its three-year course, as did the friendship of another Yale classmate, Chris Seger. Sallie Duell's insight and vision set the stage, and out of this nucleus emerged a cast of contributors. Linking them all were the bonds of friendship and the power of place.

As I began my research, Charles and the Middleton Place Foundation board had already passed the baton to Tracey Todd. Not only was Charles ready to reflect on his long and productive life, he was also prepared to examine it with candor and humility. The journey took us through myriad joys and trials of stewarding and sustaining a National Historic Landmark. Characteristically, Charles' unfailing focus and energy prevailed.

For the last 50 years, Charles has had the foresight to put in place an expert and devoted team of historians and archivists. Through the decades, the affairs and lives of the Middleton family have been systematically documented and revealed — beginning with the work of Cheves Leland and Sarah Lytle, and carried on by Barbara Doyle, Tracey Todd, Mary Edna Sullivan, Dottie Stone and Jeff Neale. This book is based on their research, scholarship and writings. I was tasked with the challenge of composing a comprehensive narrative that accurately places Charles' life and work in the context of his family and Middleton Place — as well as the expanded social order that has so appropriately become a focus of the foundation.

Fortunately, these scholars were paying close attention to the lives and work of the enslaved community. Beginning in the 1980s their diligent and meticulous research laid the foundation for a groundbreaking program of African American historical interpretation and outreach. Today the professional interpreters and volunteer guides at Middleton Place are integrating the stories of the Black and White protagonists, while research staff continue to chronicle heretofore hidden lives of women and other marginalized groups. To Charles and each of the scholars and educators at Middleton Place, I owe a tremendous debt.

Undergirding it all is a dedicated board of trustees and a team of loyal administrators, many of whom are interviewed in this book and have been associated with Middleton Place for decades. Early on, Vice President of Accounting Ileen Grange and Executive Assistant Sue Braund provided me with valuable guidance and assistance, as did Vice President of Horticulture Sidney Frazier. Many family members, friends and supporters of Middleton Place also shared their knowledge. Their names appear throughout the book and in the References section.

Charles often refers to the teachers, friends and family who have served as important influences in his life, beginning with an ancestor who had a direct impact on him, but whom he never met — his great-grandfather Judge H.A.M. Smith — followed by Charles' inspirational grandmother Heningham Ellet Smith, his beloved mother Josephine Smith Duell, and his devoted uncle Holland Duell. Later, professors and college classmates would exert similar influence, as would the luminaries he encountered on his travels around the world, and the historic preservationists he enlisted to help him revive Middleton Place.

It has been my good fortune to call on many of these mentors and their successors — especially in the historic preservation arena — for advice and insight into telling this essential and complex American story. In particular, the account of the rebirth of St. Giles House by the 12th Earl of Shaftesbury (author of the Foreword) was an inspiration, as were the extensive interviews with Charles Duell conducted by historian Walter Edgar. Christopher Madsen's meticulous research on the Duell family was another helpful guide, as were Rod Duell's remembrances. While you will find the commentary and writings of numerous scholars and preservationists quoted throughout *American Landmark*, any errors contained herein are mine alone.

Thanks go to our publishing partner Evening Post Books (EPB), founded by Pierre Manigault and John Burbage in 2008. As Middleton descendants and guardians of Lowcountry culture, the Manigault family continues to serve on the Middleton Place Foundation board and to advocate for historic preservation and land conservation. The talented EPB editorial and design team of John Burbage, Michael Nolan, Elizabeth Hollerith and Gill Guerry — combined with the photographic expertise of Rick Rhodes — bring forth books of beauty and consequence to the community.

I also wish to express my gratitude to those family members and laborers — especially in the aftermath of the Civil War — who maintained and saved the estate under difficult conditions and with limited resources. Whether Black or White, landed or penniless, they were stewards all.

As the journey of *American Landmark* comes to a close, I reflect on those recurrent, related guideposts: the bonds of friendship and the power of place. From the beginning, Sallie and Charles Duell extended their trust, hospitality and amity to me, as they have done with countless old and new acquaintances over the years. Tracey Todd and the foundation staff did the same, welcoming this newcomer into their midst and helping me grasp a story they already knew, yet was still evolving. Others connected to the Duells and Middleton Place, both near and far, generously assisted as well.

My husband, Dana, and I have lived in the South Carolina Lowcountry for nearly 40 years, raising our family here and devoting ourselves to preserving its unique landscape. While I was well aware of Middleton Place's significance in the pantheon of American landmarks, I can't say that I fully understood it. I found it both compelling and intriguing that, almost to a person, the foundation staff loved where they worked and were invested in the historic site's well-being. As the months progressed and I spent more and more time roaming the gardens, listening to interpreters, talking with staff and supporters, observing and interviewing visitors, and delving into the archives, I too grew attached.

Then the events of 2020 unfolded. I saw Middleton Place adjust to new realities and embrace hard truths — its firm foundation of truth seeking a ready platform for overcoming seemingly insurmountable differences. Could we bridge the divide? Three years ago, I might not have believed it possible. I do now, with a renewed appreciation for the prospect of friendship and potential of place.

– Virginia C. Beach

APPENDIX

MIDDLETON PLACE FOUNDATION BOARD OF TRUSTEES

CHAIRMAN

    Sallie M. Duell . . . . 2018 – present

CURRENT TRUSTEES

    Olivia Mitchell Brock . . . . 2015 – present
    Ascanio Serena di Lapigio . . . . 2020 – present
    Caroline M. Duell. . . . . 1996 – 2005; 2012 – present
    Charles H. P. Duell (President Emeritus) . . . . 1974 – present
    Sallie M. Duell . . . . 2005 – present
    Jonathan Green. . . . . 2016 – present
    Hank Holliday . . . . 2016 – present
    James Kuyk. . . . . 2015 – present
    Michael Laughlin . . . . 2013 – present
    Richard A. Leadem . . . . 2014 – present
    Pierre Manigault . . . . 1998 – present
    Earl McMillen III . . . . 2016 – present
    Caroline T. Palmer . . . . 2018 – present
    Lee Pringle . . . . 2016 – present
    W. Mason Smith III . . . . 2012 – present
    Anne Gaud Tinker . . . . 2010 – present
    M. Tracey Todd . . . . 2018 – present
    June Waterman . . . . 1995 – present

EMERITUS TRUSTEES

- T. Heyward Carter, Jr .... 1984 – 2005
- Jane Pinckney deButts .... 1990 – 2009
- Francis G. Middleton .... 1985 – 2010
- J. Rutledge Young, Jr. .... 1984 – 2004

FORMER TRUSTEES

- E. Milby Burton* .... 1976 – 1978
- Jane Carter* .... 2009 – 2012
- Thomas L. Chrystie* .... 1984 – 2005
- C. Stuart Dawson III .... 2003 – 2012
- Ted Dintersmith .... 2006 – 2007
- Carol Duell .... 1979 – 1985
- C. Holland Duell .... 2001 – 2009; 2011 – 2018
- Roderick Duell .... 2005 – 2016
- James L. Ferguson* .... 1989 – 2006
- Rachel MacRae Gray .... 1986 – 1989
- Lee Harwood* .... 1984 – 1991
- S. Colby Hollifield .... 2010 – 2014
- Philip Lader .... 2007 – 2014
- Peter Manigault* .... 1978 – 1998
- Tina Mayland .... 2011 – 2015
- Elizabeth Wright McMillen .... 2012 – 2016
- Earl Middleton* .... 1996 – 2003
- Henry Enrico B. Middleton* .... 1989 – 1998
- Kenneth E. Middleton .... 2003 – 2016
- Lane Middleton .... 1978 – 1981
- B. Allston Moore III .... 2005 – 2014
- Heningham Anne Duell Morgan* .... 1984 – 1988
- Josephine Clark Duell Routh .... 2005 – 2008
- Michelle Sinkler .... 2015 – 2020
- Irvin Slotchiver .... 1978 – 1984
- Zoe L. Stephens .... 2011 – 2020
- Charles H. Waters* .... 1976 – 1978
- J. Rutledge Young III .... 2004 – 2012

*Deceased

NOTES

Citations are keyed to the References section by author (or source) and year.

Prologue: COLORADO (p. 1)

1. Duell 2008a; Duell C. 2018a
2. Duell 2008a
3. Duell C. 2019a
4. Parker 2014
5. Duell C. 2019b
6. *Pueblo Star-Journal & Chieftain* 1962
7. Colorado City Development Co. 1963; Duell C. 2019c; 2019a

One: BETWEEN TWO WORLDS (p. 5)

1. Madsen 2015, 194
2. Madsen 2015, 206-207, 213
3. Madsen 2015; Duell R. 2019
4. Fenyvesi 1986
5. Seger 2019
6. *The New York Times* 1933; Weyeneth 2000
7. Fenyvesi 1986; Duell C. 2018b; Duell R. 2019; Duell 2008a
8. Duell C. 2018a
9. Duell 2008a
10. Duell C. 2018a
11. Schiferi 2020, Garrett 2020
12. Duell 2008a
13. Duell C. 2018a
14. Duell 2008a
15. Duell 2008a; Duell C. 2019a
16. Duell R. 2019
17. Duell C. 2019c
18. Snyder 2019
19. Duell C. 2019a; Duell S. 2019
20. Seger 2019
21. Snyder 2019; Seger 2019
22. Duell 2008a
23. Duell C. 2019e; 2019a
24. Duell C. 2019a
25. Duell C. 2019e; 2019a
26. Duell 2008a
27. Duell C. 2019e
28. Duell 2008a
29. Duell 2008a
30. Duell 2008a
31. Duell 2008a; Duell C. 2019a
32. Duell 2008a; Duell C. 2019a

Two: EMPIRE and REBELLION (p. 27)

1. Todd 2010a; Alleyne and Fraser 2016, 10-12; Edgar 2006, 47-48
2. Alleyne and Fraser 2016, 10-12; Todd 2010; Edgar 1998, 37
3. Edgar 1998, 48-49
4. Todd 2010; Alleyne and Fraser 2016, 22, 38; Edgar 2006, 566-567
5. Edgar 1998, 44
6. Edgar 1998, 42-43, 46; Beach 2019, 216-217
7. Todd 2010; Edgar 1998, 83-84, 97, 100, 102-103, 105, 107, 137; Edgar 2006, 568; Duell 2016
8. Todd 2012; Duell 2016, 12; Todd 2017
9. Stone 2014a; Todd 2017; Smith 1919
10. Stone 2014a; Duell 2016
11. Duell 2016; Todd 2017; Doyle, Sullivan and Todd 2008
12. Todd 2017; Duell 2016
13. Todd 2017
14. Stone 2014a; Todd 2017/2018
15. *Lloyd's Evening Post* 1765; Sullivan 2021

16 Stone 2014a
17 Todd 2017/2018
18 Stone 2014b; Todd 2017/2018
19 Todd 2017/2018; Edgar 2006, 627
20 Doyle 2012
21 Neale 2021
22 Doyle, Sullivan and Todd 2008
23 Stone 2014c; Mack and Savage 1999, 28-29; Duell 2016
24 Duell 2016; Edgar 2006, 626; Doyle 2012; Rubenstein 2019, 59
25 Stone 2014c; Doyle 2012; Edgar 2006, 626
26 Stone 2014c; Doyle 2012
27 Stone 2014c; Doyle 2012; Edgar 2006, 626
28 Doyle 2012; Stone 2014c
29 Stone 2014c; Doyle 2012; Edgar 2006, 627
30 Doyle, Sullivan and Todd 2008
31 Stone 2014c; Edgar 2006, 627
32 Stone 2014c
33 Doyle, Sullivan and Todd 2008; Noren 2005
34 Edgar 2006, 627-628; Doyle 2001
35 Duell 2016; Edgar 2006, 627-628; Stone 2017a

Three: DREAMS and DESPAIR (p. 57)

1 Neale 2021; Doyle, Sullivan and Todd 2008
2 Stone 2015a; Todd 2010b; Doyle 2000; Duell 2016; Stone 2017a; Doyle 2008; Doyle 2010
3 Wooster 1954, 185-197; Rowland and Hoffius 2011, 4-9; Edgar 1998, 351-353; Beach 2014
4 Sanders 1997; Edgar 2006, 852; Beach 2014
5 Lesser 1996, 1, 10, 25; Beach 2014; Calcutt 2006; Edgar 2006, 181, 852-853; Edgar 1998, 351-353; Stone 2014d
6 Wainwright 1967, 309
7 Doyle 2013/2014; Doyle 2010; Doyle 1990; Stone 2017
8 Beach 1999; Edgar 2006, 337

9 Lewis and Haskell 1981, 15
10 Doyle 2005a
11 Doyle 2013/2014; Stone 2015a; Duell 2016
12 Doyle 2013/2014
13 Cobb 2013; Bloom 2019
14 Beach 2014
15 Sherman 2019; Bloom 2019; Doyle, Sullivan and Todd 2008
16 Doyle, Sullivan and Todd 2008; Porcher and Judd 2014, 297; Beach 2014
17 Stone 2017b
18 Todd 2001; Stone 2015b; Doyle, Sullivan and Todd 2008
19 Stone 2019c
20 Stone 2019a; Doyle, Sullivan and Todd 2008; Stone 2019b
21 Doyle 2005a; Stone 2015b
22 Doyle 1990; Doyle 2006
23 Doyle 2008; Kilbride 2006, 154
24 Beach 2014; Porwoll 2014; McKinley 2014, 48; Shick and Doyle 1985
25 Johnson and Behre 2019; Doyle, Sullivan and Todd 2008
26 Doyle 1995a
27 Doyle 1995a
28 Sherman 2019; McKinley 2014, 162-163; Doyle 1995a
29 Doyle, Sullivan and Todd 2008
30 Doyle 2005b; Middleton 1871, 1875; Lewis and Haskell 1981, 15
31 Beach 2014; Woolson 1875, 8-9
32 Lewis and Haskell 1981, 15; Pinckney 1991; Doyle 2006
33 Duell 2016; Doyle, Sullivan and Todd 2008

Four: WHERE FLOWERS BLOOM (p. 91)

1. Stone 2016; Peterson 2019; Bloom 2019
2. Williams and Hoffius 2011, xiii, xiv, 19, 108; Conroy 1981
3. Stone 2016; Peterson 2019; Bloom 2019
4. Severens 1993, 76, 79-80, 82, 123
5. Stone 2016; Peterson 2019; Bloom 2019
6. Severens 1993, 76, 79-80, 82, 123
7. Lewis and Haskell 1981, 15
8. Heyward 1902
9. Begg 1994
10. Begg 1994; Heyward 1906
11. Pinckney 1991; Lowell 1955, 450
12. Begg 1994; Duncan 1906
13. Begg 1994; Duncan 1910
14. Begg 1994; Doyle 2003
15. Doyle 2003; Fox 1963; Otis 2002, 86; Todd 2020a; Doyle 1988
16. Howard 2007; Rogers 2001, 227; Lockwood 1934; Wulf 2008
17. Williams 2002; Porcher and Rayner 2001, 26-27
18. McMillan 1986
19. Doyle 2003; Pinckney 1991; Duell 2016; Dolan 1881, 1882; Fisher 1883
20. *The News and Courier* 1915
21. Heyward 1913
22. Heyward 1916; Sullivan 2021
23. Duell S. 2019; Stone 2019c; Doyle 1998a; Bellows 2020; Smith 1982
24. Doyle 1991a; Pinckney 1991; Doyle 1994a; Bonney 1934; Duell 2008b
25. Doyle 1998b; Doyle 2002a
26. Doyle 2001b; Pinckney 1991
27. Smith Family 1925; Shaffer 1926; Hutchisson and Greene 2003, 176; Blanc 1999
28. Doyle 1981, 2008, 1994a; Roosevelt 1941; Sheppard 1984; Anderson 1977
29. Pinckney 1991

Five: HERITAGE TOURISM (p. 129)

1. Duell 2008c; Duell C. 2019a; Doyle 1990b
2. Duell 2008c; Duell C. 2019a, 2019e; May 1971
3. Duell C. 2019a; Duell 2008b, 2008c; May 1971; Sanders and Anderson 1999, 166-167
4. Hutchisson and Greene 2003, 74, 202, 206; Duell 2008c; Duell C. 2018a
5. May 1971; CLPC 1974; Stone 2016/2017a, 2016/2017b; *The Post and Courier* 1994; Doyle, Sullivan and Todd 2008; Highfield 2014
6. Duell C. 2019e; Leland 2019; Duell 2008c; Doyle 1984a; Doyle 1985; Doyle 2004; Stone 2015c, 2015d
7. Duell C. 2019e; Duell 2008c; Stone 2015d; Williams 1978; *The Charleston Evening Post* 1975; Stockton 1975; Stone 2015e
8. Sullivan 2021
9. Sullivan 1986, 2008, 2009/2010, 2010, 2011; Duell C. 2019e; Duell 2008b, 2008d; Parker 2014
10. Duell 2008c; Duell C. 2019a; deButts 2019; Weyeneth 2000, 70-71, 231; HCF 1985
11. McDaniel 2019
12. Collier 1970; Whaley and Baldwin 1997, 181-182; Hall 1976; Weyeneth 2000, 147-152, 241 n.21
13. Jenrette 2000, 27-29; PSC 2020; Handal 2019, 108-111; Duell C. 2018a, 2019e; Duell 2008b; Parker 2014

Six: MARSHALING the ASSETS (p. 159)

1. Duell C. 2019e; Duell 2008c; Jacobson, Raub and Johnson, 118-124
2. Doyle 1995b
3. Doyle 1984b
4. Carter 2019
5. Duell 2008e; Duell C. 2018a; CLPC 1974; Seger 2019; Behre 2018
6. Duell 2008e; Duell C. 2019e

7. Raskin 2016; Stone 2014/2015, 2017c; Doyle 1992
8. Duell 2008c; Doyle 2003/2004; Braswell 2011; *The News and Courier* 1975; *The Charleston Evening Post* 1975; Duell C. 2018a, 2019e
9. Duell C. 2018a, 2019a, 2019e; Duell 2008c; *Yale News* 2017; McCarter 2019, 8-10, 18-27, 38, 245; Cobb 2012; Behre 2011
10. Young 2019
11. Young 2019; Beach and Beach 2019; McCarter 2019, 27
12. Duell 2008e; Doyle 1989a, 1990c; Lytle 1990; Stone 2019d

Seven: TO BEGIN AGAIN (p. 181)

1. Doyle 1989b, 1989c, 1991b; Lytle 1990; Drayton Hall 2020
2. Hoffius 2014; Grimes 2009; Wood 1974; Donaldson 2020; Highfield 2014
3. Duell 2008f; Doyle, Sullivan and Todd 2008; Lytle 1990; Doyle 1993, 1994b, 1995c, 1996a; Middleton and Barnes 2008, 142, 144-146; Stone 2017c
4. Neale 2021; Jervey 1957
5. Doyle 1998c; Doyle, Sullivan and Todd 2008; Doyle, Sullivan and Todd 2019; Zauzmer 2019; Harvard 2020
6. Sullivan 2019; Sullivan 2005; Doyle, Sullivan and Todd 2008
7. Sullivan 2021
8. Doyle 2002b, 2004/2005; Sullivan 2005; Doyle, Sullivan and Todd 2008; Middleton and Barnes 2008, 4; Edgar 2017
9. Frazier 2019a; Doyle 2002c, 2002d
10. Frazier 2018, 2019a, 2019b; Green 2018; Bertauski 2016; Lotz 2018/2019
11. Duell 2006/2007; MPF 2006; Doyle 2006/2007; Parker 2006; Garvin 1894-1987; Tinker 2019; Collins 2017; Duell 2008b; Duell S. 2019
12. Stone 2019e; Bellinger 2019; Middleton and Barnes 2008, 3-5; Butler 2018; Grant 2019; Nunez 2019
13. Stone 2020
14. Sullivan 2021
15. DeWeese Family 2019; Doyle 1994c; Stone 2016/2017b; Sullivan 2019; Du Bois 1903

Eight: A NEW CENTURY (p. 219)

1. Williams 2020; Todd 2020b
2. Luongo 2020
3. Parker 2020a; Todd 2020b
4. Parker 2020b; Todd 2020c
5. Todd 2020c; Behre 2017
6. Parker 2020c; Neale 2020
7. Green 2017
8. MBMA 2015; Wall 2014
9. Green 2018
10. Parker 2017; Green 2021
11. Pringle 2019; Stone 2019c
12. Pringle 2019
13. Pringle 2019; Pringle 2020; Cotz 2019
14. Hall 2021
15. Neale 2019, 2020; Todd 2017/2019, 2020d
16. Pringle 2020; Todd 2020d
17. McDaniel 2019
18. Beach 1993a, 1993b, 1993c, 2014; Duell 1995; Doyle 1996b, 2001c; McDaniel 2018; Beach and Beach 2019; Duell H. 2019
19. Duell C. 2018a
20. Duell C. 2018a; Stone 2015f
21. Duell 2020a, 2020b; Todd 2019, 2020c; Parker 2018; Grange 2019
22. Duell S. 2018, 2019; Duell C. 2018a, 2018b; Spoleto 2019; Nelson Byrd Woltz 2013
23. Bradham 2019; Parker 2014
24. Leadem 2019
25. Duell 2020a
26. Duell 2020a; Todd 2020c
27. Moore 2021

REFERENCES

Abbreviations:

    HCF: Historic Charleston Foundation
  MBMA: Myrtle Beach Museum of Art
    MPF: Middleton Place Foundation
    PSC: Preservation Society of Charleston
  SCETV: South Carolina Educational Television

Alleyne, Warren and Henry Fraser. 2016. *The Barbados-Carolina Connection*, 2nd edition. Wordsmith International, pp. 10-12, 22, 38.

Anderson, Jean. 1977. "Grass Roots Cooking From a Low-Country Plantation." *Family Circle,* February.

Ashley-Cooper, Nicholas (The Earl of Shaftesbury) and Tim Knox. 2018. *The Rebirth of an English Country House: St. Giles House.* New York: Rizzoli.

Beach, Virginia. 1993a. "Land Trust Preserves Middleton Vista." *Views & Vistas,* Lowcountry Land Trust, vol. 3, no. 1.

Beach, Virginia. 1993b. "Buffer Easements: Preserving Scenic Byways." *Views & Vistas,* Lowcountry Land Trust, vol. 3, no. 2.

Beach, Virginia. 1993c. "Conservation Easements Donated Along the Ashley River Road." *Views & Vistas,* Lowcountry Land Trust (spring).

Beach, Virginia Christian. 1999. *Medway.* Charleston, S.C.: Wyrick and Co., p. 23.

Beach, Virginia Christian. 2014. *Rice and Ducks: The Surprising Convergence that Saved the Carolina Lowcountry.* Charleston, S.C.: Evening Post Books, pp. 35-39, 51-53, 90-91, 198-199.

Beach, Virginia and Dana Beach. 2019. *A Wholly Admirable Thing: Defending Nature and Community on the South Carolina Coast.* Charleston, S.C.: Evening Post Books, pp. 17, 149-150, 154-155, 158-159, 160-161, 165, 167, 216-217.

Begg, Virginia Lopez. 1994. "Charleston Gardens: A Turn of the Century View." *Magnolia*, Bulletin of the Southern Garden History Society, vol. XI, no. I (fall).

Behre, Robert. 2011. "Inn at Middleton Place has proven architects . . . " *The Post and Courier,* 30 October.

Behre, Robert. 2017. "Historian sheds new light on how many slaves might have been quarantined on Sullivan's Island, but no one knows for sure." *The Post and Courier,* 25 August.

Behre, Robert. 2018. "Middleton Place's new pavilion stands out by blending into a famous landscape." *The Post and Courier,* 7 July.

Bellinger, Robert. 2019. Interview by author. Middleton Place, S.C. 29 July.

Bernstein, Fred. 2018. "Robert Venturi, Architect Who Rejected Modernism, Dies at 93." *The New York Times,* 19 September.

Bertauski, Tony. 2016. "Lessons from Middleton Place." *The Post and Courier,* 22 July.

Bland, Sidney. 1999. *Preserving Charleston's Past, Shaping Its Future: The Life and Times of Susan Pringle Frost*. Columbia, S.C.: University of South Carolina Press.

Bloom, Carin. 2019. "Wondering What Might Have Been." MPF *Notebook*, vol. 41, no. 1 (winter/spring).

Bonney, Louise. 1934. "Spring in Charleston." *House and Garden*, April.

Bradham, June. 2019. Interview by author. Charleston, S.C. 14 November.

Braswell, Tommy. 2011. "Racing tradition returns at full gallup." *The Post and Courier*, 6 October, p. 1-A.

Braund, Sue. 2019. Interview by author. Middleton Place, S.C. 9 January.

Butler, Nic. 2018. "The S.C. Constitutional Convention of 1868." Charleston-Time-Machine/Charleston County Public Library website, 2 March.

Calcutt, Becky. 2006. "An Honorable Death." MPF *Notebook*, vol. 28, no. 1 (spring).

Carter, Heyward. 2019. Interview by author. Charleston, S.C. 18 January.

The Charleston Evening Post. 1975. "Portraits on Loan to Museum." 8 January, p. 1-C.

The Charleston Evening Post. 1975. "Coaching Day set for Middleton Place April 12." 11 April.

CLPC of Hilton Head Island, Ltd. 1974. "Middleton Place Development Project."

Cobb, Warren. 2012. "The Inn At Middleton Place Celebrates 25 Years." MPF *Notebook*, vol. 34, no. 2 (summer).

Cobb, Warren. 2013. "What Might Have Been . . . Modernizing Middleton Place in 1863." MPF *Notebook*, vol. 35, no. 2 (summer).

Collier, Bernard. 1970. "South Carolina: A Yankee View." *The New York Times*, 21 June.

Collins, Ty. 2017. Interview. "Beyond the Fields: Slavery at Middleton Place." SCETV, 1 October.

Colorado City Development Co. 1963. *Colorado City Call*, October.

Conroy, Pat. 1981. "Shadows Of the Old South." GEO, May.

Cotz, Christian. 2019. Interview by author. Montpelier, Va. 8 May.

deButts, Jane P. 2019. Interview by author. Marshall, Va. 9 May.

DeWeese Family. 2019. Interview by author. Middleton Place, S.C. 19 June.

Dolan, Patrick. 1881. Letter to Williams Middleton. Middleton Place Archives, 10 November.

Dolan, Patrick. 1882. Letter to Williams Middleton. Middleton Place Archives, 3 December.

Donaldson, Robert. 2020. Interview by Walter Edgar. "SCETV: Walter Edgar's Journal." 30 January.

Doyle, Barbara. 1981. "The Glory of the Garden . . . Shall Never Pass Away." MPF *Notebook*, vol. 3, no. 2 (spring).

Doyle, Barbara. 1984a. "What is a National Historic Landmark?" MPF *Notebook*, vol. 6, no. 4 (winter).

Doyle, Barbara. 1984b. "Landmark Gift Caps Foundation's First Decade." MPF *Notebook*, vol. 6, no. 4 (winter).

Doyle, Barbara. 1985. "1975-1985: Getting Here from There." MPF *Notebook*, vol. 7, no. 1 (spring).

Doyle, Barbara. 1988. "Henry Middleton's Garden of Landscapes," MPF *Notebook*. vol. 10, no. 4 (winter).

Doyle, Barbara. 1989a. "Middleton Place Weathers Storm Of The Century." MPF *Notebook*, vol 11, no. 4 (winter).

Doyle, Barbara. 1989b. "Foundation Expanding Stableyards Interpretation." MPF *Notebook*, vol. 11, no. 3 (fall).

Doyle, Barbara. 1989c. "Eliza Leach." MPF *Notebook*, vol. 11, no. 3 (fall).

Doyle, Barbara. 1990a. "Of Summer in the City . . ." MPF *Notebook*, vol. 12, no. 2 (summer).

Doyle, Barbara. 1990b. "Foundation Enlarges Administrative Responsibility." MPF *Notebook*. vol. 12, no. 1 (spring).

Doyle, Barbara. 1990c. "Hurricane Hugo Report." MPF *Notebook,* vol. 12, no. 1 (spring).

Doyle, Barbara. 1991a. "Remembering Earlier Days." MPF *Notebook,* vol. 13 (special anniversary issue, fall/winter).

Doyle, Barbara. 1991b. "Eliza's Housewarming." MPF *Notebook,* vol. 13 (special anniversary issue, fall/winter).

Doyle, Barbara. 1992. "Symposium Salutes Southern Cooking." MPF *Notebook,* vol. 14, no. 4 (winter).

Doyle, Barbara. 1993. "July Jubilation." MPF *Notebook,* vol. 15, no. 2 (summer).

Doyle, Barbara. 1994a. "Mary Sheppard 1906-1994." MPF *Notebook,* vol. 16, no. 2 (summer).

Doyle, Barbara. 1994b. "Rhythms Along the Ashley River." MPF *Notebook,* vol. 16, no. 3 (fall).

Doyle, Barbara. 1994c. "Martha DeWeese: 1909-1994." MPF *Notebook,* vol. 16, no. 4 (winter).

Doyle, Barbara. 1995a. "The Dear Old Wreck . . ." MPF *Notebook,* vol. 17, no. 4 (winter).

Doyle, Barbara. 1995b. "Foundation Celebrates Twenty Years." MPF *Notebook,* vol. 17, no. 1 (spring).

Doyle, Barbara. 1995c. "Rhythms Along the Ashley River." MPF *Notebook,* vol. 17, no. 2 (summer).

Doyle, Barbara. 1996a. MPF *Notebook,* vol. 18, no. 4, p. 5 (winter).

Doyle, Barbara. 1996b. "An Essential Corridor: The Ashley River Historic District." MPF *Notebook,* vol. 18, no. 4 (winter).

Doyle, Barbara. 1998a. "Faith and Courage . . ." MPF *Notebook,* vol. 20, no. 3 (fall).

Doyle, Barbara. 1998b. "Do You Know Your Middleton Place . . .?" MPF *Notebook,* vol. 20, no. 1 (spring).

Doyle, Barbara. 1998c. "Preserving the Spring House." MPF *Notebook,* vol. 20 no. 4 (winter).

Doyle, Barbara. 2000. "The House on Boundary Street." MPF *Notebook,* vol. 22, no. 3 (fall).

Doyle, Barbara. 2001a. "When Presidents Come Calling." MPF *Notebook,* vol. 23, no. 2 (summer).

Doyle, Barbara. 2001b. "The Jewel in the Woods." MPF *Notebook,* vol. 23, no. 1 (spring).

Doyle, Barbara. 2001c. "Easements Given to Foundation." MPF *Notebook,* vol. 23, no. 1 (spring).

Doyle, Barbara. 2002a. "To Increase Understanding of Plantation Life . . ." MPF *Notebook,* vol. 24, no. 4 (winter).

Doyle, Barbara. 2002b. "Foundation Receives Grant." MPF *Notebook,* vol. 24, no. 3 (fall).

Doyle, Barbara. 2002c. "Going For The Gold: Carolina Gold, That Is." MPF *Notebook,* vol. 24 no. 2 (summer).

Doyle, Barbara. 2002d. "Going For The Gold: Carolina Gold, That Is." MPF *Notebook,* vol. 24 no. 3 (fall).

Doyle, Barbara. 2003. "Middleton Place and the Two Andres." MPF *Notebook,* vol. 25, no. 1 (spring).

Doyle, Barbara. 2003/2004. "The Races! The Races! Horse-racing Memorabilia on Display." MPF *Notebook,* vol. 25, no. 4 (winter).

Doyle, Barbara. 2004. "Happy Anniversary, Middleton Place Foundation!" MPF *Notebook,* vol. 26, no. 3 (fall).

Doyle, Barbara. 2004/2005. "New African American Exhibit Opens." MPF *Notebook,* vol. 26, no. 4 (winter).

Doyle, Barbara. 2005a. "Life is Real, Life is Earnest . . . An Incident From a Diary." MPF *Notebook,* vol. 27, no. 3 (fall).

Doyle, Barbara. 2005b. "Foundation Makes Exciting Find!" MPF *Notebook,* vol. 27, no. 2 (summer).

Doyle, Barbara. 2006. "To Relax The Heart." MPF *Notebook,* vol. 28, no. 3 (fall).

Doyle, Barbara. 2006/2007. "Coming Together: A Place to Begin." MPF *Notebook,* vol. 28, no. 4 (winter).

Doyle, Barbara. 2008. "Coming Home." MPF *Notebook*, vol. 30, no. 3 (fall).

Doyle, Barbara. 2010. "Remembering the Rebellion." MPF, *Notebook,* vol. 32, no. 3 (winter).

Doyle, Barbara. 2012. "Exiled to Congress." MPF *Notebook,* vol. 34, no. 3 (fall).

Doyle, Barbara. 2013/2014. "The Devoted Service of Williams Middleton." MPF *Notebook*, vol. 35, no. 4 (winter).

Doyle, Barbara, Mary Edna Sullivan, and Tracey Todd. 2008. *Beyond the Fields: Slavery at Middleton Place.* Middleton Place Foundation, pp. 24, 26-27, 33-36, 38, 40-41, 62-63, 65-68.

Doyle, Barbara, Mary Edna Sullivan, and Tracey Todd. 2019. Middleton Place Plantation Chapel exhibit.

Drayton Hall, 2020. Caretaker's House Exhibit.

Du Bois, W.E.B. 1903. *The Souls of Black Folk.* Chicago: A.C. McClurg & Co., chapter 10, par 3, lines 3-4.

Duell, Charles. 1995. "President's Message." MPF *Notebook,* vol. 17, no. 4 (winter).

Duell, Charles. 2006/2007. "President's Message." MPF *Notebook,* vol. 28, no. 4 (winter).

Duell, Charles. 2008a. Interview by Walter Edgar. Charleston, S.C., DVD #3, transcript pp. 31-34, 39, 40, 41, 43, 44-45, 47-50.

Duell, Charles. 2008b. Interview by Walter Edgar. Charleston, S.C. DVD #6, transcript pp. 93-94, 95-96.

Duell, Charles. 2008c. Interview by Walter Edgar. Charleston, S.C. DVD #4, transcript pp. 50-59, 61-62.

Duell, Charles. 2008d. Interview by Walter Edgar. Middleton Place, S.C. DVD #1, transcript pp. 15-16.

Duell, Charles. 2008e. Interview by Walter Edgar. Charleston, S.C. DVD #5, transcript pp. 65-69.

Duell, Charles. 2008f. Interview by Walter Edgar. Charleston, S.C. DVD #2, transcript p 25.

Duell, Charles. 2016. *Middleton Place: A Phoenix Still Rising.* Columbia, S.C.: R.L. Bryan and Co., p. 12, 14-17, 22-24, 30, 63.

Duell, Charles. 2018a. Interview by author. Middleton Place, S.C. 17 December.

Duell, Charles. 2018b. Interview by author. Charleston, S.C. 11 July.

Duell, Charles. 2019a. Interview by author. Middleton Place, S.C. 7 June.

Duell, Charles. 2019b. Interview by author. Charleston, S.C. 26 April.

Duell, Charles. 2019c. Interview by author. Charleston, S.C. 8 April.

Duell, Charles. 2019d. Interview by author. Middleton Place, S.C. 3 June.

Duell, Charles. 2019e. Interview by author. Middleton Place, S.C. 4 February.

Duell, Charles. 2020a. Interview by author. Middleton Place, S.C. 17 July.

Duell, Charles. 2020b. Telephone interview by author. 24 March.

Duell, Holland. 2019. Interview by author. Middleton Place, S.C. 8 March.

Duell, Rod. 2019. Interview by author. Middleton Place, S.C. 21 February.

Duell, Sallie. 2018. Interview by author. Charleston, S.C. 11 July.

Duell, Sallie. 2019. Interview by author. Charleston, S.C. 21 January.

Duncan, Frances. 1906. Letter to R.W. Gilder. The New York Public Library: Century Company Records, 29 April.

Duncan, Frances. 1910. "An Old-Time Carolina Garden." *The Century Magazine,* vol. LXXX, no. 6 (October).

Edgar, Walter. 1998. *South Carolina: A History.* Columbia: University of South Carolina Press, pp. 37, 42-43, 44, 46, 48-49, 83-84, 97, 100, 102-103, 105, 107, 137, 351-353.

Edgar, Walter, ed. 2006. *The South Carolina Encyclopedia.* Columbia, S.C.: University of South Carolina Press, pp. 37, 47-48, 181, 337, 566-568, 626-628, 852-853.

Edgar, Walter. 2017. Interview. "Beyond the Fields: Slavery at Middleton Place." SCETV, 1 October.

Fenyvesi, Charles. 1986. "The Enduring Mystery of Middleton Place." *Historic Preservation*, April, p. 34.

Fisher, Eliza. 1883. Letter to Susan Middleton. Middleton Place Archives, 10 April.

Fox, Helen. 1963. *Andre Le Notre: Garden Architect to Kings*. New York: Crown, ch. 1.

Frazier, Sidney. 2018. Interview by author. Middleton Place, S.C. 17 December.

Frazier, Sidney. 2019a. Interview by author. Middleton Place, S.C. 22 February.

Frazier, Sidney. 2019b. Interview by author. Middleton Place, S.C. 7 March.

Garvin, Mamie E. 1894-1987. "Inventory of the Mamie E. Garvin Fields Papers, 1894-1987." Avery Research Center for African American History and Culture, College of Charleston.

Garrett, Margaret. 2020. "C of C decision ignores Robert Smith's vast contributions." *The Post and Courier*, 6 November, p. A-11.

Grange, Ileen. 2019. Interview by author. Middleton Place, S.C. 10 January.

Grant, Andrea. 2019. "Reinterpreting Life On A Southern Plantation." Suffolk University website/News & Features, 3 September.

Green, Bill. 2018. Interview by author. Middleton Place, S.C. 17 December.

Green, Jonathan. 2017. Interview. "Beyond the Fields: Slavery at Middleton Place." SCETV, 1 October.

Green, Jonathan. 2018. "Sustaining The Future of Middleton Place," MPF Charles Duell Legacy Fund brochure.

Green, Jonathan. 2021. Email communication with author. 5 February.

Grimes, William. 2009. "Philip Curtin, 87, Scholar of Slave Trade, is Dead." *The New York Times*, 16 June.

Hall, Basil. 1976. "Keeping Posted." *The Charleston Evening Post*, 22 April.

Hall, Jamal. 2021. "Let's Talk Tuesday" interview with Carin Bloom and Jeff Neale. "Plugged into History." Middleton Place, S.C. 12 March.

Handal, Leigh Jones. 2019. *Lost Charleston*. London: Pavilion Books, pp. 108-111.

Harvard University. 2020. "The Pluralism Project." Cambridge, Mass.

HCF/Historic Charleston Foundation. 1985. "Edmunds Rated Most Influential Woman." *Historic Charleston Reproductions* newsletter, fall.

Heyward, Elizabeth M. 1902. Letter to Emeline Middleton. Middleton Place Archives, 12 April.

Heyward, Elizabeth M. 1906. Letter to Wilhelm Miller. Middleton Place Archives, May.

Heyward, Elizabeth M. 1913. Will. Middleton Place Archives, box 35, file 6 (22 March).

Heyward, Julius H. 1916. Deed to J.J. Pringle Smith. Middleton Place Archives, box 35, file 7 (20 March).

Highfield, Elaura. 2014. "Public History and the Fractured Past: Colonial Williamsburg, the Usable Past, and the Concept of an American Identity." Master's Thesis. Middle Tennessee State University.

Hoffius, Stephen. 2014. "A Smash Hit. Again." *Amherst Magazine* (fall).

Howard, Hugh. 2007. *Houses of the Founding Fathers*. New York: Artisan.

Hutchisson, James and Harlan Greene, eds. 2003. *Renaissance in Charleston: Art and Life in the Carolina Low Country, 1900-1940*. Athens: University of Georgia Press, pp. 74, 176, 202, 206.

Jacobson, Darien and Brian Raub, and Barry Johnson. "The Estate Tax: Ninety Years and Counting." www.irs.gov, pp. 118-124.

Jenrette, Richard. 2000. *Adventures with Old Houses*. Charleston: Wyrick & Co., pp. 27-29.

Jervey, Henrietta and Dalcho Historical Society. 1957. "The Private Register of the Rev. Paul Trapier." *South Carolina Historical Magazine*, vol. 58, no. 4, p. 247.

Johnson, Chloe and Robert Behre. 2019. "Charleston's phosphate era unearthed riches, left scars." *The Post and Courier*. 23 June, p. A-1.

Kilbride, Daniel. 2006. *An American Aristocracy: Southern Planters in Antebellum Philadelphia*. Columbia, S.C.: University of South Carolina Press, p. 154.

Leadem, Rich. 2019. Interview by author. Charleston, S.C. 18 November.

Leland, Cheves. 2019. Interview by author. Charleston, S.C. 26 March.

Lesser, Charles. 1996. *Relic of the Lost Cause*. South Carolina Department of Archives and History, 2nd edition, revised, pp. 1, 10, 25.

Lewis, Kenneth and Helen Haskell. 1981. Letter of T.B. Bennett to Williams Middleton, 28 October, 1864. *The Middleton Place Privy: A Study of Discard Behavior and The Archeological Record*, Institute of Archeology and Anthropology, University of South Carolina, August, p. 15.

Ibid. Letter of A.C. Shaffer to Williams Middleton. 25 February, 1875.

Ibid. Letter of J.D. Edwards to Williams Middleton. 16 May, 1881.

Ibid. Lease agreement betw/ Elizabeth M. Heyward and United Timber Co. 6 July, 1915.

Lloyd's Evening Post. 1765. "Death Notice Mrs. Sarah Middleton, relict of the Hon. Arthur Middleton . . ." London, England. 23 December.

Lockwood, Alice G.B., ed. 1934. "Middleton Place Gardens: An Introductory Survey." *Gardens of Colony and State: Gardens and Gardeners of the American Colonies and of the Republic Before 1840*. New York: Charles Scribner's Sons for the Garden Club of America.

Lotz, C.J. 2018/2019. "Meet The King of Camellias." *Garden & Gun* (December/January).

Lowell, Amy. 1955. "Charleston, South Carolina" and "The Middleton Place." *Complete Poetical Works of Amy Lowell*. New York: Houghton Mifflin, p. 450.

Luongo, Michael. 2020. "Despite Everything, People Still Have Weddings at 'Plantation' Sites." *The New York Times*, 17 October.

Lytle, Sarah. 1989. "The Director Notes: What was it like?" MPF *Notebook*, vol 11, no. 4 (winter).

Lytle, Sarah. 1990. "The Director Notes." MPF *Notebook*, vol. 12, no. 2 (summer).

Mack, Angela and J. Thomas Savage. 1999. *In Pursuit of Refinement: Charlestonians Abroad 1740-1860*. Columbia, S.C.: University of South Carolina Press, pp. 28-29.

Madsen, Christopher. 2015. *Rowdy*. Santa Barbara, CA, pp. 194-195, 206-207, 213.

May, Jean. 1971. "Middleton Place Plantation Stableyards." *Sandlapper: The Magazine of South Carolina*. Columbia, S.C.: Sandlapper Press.

MBMA/Myrtle Beach Museum of Art. 2015. "Rice: Paintings by Jonathan Green." Press release, 29 September.

McCarter, Robert. 2019. *Place Matters: The Architecture of WG Clark*. Charlottesville: Oro Editions, pp. 8-10, 18-27, 38, 245.

McDaniel, George. 2018. "Standing at the Crossroads." *The Southern Edge*, pp. 62-66 (winter).

McDaniel, George. 2019. Interview by author. Summerville, S.C. 5 March.

McKinley, Shepherd. 2014. *Stinking Stones and Rocks of Gold*. Gainesville: University Press of Florida, pp. 48, 162-163.

McMillan, George. 1986. "South Carolina's Great Colonial Garden." *The New York Times*, 30 March.

Middleton, Earl and Joy Barnes. 2008. *Knowing Who I Am: A Black Entrepreneur's Struggle and Success in the American South.* Columbia, S.C.: University of South Carolina Press, pp. 3-5, 142, 144-146.

Middleton, Williams. 1871. Letter to Hal Middleton. Middleton Place Archives.

Middleton, Williams. 1875. Letter to Eliza Middleton. Middleton Place Archives, 30 January.

Moore, Alexander. 2021. Email communication with Tracey Todd. 7 February.

MPF/Middleton Place Foundation. 2006. Reunion Planning Committee letter. 8 March.

Neale, Jeff. 2019. Interview by author. Middleton Place, S.C. 17 January.

Neale, Jeff. 2020. Interview by author. Middleton Place, S.C. 17 July.

Neale, Jeff. 2021. Email communication with author. 8 January.

Nelson Byrd Woltz. 2013. *Garden Park Community Farm.* New York: Princeton Architectural Press.

The New York Times. 1933. "Josephine Smith Becomes a Bride — Charleston Girl is Married to Charles Halliwell Duell of New York." 22 October.

The News and Courier. 1915. Obituary notice for Elizabeth M. Heyward. 18 June.

The News and Courier. 1975. "Coaching Day is Scheduled at Middleton." 11 April, p. 11-B.

Noren, Clint. 2005. "South Carolina Slaves and the Revolution — A Brief Overview." MPF *Notebook*, vol. 27, no. 2 (summer).

Nunez, Nick. 2019. "The Mill House and The Enslaved Watermen." Presentation. Middleton Place, S.C., 29 July.

Otis, Denise. 2002. *Grounds for Pleasure: Four Centuries of the American Garden.* New York: Abrams, p. 86.

Parker, Adam. 2006. "Past meets future: Middleton Place reunion brings history to bear on its descendants." *The Post and Courier,* 12 November.

Parker, Adam. 2014. "Steward of Middleton Place." *The Post and Courier*, 26 December.

Parker, Adam. 2017. "Requiem for Rice: Programs to honor contributions of 'unmourned' slaves." *The Post and Courier,* 15 October, G-2.

Parker, Adam. 2018. "Historic Middleton Place led by someone outside family for first time in 300 years." *The Post and Courier,* 8 July, p. F-1.

Parker, Adam. 2020a. "Catastrophic: Drayton Hall and other historic sites make an urgent call for help as funds dry up amid coronavirus shutdown." *The Post and Courier,* 26 April, p. F-1.

Parker, Adam. 2020b. "Museums, historic sites go virtual," *The Post and Courier,* 24 May, p. F-1.

Parker, Adam. 2020c. "Plantation politics: Under scrutiny, historic Lowcountry sites consider their role in an expanding dialogue on race." *The Post and Courier,* 5 July, p. F-1.

Peterson, Bo. 2019. "Researchers hunt for 'buried' SC faults that could cause next 'great' quake." *The Post and Courier,* 20 May.

Pinckney, Elise. 1991. "Still Mindful of the English Way: 250 Years of Middleton Place on the Ashley." *South Carolina Historical Magazine*, vol. 92, no. 3, p. 158 (July).

Porcher, Richard and William Judd. 2014. *The Market Preparation of Carolina Rice.* Columbia, S.C.: University of South Carolina Press, p. 297.

Porcher, Richard and Douglas Rayner. 2001. *A Guide to the Wildflowers of South Carolina.* Columbia, S.C.: University of South Carolina Press, pp. 26-27.

Porwoll, Paul. 2014. *Against All Odds: History of St. Andrew's Parish Church, Charleston, 1706-2013.* WestBow Press.

The Post and Courier. 1994. "Mary Sheppard, retired cook, dies." 12 May, p. 2-B.

Pringle, Lee. 2019. Interview by author. Charleston, S.C. 11 March.

Pringle, Lee. 2020. Facebook Live interview by Carin Bloom and Tracey Todd. "Plugged into History." Middleton Place, S.C. 2 June.

PSC/Preservation Society of Charleston. 2020. "St. Mary's Hotel, Planter's Hotel, Mills House, St. Johns." *Alfred O. Halsey Map 1949,* #29 (website).

Pueblo Star-Journal & Chieftain. 1962. October.

Raskin, Hannah. 2016. "Lowcountry Sojourn: Renowned chef Edna Lewis spent only three years at Middleton Place but left a rich legacy." *The Post and Courier,* 13 January, p. D-1.

Rockefeller, Barbara Bellows. 2020. Email communication with author. 24 January.

Rogers, Elizabeth Barlow. 2001. *Landscape Design: A Cultural and Architectural History.* New York: Harry N. Abrams, p. 227.

Roosevelt, Eleanor. 1941. "My Day." *Richmond News Leader.* 19 March.

Rowland, Lawrence and Stephen Hoffius, eds. 2011. *The Civil War in South Carolina.* Charleston, S.C.: Home House Press, pp. 4-9.

Rubenstein, David. 2019. *The American Story: Conversations with Master Historians.* New York: Simon and Schuster, p. 59.

Sanders, Albert and William Anderson. 1999. *Natural History Investigations in South Carolina: From Colonial Times to the Present.* Columbia, S.C.: University of South Carolina Press, pp. 166-167.

Sanders, Betty Jean. 1997. "To Dissolve the Union . . ." MPF *Notebook,* vol. 19, no. 1 (spring).

Schiferi, Jenna. 2020. "College of Charleston launches virtual history site that aims to uncover hidden stories." *The Post and Courier,* 13 April, p. A-3.

Seger, Chris. 2019. Telephone interview by author. 24 July.

Severens, Martha. 1993. *Alice Ravenel Huger Smith: An Artist, A Place and a Time.* Charleston: Carolina Art Association, pp. 76, 79-80, 82, 123.

Shaffer, E.T.H. 1926. "The Ashley River and Its Gardens." *National Geographic.* Washington D.C.: National Geographic Society, vol. XLIX, no. 5 (May).

Sheppard, Mary. 1984. Interview by Barbara Doyle. Middleton Place, S.C. August.

Sherman, Bob. 2019. Interview by author. Middleton Place, S.C. 17 July.

Shick, Tom and Don Doyle. 1985. "The South Carolina Phosphate Boom and the Stillbirth of the New South, 1867-1920." *The South Carolina Historical Magazine,* vol. 86, no. 1 (January).

Smith Family. 1925. Scrapbook. Middleton Place Archives, box B.

Smith, Heningham. 1982. "My Little World." Memoir published in MPF *Notebook,* vol. 4, no. 3 (fall).

Smith, Henry A.M. 1919. "The Ashley River: Its Seats and Settlements." *The South Carolina Historical and Genealogical Magazine,* vol. 20, no. 2, pp 115-122 (April).

Snyder, Stephen. 2019. Interview by author. Cashiers, N.C. 10 August.

Spoleto Festival USA. 2019. "Spoleto Festival USA honors Sallie M. Duell, Susan W. Ravenel, and Kathleen Rivers." Press release, 3 April.

Stockton, Robert. 1975. "Ancestral Portraits Returned to Middleton Place." *The News and Courier,* 13 January.

Stone, Dottie. 2014a. "The Middleton Marys: Henry's Marys." MPF *Notebook,* vol. 36, no. 1 (spring/summer).

Stone, Dottie. 2014b. "Henry Middleton, "Actual Rebel." MPF *Notebook,* vol. 36, no. 2 (fall).

Stone, Dottie. 2014c. "The Middleton Marys: Mary Izard." MPF *Notebook,* vol. 36, no. 2 (fall).

Stone, Dottie. 2014d. "The Price They Paid." MPF *Notebook,* vol. 36, no. 1 (spring/summer).

Stone, Dottie. 2014/2015. "Edna Lewis, 'Grande Dame of Southern Cooking.' " MPF *Notebook,* vol. 36, no. 3 (winter).

Stone, Dottie. 2015a. "Middleton Brothers And The Civil War." MPF *Notebook,* vol. 37, no. 2 (summer).

Stone, Dottie. 2015b. "February 22, 1865: The 'Wanton Destruction . . . Was Sad In The Extreme." MPF *Notebook,* vol. 37, no. 1 (spring).

Stone, Dottie. 2015c. "Happy Birthday Middleton Place Foundation!" MPF *Notebook,* vol. 37, no. 1 (spring).

Stone, Dottie. 2015d. "Opening Day at the House Museum." MPF *Notebook,* vol. 37, no. 1 (spring).

Stone, Dottie. 2015e. "Family Portrait Home to Stay." MPF *Notebook,* vol. 37, no. 1 (spring).

Stone, Dottie. 2015f. "President Charles Duell Honored." MPF *Notebook,* vol. 37, no. 1 (spring).

Stone, Dottie. 2016. "Middleton Place and the Earthquake of 1886." MPF *Notebook,* vol. 38, no. 1 (spring).

Stone, Dottie. 2016/2017a. "The Middleton Marys: Mary Sheppard." MPF *Notebook,* vol. 38, no. 3 (winter).

Stone, Dottie. 2016/2017b. "Who is Anna Perry?" MPF *Notebook,* vol. 38, no. 3 (winter).

Stone, Dottie. 2017a. "Down Along the Combahee." MPF *Notebook,* vol. 39, no. 1 (spring).

Stone, Dottie. 2017b. "Nothing But Smoldering Ruins . . . The Combahee Ferry Raid." MPF *Notebook,* vol. 39, no. 2 (summer).

Stone, Dottie. 2017c. "Top Chef Comes to Middleton Place," MPF *Notebook,* vol. 39, no. 1 (spring).

Stone, Dottie. 2017d. "Earl Middleton, Tuskegee Airman." MPF *Notebook,* vol. 39, no. 2 (summer).

Stone, Dottie. 2019a. "Moro Brewer, abt. 1821-1890." MPF monograph.

Stone, Dottie. 2019b. "The Wood Nymph — A Middleton Survivor." MPF *Notebook.* vol. 41, no. 3 (fall).

Stone, Dottie. 2019c. Interview by author. Middleton Place, S.C. 15 July.

Stone, Dottie. 2019d. "Remembering Hurricane Hugo." MPF *Notebook,* vol. 41, no. 3 (fall).

Stone, Dottie. 2019e. "A Summer of Learning." MPF *Notebook,* vol. 41, no. 3 (fall).

Stone, Dottie. 2020. "Connecting to Shared History: Conversations with Middleton Place Descendants." MPF *Notebook,* vol. 42, no. 2 (fall).

Sullivan, Mary Edna. 1986. "Candlesticks Add Luster to Foundation Collection." MPF *Notebook,* vol. 8, no. 2 (summer).

Sullivan, Mary Edna. 2005. "Developing a Vision — Beyond the Fields: Slavery at Middleton Place." MPF *Notebook,* vol. 27, no. 1 (spring).

Sullivan, Mary Edna. 2008. "Foundation Receives Important Gift." MPF *Notebook,* vol. 30, no. 3 (fall).

Sullivan, Mary Edna. 2009/2010. "Reuniting Heirlooms." MPF *Notebook,* vol. 31, no. 4 (winter).

Sullivan, Mary Edna. 2010. "Carolina Gold, English Silver, and Jewels of the Past: Notes on a Special Exhibit." MPF *Notebook,* vol. 32, no. 1 (spring/summer).

Sullivan, Mary Edna. 2011. "Recent Additions at Middleton Place." *Antiques & Fine Art,* January.

Sullivan, Mary Edna. 2019. Interview by author. Middleton Place, S.C. 19 June.

Sullivan, Mary Edna. 2021. Email communication with author. 2, 8, 15 February.

Tinker, Anne Gaud. 2019. Interview by author. Charleston, S.C. 27 February.

Todd, Tracey. 2001. "Setting The Record Straight." MPF *Notebook,* vol. 23, no. 4 (winter).

Todd, Tracey. 2010a. "Barbados: Notes From a Working Vacation." MPF *Notebook*, vol. 32, no. 2 (fall).

Todd, Tracey. 2010b. "Divided Nation And Divided Brothers: The Sesquicentennial of Secession." MPF *Notebook*, vol. 32, no. 3 (winter).

Todd, Tracey. 2012. "Further Notes From Barbados." MPF *Notebook,* vol. 34, no. 1 (spring).

Todd, Tracey. 2017. "Notes on the Life of Henry Middleton, Part One." MPF *Notebook,* vol. 39, no. 1 (spring).

Todd, Tracey. 2017/2018. "Notes of the Life of Henry Middleton, Part Two." MPF *Notebook,* vol. 39, no. 3 (winter).

Todd, Tracey. 2019. Interview by author. Middleton Place, S.C. 17 January.

Todd, Tracey. 2020a. Interview by author. Middleton Place, S.C. 21 February.

Todd, Tracey. 2020b. Zoom interview by author. 13 July.

Todd, Tracey. 2020c. Interview by author. Middleton Place, S.C. 17 July.

Todd, Tracey. 2020d. Interview by author. Middleton Place, S.C. 9 September.

Wainwright, Nicholas, ed. 1967. *A Philadelphia Perspective: The Diary of Sidney George Fisher.* Philadelphia: Historical Society of Pennsylvania, p. 309.

Wall, Pam. 2014. "Rice in the Lowcountry: The Art of Jonathan Green and Alice Ravenel Huger Smith." Gibbes Museum of Art website, 17 October.

Weyeneth, Robert. 2000. *Historic Preservation for a Living City: Historic Charleston Foundation 1947-1997.* Columbia, S.C.: University of South Carolina Press, pp. 59, 70-71, 145, 147-152, 156, 231, 241 (n.21).

Whaley, Emily and William Baldwin. 1997. *Mrs. Whaley and Her Charleston Garden.* Chapel Hill: Alqonquin Books, pp. 181-182.

Williams, Charlie. 2002. "Andre Michaux, A Biographical Sketch." Andre Michaux International Symposium.

Williams, Emily. 2020. "Plantation weddings spur dialogue on national stage." *The Post and Courier,* 9 January, p. A-1.

Williams, Roger. 1978. "Middleton Place: Assembling the Evidence of History." *Americana*, vol. 6, no. 1 (March/April).

Williams, Susan Millar and Stephen Hoffius. 2011. *Upheaval in Charleston: Earthquake and Murder on the Eve of Jim Crow.* Athens: University of Georgia Press, pp. xiii, xiv, 19, 108.

Wood, Peter. 1974. *Black Majority: Negroes in Colonial South Carolina from 1670 through the Stono Rebellion.* New York: Alfred A. Knopf.

Woolson, Constance Fennimore. 1875. "Up the Ashley and Cooper." *Harper's New Monthly Magazine*, vol. 52, no. 307, pp. 8-9 (December).

Wooster, Ralph. 1954. "Membership of the South Carolina Secession Convention." *The South Carolina Historical Magazine*, vol. 55, no. 4, pp. 185-197.

Wulf, Andrea. 2008. *The Brother Gardeners.* New York: Random House.

Yale News. 2017. "In memoriam: Vincent Scully, beloved teacher 'helped shape a nation.' " 1 December.

Young, Rutledge. 2019. Interview by author. Charleston, S.C. 31 January.

Zauzmer, Julie. 2019. "The Bible was used to justify slavery. Then Africans made it their path to freedom." *The Washington Post,* 30 April.

INDEX

— A —

Abraham (enslaved person), 70, 191
Adams, John, 39, 228
Adventures with Old Houses (Jenrette), 155
African American Focus Tour, 197, 199, 204
African American history. *see* history, African American; interpretation of African American history
African American interpretive center, 85. *see also* Eliza's House
African Americans. *see also* enslaved people; slavery; slaves, Middleton
    Ashley's Sack, *233*, 251
    disenfranchisement, 92
    freedom, 71–79
    loyalists, 50–51
    religion and, 190–193
African Americans associated with Middleton family, 181–217. see also *Beyond the Fields: Slavery at Middleton Place*; enslaved people; history, African American; interpretation of African American history; reunions; slavery; slaves, Middleton
    descendants of, 230–231
    endowed scholarship program for descendants of, 219
    plantation chapel (and spring house), 189–190, *191*, *192*
    research on, xii, 159, 189, 193–195, 205, 225–226
    reunions of, 205–207, *208–209*, 210, 217, 226
    tracing ancestry of, 226
Agrippa (enslaved worker), 206
All God's Dangers (Rosengarten), 183
alliances, family, 38
Alston, Anthony, 78, 85
Alston, Charles, 130

Alston, Susan, 130–131
American Aristocracy, An (Kilbride), 79
American Institute of Architects, 174
American Tobacco, 7
Americana magazine, 142
Amory, Sarah, 31. see also Middleton, Sarah Amory
Andover (Phillips Academy), 14–15
Andrew (enslaved person), 70
Angell, Herbert, 99–100
annexation war, 237–238
architecture. *see also* buildings of Middleton Place
    Eliza's House and, 183
    Inn at Middleton Place, 171–176
    Le Corbusier, 19, 171
    modernist design, 19
art collection at Middleton Place, 36, 42, *144*, *145*, *154*. see also portraits
Articles of Confederation, 45
Ashley Cooper, Earl Anthony, viii–ix, 29, 30
Ashley Phosphate Mining Company, 80–81, 83
Ashley River corridor, 235–240, *237*
Ashley River Road (Highway 61), 150, *221*, 236
Ashley, Bud, 118
Ashley's Sack, *233*, 251
Ashley-Cooper, Anthony (12th Earl), viii–ix, 254
Asia, 17–18
Aspin, Les, 15
Atlantic Slave Trade, The (Curtin), 184
authenticity, 16, 138, 163
Avery Research Center, 181
azaleas, 111, 112, 117, 123

— B —

Baker, Mary, 34. *see also* Williams, John
Banbury, John, 51
Banbury, Lucy, 51
Barbados, 27–28, *28*, 29
barbed wire, 71
Barnes, Joy, 205, 211
Batavia, 49
Beckett, Ted, 202
Begg, Virginia Lopez, 99, 103, 104, 105
Behre, Robert, 162
Bellinger family, 205
Bellinger, Edmund C., 210, 211
Bellinger, Robert, 181, 210–213, *211*
Bennet, Jefferson, 66
Betts, Ann Whelan, 103
Beyond the Fields: Slavery at Middleton Place (book; documentary; exhibit), 197–198, 204, 205, 206, 213–214, 217
Black History Month, 232
Black Majority (Wood), 184
Bloom, Carin, 212, 213, 220–221, 222
boats, 5
    Obsession, 4
    Rowdy, 5
    schooner, 70–71, 212–213
Boissonnas, Rémi, 20
Bosque, 37
Bowen, Racena, 232
Boyce, W.W., 60
Brackville, Eleanor Phillips, 148
Bradham, June, 245
Brantley, Donna, 235
Braund, Sue, 254
Brewer, Moro, *75*, 76–77, 88, 143
    great-great-grandson of, 230–231
Brewer, Rachel, 88
bricks, 65–66, 68
Brock, Olivia Mitchell, 256
Brooklyn Botanic Garden, 178
Brooks, Eric, 165–166, 171
Brown, Catherine, 85, 92
Brown, Chloe, 85, 88, 92
Brown, Ned, 85, 88, 92
buffers, vegetative, 235, 236
buildings of Middleton Place. *see also* Eliza's House; house museum; south flanker
    destruction of, 54, *56*, 57, 76, 77–79, 103. *see also* Middleton Place, repairs to; Middleton Place, survival of houses, 34–35, 36, *37*, 42, *54*, 81
    LaFarge's, 119–120, *119*
    spring house/chapel, 189–190, *191*, *192*, 216
    stableyards, *119*, 132–134, 137, 159, *160*
Bull, Maria Henrietta, 37, 38. *see also* Middleton, Henry (Governor)
Bunting, Ethel-Jane, 18
Bunting, Fred, 18
Burton, E. Milby, *132*, 133, 136, 141, 257
Burwell, Carter, 108
Bush, William, 15
Butler, Nic, 223
Butterfly Lakes, *70*, *98*, 99, 106, 157. *see also* gardens at Middleton Place

— C —

Caesar (enslaved person), 232
Caffrey, Kathy, 142
Calhoun, John C., 52, 222
Calvary Church, 191
Cambodia, 18
camellias, *90*, 109, 110, 111, 117, 118, *203*
candlesticks, 146–148, *147*, *148*
Carolina colony. *see also* South Carolina
    Commons House, 35
    connection to Barbados, 28
    economy of, 30. *see also* indigo; rice
    Fundamental Constitutions, 30
    government of, 29–30
    Middletons' arrival in, 29
Carolina Gold Rice Foundation, 199
Carolina Housewife, The (Rutledge), 166
Carolina Rice Plantation, A (Smith), *204*, 225
Carpenter, Caesar, 206
Carter family, 239
Carter, Jane, 257
Carter, T. Heyward, Jr., 161, 236, 257
Castiglioni, Luigi, 42
Catesby, Mark, *154*
Cavel, Sando, 71
Cedar Grove, 48, 49
Center for Historic Plants, 178
Center for the Study of Slavery, 220, 241
Century Magazine, *101*, 103

chapel, 189–190, *191*, *192*, 216
Chapman, Ben, 141, *144*, 201–202, 216
Charleston
    annexation war and, 237–238
    arts community in, 133–135
    during Civil War, 67, 68, 69, 74, 155
    in Duell's childhood, 10
    economy of, 83, 156
    growing interest in, 103
    hospital workers strike, 135
    industrialization in, 83
    preservation community in, 133
    promotion of, 120
    racial unrest in, 222–224
    relation with past, 151–153
    during Revolution, 40, 45–47
    as tourist destination, 123, 150–157
Charleston Associates, 155
Charleston Courier, 109–110
Charleston Daily Courier, 49, 53
Charleston Evening Post, 143
Charleston Gospel Choir, 228
Charleston green, 162, 174
Charleston Mercury, 61
Charleston Mining and Manufacturing Company, 80
Charleston Museum, 133, 136
Charleston Renaissance, 123, 134–135
Cheves, Langdon, 34
Christianity, 190–193
Chrystie, Thomas L., 257
Churchill, Winston, 249
Circular Congregational Church (Charleston), *61*, 62
City of North Charleston, 237–238
Civil War, U.S.
    African American soldiers in, *58*, 71, 74, 75
    Charleston in, 67, 68, 69, 74, 155
    devastation of Middleton Place in, 54, 56, 57, 76, 77–79, 103
    enslaved people freed during, 71–74
    Middleton family's military service in, 63, 67
    Middleton loyalties during, 58
    Middletons' physical divisions during, 59
    Williams Middleton in, 63, 66–67
    occupation of Middleton family lands, 71
    South Carolina Secession Convention, 60–63
    valuables hidden during, 76–77, 122, 143, 144–145
Clark and Menefee, 172
Mark Clark Expressway (Interstate 526), 150
Clark, W.G., 159, 162, 172–175, *172*, 177
Clement, Priscilla, 142
Coaching Day, 169–170
Coastal Conservation League, 238
Coleman, Peter, 197, 198
collections. *see also* library at Middleton Place; portraits
    Ashley's Sack, *233*, 251
    candlesticks, 146–148, *147*, *148*
    house museum, 143–149
    portraits, *26*, *38*, *45*, 77, 143, 144–146, *144*, *145*, *147*
College of Charleston, 240
    Avery Research Center, 181
    Center for the Study of Slavery, 220, 241
    founding of, 11
Colleton, John, 29
Collier, Bernard, 150–152
Collins, Ty, 205, 207, 210
Colonial Williamsburg, 138, 142
    assistance from after Hugo, 177–178
    interpretation at, 185
Colonial Williamsburg Foundation, 133
colonoware, 185, *189*
Color of Change, 219
Colorado, 1–3, 15
Colour of Music Festival, 228
Combahee River, Union raid on, 72–74
Confederate States of America, 62. *see also* Civil War, U.S.
Conroy, Pat, 92
conservation development, 169, 170–171
conservation easements, 235, 236, 239
Conservation Fund, The, 239
Cooper-Murray, Sharon, 186
Cornwallis, Charles, 45
cotton production, 69–70
Cotz, Christian, 230
Country Life, 99–100
COVID-19, 220–222
Crow Ranch, 1–3
Crowfield, 34

274

Crowfield Hall (U.K.), 36
culinary heritage, 163–164
Curtin, Philip, 184
Curtis and Davis, 155
Cypress Lake, 178–179

— D —

d'Argenville, Dezalier, 106
Dawson, C. Stuart III, 257
De Saumarez, Lord, 143
Deane, Silas, 39
debts
   of Henry Middleton, 54, 57, 58
   of Williams Middleton, 82
deButts, Jane Pinckney, 257
Declaration of Independence, 43, *44*, 45, *46*
"Declaration of Rights and Grievances", 39
Descartes, René, *107*
destruction of Middleton Place, 54, *56*, 57, 76, 77–79, 103. *see also* Middleton Place, repairs to; Middleton Place, survival of
development, 235–236
   annexation war and, 237–238
   Mark Clark Expressway (Interstate 526), 150
   Crow Ranch and, 3
   threats of, 150, 167
DeWeese, Martha, 138, *212*, 214, *215*
   descendants of, 213–217, *215*
DeWeese, Solomon, 214, 216
di Lapigio, Ascanio Serena, 256
Diep, Xuan-Chi, 19–20, *20*
digital programming, 221–222
Dintersmith, Ted, 257
Doctor (enslaved person), 51
Dolan, Mary, 112
Dolan, Patrick, 92, *93*, 112, 113
Dolan, Susie, 112
donations. *see also* collections
   Ashley's Sack, *233*, 251
   Middleton Place Foundation and, 139
   nonprofit status and, 159
Donnelley Foundation, 238
Dorchester County, 196, 197, 237
dowry, law and, 34–35
Doyle, Barbara, xii, 59, 81–82, 83, 124, 193–195, *195*, *210*, 242, 247, 253

Barbara Doyle History and Archives Center, 247–248
Doyle, Don, 81
Drayton Hall, 221, 234, 235, 236
Drayton, Charles, 38
Drayton, John, 57, 86, 99
Drinker, Henry Middleton, 143
Du Bois, W.E.B., 216
Dubrow, Elbridge, 18
Ducks Unlimited, 238
Charles Duell Legacy Fund, xiii
Duell, Anne. *see* Morgan, Heningham Anne Duell
Duell, Carol Wood, 20–21, *130*, 131, 257
Duell, Caroline Middleton (daughter of Charles Halliwell Pringle Duell), 239, 246, 256
Duell, Charles Halliwell (father of Charles Halliwell Pringle Duell), 8–9, *8*, 13–14, 119
Duell, Charles Halliwell Pringle, viii, xi, 5, 9, 27, 53, 130, 159, 183, 205, 253, 255, 256
   architecture, study and patronage of, 171–174
   career of, 21, 24, 131, 156–157, 250–251
   Charleston Associates, 155
   childhood at Middleton Place, 118
   children of, *130*, 131, 239
   in Colorado, 1–3
   commendations and awards, *238*, 241
   connections of, 14, 18
   education of, 1–2, 14–16, *15*, 19, 171
   establishment of Middleton Place Foundation, 139, 143, 159–161
   grandchildren of, *250*
   inheritance of Middleton Place, 24–25, 126, 131
   international travel by, 16–19
   on joint reunion, 207
   language study by, 17, 19
   mentors. *see* Burton, E. Milby; Edmunds, Frances; Hastie, Norwood; Humelsine, Carl; Jenrette, Dick
   at Phillips Academy, 14
   A Phoenix Still Rising, 53
   photographs of, *xiv*, *4*, *8*, *10*, *12*, *17*, *20*, *130*, *144*, *154*, *168*, *225*, *234*, *238*, *243*,

246, *248*, *250*
President's Award, *238*, 241
retirement of, 240
sisters of, 9, *10*, *13*, 24–25, 118, 130
at Yale, 14, *15*, 171
Duell, Charles Holland (great-grandfather of Charles Halliwell Pringle Duell), 5–7
Duell, Halliwell "Wally", 1
Duell, Holland "Holly", 1–3, 254
Duell, Holland (son of Charles Halliwell Pringle Duell), 131, 186, *195*, 239, 257
Duell, Holland Sackett (grandfather of Charles Halliwell Pringle Duell), 5–6, *6*, 7
Duell, Josephine (daughter of Charles Halliwell Pringle Duell). *see* Routh, Josephine Duell
Duell, Josephine Scott Smith (mother of Charles Halliwell Pringle Duell), *7*, *8*, 13, 113, 254
    death of, 14, 129
    education of, 13
    gardens and, 118
    marriage of, 8
    "Miss Josephine Smith in Oak with Peacock" (Smith), *95*
Duell, June (daughter of Charles Halliwell Pringle Duell). *see* Waterman, June Duell
Duell, Mable Halliwell (grandmother of Charles Halliwell Pringle Duell), 6–7
Duell, Roderick, 174, *246*, 254, 257
Duell, Sallie McPherson, 205, *225*, *234*, 243–245, *243*, *246*, 253, 255, 256
Duell, Scottie, 9, *10*, 15, 118, 130
Duell, Sloan and Pearce Publishing Company, 9, 19
Duke, James Buchanan, 7
Duncan, Frances, *101*, *102*, 103–105

— E —
Eady, Brittney, 214, *215*, 216
Eady, Jalye, 214, *215*
Eady, Justin, Jr., 214, *215*
earthquake (1886), 91, 92–95
easements, 235, 236, 239
Nine East Battery (Roper House), 155
21 East Battery. *see* Edmondston-Alston House
Easter, Steve, *15*, 19

economy, South Carolina, 30, 31, 39, 41, 69–71. *see also* indigo; rice
Edgar, Walter, 28, 29–30, 31, 40, 45, 52, 60, 254
Edmondston, Charles, 131
Edmondston-Alston House (21 East Battery), 10, *11*, 16, *151*
    creation of house museum, 149–150
    during Duell's childhood, 12–13
    Duell's inheritance of, 25
    given to Middleton Place Foundation, 247
    history of ownership, 11, 130–131
    living with, 243–244
    management of, 241
    taxes on, 131
Edmunds, Frances, 149, 150, 152–153, *152*. *see also* Historic Charleston Foundation
Edmunds, Henry, 150
Edwards, Clementina Rutledge, 147
Edwards-Jackson-Prioleau families, 205
Eliza's House, 85, 98–99, 119, 138, 181–183, 204
    exhibit area in, 195–196
    new location, *183*
    original location, 99, *182*
    Sheppard and, 138
Elwig, William, 191
emeritus trustees. *see* trustees of Middleton Place Foundation
Enlightenment, 30, 108
enslaved people. *see also* African Americans; African Americans associated with Middleton family; history, African American; interpretation of African American history; slavery; slaves, Middleton
    building of Middleton Place and, 35, 36
    colonoware, 185, 189
    cotton production and, 69–70
    death of slave owner and, 198
    dwelling at Hobonny, *73*
    families of, 190–191, 198
    formerly enslaved people, 81, 83, 85, 88, 92–93, 112. *see also* Eliza's House
    freed during Civil War, 71–74
    freedmen, 83, 85
    Fundamental Constitutions and, 30

in historic interpretation, 138, 219. *see also* interpretation of African American history; interpretation, historic
identity of, 205
imported by Middletons, 29
in Mary Izard's inheritance, 48–49
list of names, 197–198, 206
marriages of, 190–191
monetary value of, 41
Native Americans, 30–31
religion and, 190–193
in Revolutionary period, 49–51
in Susan Smith's inheritance, 85
trade in, 27–28, *29*, 223, *227*
wealth and, 29, 35–36, 41, 65
Epps family, 205
estate taxes, 22, 25, 130
"Everybody's Garden" (Gladwin), 96

— F —

family alliances, 38
Family Circle magazine, 207
FEMA, 179
Ferguson, James L., 257
fertilizer, 79–81
Festival of Houses and Gardens, 153
Fields family, 205
Fields, Karen, 206
Fields, Mamie Garvin, 187, 206
First Baptist Church (Summerville), 85
First Continental Congress, 39
Fishburne, Julien, 83
Fisher, Eliza Middleton (sister of Williams), 58–59, *65*, 88, 143, 145–146
Fisher, J. Francis, 58, 59, 64, *65*, 78, 83, 88, 145–146
Fisher, Sidney, 64
Floyd, George, 222
food, 163–167. *see also* Sheppard, Mary Washington
Food Network, 199
Footlight Players, 134
Foreign Service exam, 16, 19, 21
former trustees. *see* trustees of Middleton Place Foundation
Fort Sumter, 66, 71
Fox, Helen, 106

Frazier, Sidney, 178, 179, 198, 200, 201–204, *203*, 206, 242, 254. *see also* gardens at Middleton Place
Free South, 74
freedman's cottage, 85, 98–99, 138, *182*. *see also* Eliza's House
Frissell, Toni, 170
Full Faith Ministries, 203
Fundamental Constitutions, 30

— G —

Gadsden, Betty, 8–9
Gadsden, Christopher, 39
Gage, Thomas, 40
Garden & Gun, 202
Garden Club of America, 108, 125, 159
garden fever, 99, *121*, 123
Garden, Alexander, 105
gardens
  Carter's Grove, 108
  conservation easements and, 235
  interest in, 99, 103, *121*, 123
  Le Nôtre, 105–108
  at Magnolia Plantation, 86, 99, 100, 202
gardens at Middleton Place, *12*, *121*, *178–179*, 203. *see also* Alston, Anthony; Horlbeck, Ansel
  Angell's photographs of, 99–100
  azaleas, 111, 112, 117, 123
  Bosque, 37
  building of, 35, 36, 104, 106, 108–110
  Bulkley Medal, *124*, 125, *125*
  burials in, 48, 53, *75*, 113
  Butterfly Lakes, *70*, 95, *98*, 99, 106, 157
  camellias, *84*, 90, 109, 110, 111, 117, 118, *203*
  Chapman and, 141, *144*, 201–202, 216
  Cypress Lake, 178–179
  damage to during Civil War, 78. *see also* destruction of Middleton Place
  diagram of, *102*, 105
  during Duell's childhood, 12
  Duncan's article on, *101*, 103–105
  early references to, 35, 105
  earthquake damage to, 95
  formerly enslaved workers and, 112
  Frazier and, 178, 179, 198, 200,

201–204, *203*, 206, 242
future plans for, 245
Garden Club of America's assessment of, 159
Green and, 141, 201–202
Hurricane Hugo and, 177, 178–179, 202
Le Nôtre's influence on, 106
Lowell on, 100–102
main axis, *104, 158*
Michaux and, 53, 90, 108–109
Henry Middleton and, 35–36, 106, 108
Henry (Governor) Middleton and, 53, 108, 109–110, *110*
Lillie Middleton and, 98, 99–105
Mary Helen Hering Middleton and, 109
Mary Williams Middleton and, 35–36, 106, 108
Williams Middleton and, 86–88, 110–112
New Camellia Garden, 118
Newman and, 106
opened to visitors, 86–88, 118
overgrowth of, 99, 115
plant nursery, 118, 161
promotion of, 86-88, 120
as public health asset, 222
"Reine des Fleurs", *90*
restoration of, 13, 83, 100, 105, 116–118, 125–126
Alice Smith's paintings of, *70, 95,* 96
Pringle and Heningham Smith and, 12–13, 105, 116–118, 120
tomb, 37, *75, 77,* 113
250th anniversary, 126
Wood Nymph statue, *76*
Woodle and, 141, 179, 202
Gardens of Colony and State (Garden Club of America), 108
gardens, landscape, 107–108, 159
genealogy, researching, 226
George (enslaved person), 51
Giamatti, Bart, 15
Gibbes Museum of Art, 113, 225
Gilder, Richard Watson, 103
Gladwin, William Zachary, 96
Glascoe, Myrtle, 181

Goddard, Paulette, 126
Godfrey, Richard, 34
Goldberge, Paul, 171
Goodwin, William, 133
Goose Creek, 29, 40. *see also* Oaks, The
Grand Council, 31
Grand Teton Lodge Company, 157
Grange, Ileen, 242, 254
Granger, Gordon, 213
Grant, Stepney, 74
Gray, Rachel MacRae, 257
Green, Bill, 141, 201–202
Green, Jonathan, 224–226, *225,* 228, 256
Greene, Harlan, 134, 135
grist mill, 70, *70*
Grosvenor, Mel, 157
Grounds for Pleasure (Otis), 107
Guide to the Wildflowers of South Carolina (Porcher), 108
Gulla (enslaved person), 51
Gullah culture/language, 164, 166, 198, 216, 224

— H —

Haley, Nikki, 241
Hall, Jamal, *218,* 231–232
Halliwell, C. Eliezer, 7
Hanahan family, 239
Hanahan, Ross, 236
Hanckel, J. Stuart, 190
Hancock, John, 39
Hansen, Cliff, 157
Harper's New Monthly Magazine, 86
Harper's Weekly, 74
Harrigan, Violetta, 206
Harwood, Lee, 257
Hastie family, 99
Hastie, Drayton, 155
Hastie, Norwood, 118, 155
Heinz, Jack, 15
Helmer, Lee, 197
Hemmings, Sally, 188
Hercules (enslaved person), 51
Hering, Mary Helen. *see* Middleton, Mary Helen Hering
heritage tourism, 131, 153. *see also* Colonial Williamsburg; interpretation of African American history; interpretation, historic; preservation

Hessians, 51
Heyward, Anne Louise, 113, 148
Heyward, Dorothy, 134
Heyward, Dubose, 134
Heyward, Elizabeth Middleton. *see* Middleton, Lillie
Heyward, Julius, 92, 113, 148
Heyward, Mrs. Julius H. *see* Middleton, Lillie
Heyward, Thomas, 47
Hill, Marilyn, *238*
Historic Charleston Foundation, 149–150, 153, 155–156, 236, 238. *see also* preservation
historic interpretation. *see* Colonial Williamsburg; interpretation of African American history; interpretation, historic
history, African American, 181–217. *see also* African Americans; *Beyond the Fields: Slavery at Middleton Place*; enslaved people; interpretation of African American history; slavery; slaves, Middleton
  incorporation into historic interpretation, 224–234
  Juneteenth, 213, 223–224
  oral history and, 228
  plantation weddings and, 219–220
  significance of historic sites to, 224
  study and interpretation of, 181–198
Hobonny, 48, 57, 60, *72*, 73
Hoffius, Stephen, 91
Holliday, Hank, 245, 256
Hollifield, S. Colby, 257
Holmes, Francis, 79, 80
Horlbeck, Ansel, 85, 88, 92, 97, *97*, 112
Horlbeck, Molsey, 88, 98, 112
Horse Savanna, 60, 70, 85, 167
horses, 1, 2, 5, *20*, 41, *42*, 168–170, *168*, *169*, 201, 247
hospital workers strike, 135
hotels
  Inn at Middleton Place, *170*, 171–176, *172*, 247
  Mills House Hotel, 155–156, 165
house museum. *see also* buildings of Middleton Place; interpretation; Middleton Place, repairs to; south flanker
  collections, 143–149
  exhibits, 142, 232
  interpreters at, 142
  opening of, 139, 142
  restoration of, 140–142
  Sheppard and, 137
houses at Middleton Place, 34–35, 36, *37*, *54–55*, *56*, 81, *93*, *178*, *182*, *183*. *see also* south flanker
housing, for former slaves, 85, 98–99, 138, *182*, *183*. *see also* Eliza's House
Howard, Hugh, 108
Humelsine, Carl, 133, 157, 185
hunting, 5, 97, *168*, 169, 201
Hurricane Hugo, 150, 176–179, *176*, 202
hurricanes, 54
Hutchisson, James, 134, 135
hymns/spirituals, 216–217, 228

— I —

income, historic sources at Middleton Place
  diversification/experimentation in, 70
  grist mill, 70, *70*
  land, 242
  mining, 80–81, 83, 88, 97, 167, 173
  rice, 49, 70, 197, 198–201, 204–205, 212–213, 225
  schooner, 70–71, 212–213
  during Smiths' stewardship, 117–118, 131–132
  timber, 97, 167–168, 179, 242
  tours, 86, *86*, 88
Indian affairs, 31
indigo, 24, 35, 39
Ingle, Addison, *4*
inheritance of Middleton Place. *see also* Duell, Charles Halliwell Pringle; Middleton, Lillie; Middleton, Williams
  Duell's, 24–25, 126, 131
  Arthur Middleton's, 37
  Henry Middleton's, 49
  by Smith, 23–24, 113, 114, 115
  through female side of family, 34–35
inheritance taxes, 24, 130
inheritance, for women, 34–35, 48, 49
Inn at Middleton Place, *170*, 171–176, *172*, 247
Institute Hall, *61*, 62
International African American Museum, 241, *233*
internship program, 212–213

interpretation of African American history, 138, 223, 229–234, *229*. *see also* African Americans associated with Middleton family; Eliza's House; enslaved people; slavery; slaves, Middleton
- African American Focus Tour, 197, 199, 204
- Bellinger's recommendations for, 213
- *Beyond the Fields: Slavery at Middleton Place*, 197–198, 204, 205, 206, 213–214, 217
- DeWeese family and, 214
- grants for, 195–196
- inauguration of formal program, 182
- Juneteenth program, 213, 223–224
- "Moment in Time" exhibit, 232
- panel on, 181
- rice exhibit, 212–213
- rice field, 198–201, *200*, 204–205
- slavery in, 138, 219

interpretation, historic. *see also* Colonial Williamsburg; house museum; visitor experience
- cooking demonstration, *164*
- demonstration rice field, 197, 198–201, *200*, 204–205
- living history, 231
- "Moment in Time" exhibit, 232
- race and, 138, 181, 185, 223, 224–234
- stableyards, 132–134

Isaac (enslaved person), 71
Izard property, 48
Izard, Isabella Hume, 46, 48
Izard, John, 46, 48
Izard, Mary "Polly". *see* Middleton, Mary Izard "Polly"

— J —

James Island, 223
Jamison, David F., 62
Thomas Jefferson Foundation, 188
Jenny (enslaved person), 232
Jenrette, Dick, 155–156
Jim Crow laws, 92, 234
Joanna Foundation, 189
Joe Gould's Secret, 14
John (enslaved person), 51
Johnson, Ladybird, 157

Johnson, Priscilla, *74*
Johnston, Frances Benjamin, *98*, *116*
Jordan, Dan, 188
judges, federal, 7
Juneteenth, 213, 223–224
Junior League, 163, 244

— K —

Kahn, Louis, 172
Kennedy, Marion, 235
Kilbride, Daniel, 79
Knowing Who I Am (Middleton and Barnes), 211
Kuyk, James, 256

— L —

Lader, Philip, 170, 257
LaFarge, Bancel, 119–120, *119*
LaFave, Jan, 142
land, 242. *see also* Cedar Grove; Hobonny; Old Combahee
- acquired by Middletons, 29, 34, 41, 129
- Izard property, 48
- rights associated with, 29, 34–35

land protection, 235–240
Landmark designation, xiii, 138, *140*, 155, 159
landscape architecture, 105–108
landscape gardens, 107–108, 124–125, 159
Lane, G. Winston, 27
Laughlin, Michael, 245, *246*, 256
Laurens, Henry, 44
Le Corbusier, 19, 171
Le Nôtre, André, 105–108, *107*
Leach, Eliza, 85, 138, 141, 181–182, *185*, 216
Leadem, Richard A., 245, 246, *246*, 256
Lee, Robert E., 59, 69, 155
Leland, Cheves, 141–142, 253
Leland, Isabella Gaud, 141
Leland, Jack, 141
Lemon Swamp and Other Places, A Carolina Memoir (Fields), 187, 206
Lesser, Charles, 61, 63
Lester, Cairy, 223–225
Lewis, Edna, 165–167, *166*
library at Middleton Place, 36, 57, *154*

Lincoln, Abraham, 60
living history, 231. *see also* interpretation of African American history; interpretation, historic
Locke, John, 30
Logan, Sandy, 162
Lord, Mary, 18
Lords Proprietors, viii–ix, 29–30, 31
Lowcountry Land Trust, 235, 236, 238
Lowcountry Rice Culture Project, 225
Lowcountry Rice Forum, 167
Lowell, Amy, 100–102
loyalists, Black, 50–51
Lucas, Jonathan, 49
Lynch, Thomas, 39
Lynden, Patricia, 165
Lytle, Sarah, 142, 177, 242, 253

— M —

Mackenzie, Mary. *see* Middleton, Mary Mackenzie
Maddox, Luke, 190
Madison, James, 228–229
Magnolia Plantation, 86, 99, 100, 202
Major, Marty, 175, 176
Manigault, Ann, 38
Manigault, Marjorie, 205
Manigault, Peter, *20*, *152*, 247, 257
Manigault, Pierre, 246–247, 255, 256
Marcy, Henry, 57, *58*, 75, 78, 144
Martin, Steve, 14
Martin, William, 62
Martz, Randolph, 165
Marvin, Robert, 170
Mary (enslaved person), 51, 232
Mary Washington College, 181
May, Jean, 135, 136
May, Smart, 93
Mayes family, 205
Mayes, Anna Bowens, 207
Mayes, Annette, 88, 93, 99, 112, 206–207
Mayes, Bud, 207
Mayland, Tina, 257
McCarter, Robert, 173
McDaniel, George, 150, 234, *234*, 245
McGee, Peter, *152*
McKay, Jenny Sanford, *248*
McKissick Museum, 181, 186
McMillen, Earl III, 256

McMillen, Elizabeth Wright, *246*, 257
MeadWestvaco, 239
Medical College of South Carolina, 131
Medway plantation, 66
Meeks, Stephanie, 241
Number One Meeting Street, 65, *66*, 68, 77, 78
    after Civil War, 81
    during Civil War, 67
    Williams Middleton's purchase of, 63–64
    sale of, 82
26 Meeting Street, 113
Memminger, Christopher, 60, 61
Menefee, Charles, 172
Meyer, Annie, 207
Michaux, André, 53, *90*, 108–109
Middleton Equestrian Center, 169, 247
Middleton family crest, *43*
Middleton Family Tree database, 194
Middleton Inn Associates, 175–176
Middleton Oak (tree), *116*, 177
Middleton Oaks (development), 170–171
Middleton Place
    buildings of. *see* buildings of Middleton Place; Eliza's House; south flanker
    destruction of, 54, *56*, 57, 76, 77–79, 103
    during Duell's childhood, 12, 13, 118
    Duell's inheritance of, 24–25, 126, 131
    gardens of. *see* gardens at Middleton Place
    interpretation, historic, 132–134, 138, *164*, 181, 185, 197, 198–201, *200*, 204–205, 223, 224–234
    interpreters, *128*, 136, 138, 142, 185, *218*, 229, 231–232
    ownership of, 23–25, 88, 118, 142, 242
    plant nursery, 118, 161
    proposed expansion of (1863), 68–69, *68*
    repairs to, 81–83, 114–123, 137–138. *see also* Duell, Charles Halliwell Pringle; Eliza's House; house museum; Middleton Place, survival of; south flanker
    returned after Civil War, 59–60
    sketch of (circa 1842), *54–55*
    survival of, xii–xiii, 23–24, 88, 112, 131, 142, 143, 160–161, 242
    sustainability of, 129–133, 159–179, 239, 242

virtual experiences, 221–222
visitor experience, 159, 161–162, 163–167, 221–222, 231
in Mary Williams' dowry, 34–35
Middleton Place Foundation. *see also* Duell, Charles Halliwell Pringle; Todd, M. Tracey
   assets of, 161, 240
   budget of, 157, 161, 220, 240
   commendations and awards, 241
   donations and, 159
   Duell's gifts to, 160–161, 247
   Edmondston-Alston House and, 150
   establishment of, 139, 143, 159–161
   501(c)(3) status, 139, 159, 161, 179
   Hurricane Fund, 179
   memberships in, 222, 242
   Middleton Place given to, 160–161
   mission of, xii, 224, 240, 247
   need for, 139
   nonprofit status, 139, 159, 161, 179
   pandemic and, 220–222
   racial justice issues and, 219–220, 222
   strategic issues for, 245–248
   trustees. *see* trustees of Middleton Place Foundation
Middleton Place National Landmark, Inc., 138–139, *140*
Middleton Place Restaurant, 163–167, *165*
"Middleton Place, The" (Lowell), 101–102
Middleton, Abram, 210–211
Middleton, Adam, 73
Middleton, Alicia Hopton, 77
Middleton, Arthur (1648-1685)
   in Barbados, 27–28
   death of, 31
   land acquisition by, 29
   slave trade by, 27
Middleton, Arthur (1681-1737), ix
   Revolution of 1719, 31, 34
   on slavery, 198
Middleton, Arthur (1742-1787), *26*, 35–37, *38*, *44*, *45*, 108, 143, *144*, 206, 207, 250
   death of, 48
   education of, 36
   horses of, 41–42, *42*, 168
   in Revolutionary period, 40–47
   signature on Declaration of Independence, *46*
   travel by, 42
Middleton, Arthur (brother of Williams), 57, 58
Middleton, Bernice (wife of Earl), 186
Middleton, Catherine, 58
Middleton, Charles (enslaved person), 231–232
Middleton, Charles (formerly enslaved person), 51
Middleton, Earl, 186–188, *186*, 205, 257
   ancestors of, 210, 211
Middleton, Edward (1642-1685)
   in Barbados, 27–28
   death of, 31
   land acquisition by, 29
Middleton, Edward (brother of Williams), 57–60
   loyalty to Union, 58
Middleton, Eliza. *see* Fisher, Eliza Middleton
Middleton, Ellen, 58
Middleton, Emma Philadelphia, 44
Middleton, Francis G. "Frank", 206, *210*, 257
Middleton, Hal (son of Williams), 79, 92, 97
Middleton, Harry, 51
Middleton, Henrietta (daughter of Henry), 38, 39, 40
Middleton, Henry "Harry" (brother of Williams), 57, 58
Middleton, Henry (1717-1784), 34–40, *36*, 106, 143, *144*, 207. *see also* Middleton, Mary Williams
   death of, 40
   estate of, 41
   gardens and, 36, 104–108
   horses of, 168
   purchase of The Retreat, 37–38
   in Revolutionary period, 38–40
   second wife of, 37–38
   third wife of, 40
Middleton, Henry (1770-1846; Governor), *26*, 34, 35, 42, 49, *51*, 52–54, 57, 143. *see also* Middleton, Mary Helen Hering
   death of, 53
   debts of, 54, 57, 58
   gardens and, 108, 109–110

plant list, *110*
political career, 52–53
Middleton, Henry Bentivoglio "Benti" (nephew of Williams), 58, *59*, 67
Middleton, Henry Enrico B., 257
Middleton, Hester (daughter of Henry), 38
Middleton, Isabella Johannes (daughter of Arthur and Mary), 46, 47
Middleton, James B., 206
Middleton, James C., 210, 211
Middleton, John Izard (brother of Williams), 57, 58, 67, 77, 226
   South Carolina Secession Convention and, 60–63
Middleton, John Izard (son of Arthur and Mary), 48, 49
Middleton, Kenneth E. (son of Earl), 205, *246*, 257
Middleton, Lane, 257
Middleton, Lillie (Elizabeth Middleton Heyward; daughter of Williams), 23, 24, 82–83, 86, 92, 100, 103, 148
   copybook, 96
   death of, 115
   ownership of Middleton Place, 23, 24, 88, 97–99
   will of, 112–113
Middleton, Maria (sister of Williams), 58
Middleton, Maria Henrietta Bull (second wife of Henry), 37, 38
Middleton, Mary (daughter of Henry), 38
Middleton, Mary Frances, 205
Middleton, Mary Helen Hering (wife of Governor Henry), *51*, 52, 58
   gardens and, 109
Middleton, Mary Izard "Polly" (wife of Arthur), *26*, 37, 40, 42, 44, 70, 143
   during British occupation, 47–48
   death of, 49
   inheritance of, 48–49
Middleton, Mary Mackenzie (third wife of Henry), 40
Middleton, Mary Williams (wife of Henry)
   building of gardens, 36, 106, 108
   death of, 36–37
   expansion of Middleton Place, 36
   inheritance and dowry of, 34–35, 189
Middleton, Oliver Hering (brother of Williams), 57, 148

Middleton, "Rie" (daughter of John; niece of Williams), 67
Middleton, Russell, 77, 79
Middleton, Ruth, *233*
Middleton, Sarah (daughter of Henry), 38
Middleton, Sarah (formerly enslaved person), 51
Middleton, Sarah Amory (wife of Arthur Middleton; 1681-1737), 31
Middleton, Sarah Fowell (wife of Edward Middleton; 1642-1685), 31
Middleton, Septima Sexta, 48, 49, *147*
Middleton, Susan Pringle Smith (wife of Williams), 11, 63, 77, *80*, 82, 86, 92, 110, 190
   death of, 97
   inheritance of, 63
   slaves owned by, 85
Middleton, Thomas (brother of Henry), *29*, 34
Middleton, Thomas (enslaved person), descendants of, 187. *see also* Middleton, Earl
Middleton, Thomas (nephew of Williams), 67
Middleton, Thomas (son of Henry), 38, 207
   horses and, 168
Middleton, William (brother of Henry), 34, 36
Middleton, William (enslaved person), 71
Middleton, Williams (1809-1883), 11, *63*
   after Civil War, 78–79
   during Civil War, 63–67
   death of, 88, 92
   debt of, 82
   diversification/experimentation by, 70
   family portrait and, 144–146
   freedman's cottage built by, 138. *see also* Eliza's House
   gardens and, 88, 110–112
   hidden valuables and, 76–77, *76*, 122, 143, 144–145
   inheritance of Middleton Place, 57
   inheritance of Old Combahee, 57
   lifestyle of, 64–65
   Oath of Allegiance, 78
   phosphate mining and, 80–81, 173
   preservation of Middleton Place, 88
   proposed expansion of Middleton Place, 68–69

purchase of Number One Meeting Street, 63–64
repairs to Middleton Place, 81–83, 85. *see also* Middleton Place, repairs to
restoration of south flanker, *56*, 85
on rice, 201
signature on Ordinance of Secession, *62*
South Carolina Secession Convention and, 60–63
spring house/chapel expansion, 189–193
Millbrook Plantation, 236, 237, 239
Miller, Wilhelm, 100
Mills House Hotel, 155–156, 165
mining, 79–81, 83, 88, 97, 167, 173
Minton, Henry, 51
Mole, Annette, 142
"Moment in Time" exhibit, 232
Monroe, James, 52, *53*
Montgomery, James, 72
Monticello, 150, 178, 188
Montpelier, 229–230
Moore, Alex, 248
Moore, B. Allston III, 205, 257
Moore, James, 31
Morgan Guaranty Trust, 21
Morgan, Heningham Anne Duell, 9, *10*, *13*, 24–25, 118, 130, 257
Morning Star Hall Singers, 216
Morrison, William "Bo", *4*
Morse, Samuel F. B., *53*
Moulin, Edmond, 178
Mrs. Whaley and Her Charleston Garden (Whaley), 153
Murray, Edward, 146, 147
Myers, deRosset, *4*

— N —

Nash, Ogden, 8
National Geographic Magazine, 120, *121*
National Historic Landmark designation, xiii, 138, *140*, 155, 159
National Register of Historic Places, 138–139
National Trust for Historic Preservation, 150, *152*, 155, 236, *238*, 240, 241, 250
Native Americans, 30–31
Natural History of Carolina, Florida and the Bahama Islands (Catesby), *154*
Nature Conservancy, The, 238

Neale, Jeff, 212, 221, 223, 224, 231, 232, 253
Neale, Linda, 214
Negroponte, John, 15
New Bethlehem Baptist Church, 203
New York Times Magazine, The, 126
New York Times, The, 8
Charleston in, 150–152
on plantation weddings, 220
1619 Project, 211
New Yorker, 171
Newman, George, 106
Newport house, 64, *64*
News and Courier (Charleston), 120
Nieuport, 57–58, 60, 72, 73
Non Importation Association, 38
Noren, Clint, 201
North Charleston, 237–238
Nullification Doctrine, 52–53
Nunez, Nick, 212

— O —

Oaks, The, 34, 38, 40
"Obsession", *4*
Old Combahee, 48, 57, 58, 60
Opala, Joseph, 206
oral history, 181, 194, 228
Ordinance of Secession, 60–63, *62*
Otis, Denise, 106–107

— P —

Palmer, Caroline T., 246, 256
Palmer, Honorable Mrs. Llewellyn, 143
Palmetto Conservation Foundation, 236
pandemic, 220–222
Paris Institute of Political Studies, 19
Parker, Adam, 206, 207, 220, 223, 224, 240
past
Charleston's relation with, 150–153
present's relation with, 245, 248–251
Patriot, The, 178
Paycheck Protection Program, 220–221
Peacock, Scott, 167
Pearce, Charles, 9
Pearson, Al, 205
Pearson, Anita Middleton, 205
Perry, Anna, 136–137, *137*, 141, 214
Perry, Richard, 136, 216

Philadelphia, Middletons in, 64–65. *see also* Fisher, Eliza Middleton; Fisher, J. Francis
Phillips, Ruth Saunders, 206, 207, *210*
Phillis (enslaved person), 51
Phoenix Still Rising, A (Duell), 53
phosphate mining, 79–81, *79*, 83, 88, 97, 173
Piccolo Spoleto arts festival, 216
Pierce, Yolanda, 192
Pierson, George, 18
Pierson, Harriet Duell, 5–6, 18
Pierson, John H.G., 18
Pinckney, Charles Cotesworth, 38, 52, 102
Pinckney, Elise, 100, 109, 117, 126
Pinckney, Eliza Lucas, 24
Pinckney, Josephine, 153
plantation economy, 41, 69–70
plantation model, 27–28, 69. *see also* enslaved people; slavery
Plantation Singers, The, 216
plantation weddings, 219–220
Plate, Douglas, *4*
"Point-Flow, The" (Smith), *204*
Poplar Grove, 237, 239
Porcher, Richard, 108, 109
Porgy (Heyward), 134
Porgy and Bess (opera), 134, 135, 245
Porter Military Academy, 1
portraits, *26*, *38*, *45*, 77, 143, 144–146, *144*, *145*, *147*
Post and Courier (Charleston)
　account of Lester's visit, 223, 224
　on Clark's portal, 162
　on Duell's retirement, 240
　on joint reunion, 206
　on Lewis, 166
　on pandemic, 220
　on slavery in historic interpretation, 219
Powell, Alan, 141
Powers, Bernard, 220, 240–241
Pratt, Nathaniel, 80
Prentiss, Julia Middleton, 207
preservation. *see also* Colonial Williamsburg; heritage tourism; Historic Charleston Foundation; Middleton Place, survival of; National Trust for Historic Preservation
　Burton and, 133
　in Charleston, 123, 133, 150–153
　Charleston Renaissance, 123, 134–135
　Duells and, 149–150, 155–157, 160–161, *238*, 241–245, 249–251, 253–255
　Edmunds and, 149, 150, 152–153, *152*
　Jenrette and, 155–156
　Manigault family and, 255
　Woodwards and, 8–9
Preservation Act (1966), 140
preservation of Middleton Place. *see* Middleton Place Foundation; Middleton Place, repairs to; Middleton Place, survival of
President's Advisory Council on Historic Preservation, 150, 250
Pringle, Isom, 226
Pringle, Lee, *225*, 226–230, *227*, 256
Pringle, Middleton, 226
Pringletown Family Reunion, 226
Prioleau, Hercules, 85
Pullen Phillips, Harriet, 147–148

— R —

race relations
　after Civil War, 91–92
　culinary heritage and, 163–164
　hospital workers strike, 135
　Jim Crow laws, 92, 234
　plantation weddings and, 219–220
Rachael (enslaved person), 191
racial justice issues, 222–224
Rainey, Reuben, 106
Randolph, Peyton, 39
Rashford, John, 181
Raskin, Hannah, 166
Ravenel, Charles "Pug", 155, 175
Reap the Wild Wind, 126
Reid, Marion, *4*
religion, 30, 190–193, 203, 216–217, 228
Reminiscences (Smith), 93
Renaissance in Charleston (Greene and Hutchisson), 135
resort development, 167
Retreat, The, 37–38

reunions, *180*
  joint, 205–207, *208–209*, 210, 217, 226
  of Thomas Middleton's descendants, 187
  of Lee Pringle's extended family, 228
  Pringletown Family Reunion, 226
  retrieving heirlooms and, 146
Revolution of 1719, 31, 34
Revolutionary period, 39–51
Rhett, Robert Barnwell, 60–61
rice, 35–36, *199*
  Carolina Gold Rice Foundation, 199
  A Carolina Rice Plantation, *204*, 225
  demonstration rice field, 197, 198–201, *200*, 204–205
  embargo exemption, 39
  foreign competitors, 69
  Green's paintings of, 225
  Lowcountry Rice Culture Project, 225
  Middleton wealth and, 65
  "The Point-Flow", *204*
  preservation of rice landscape, 235
  rice exhibit, 212–213
rice mills, 49, 70
Richmond News Leader, 123
rights, property and, 34–35
John and Kathleen Rivers Foundation, 189
Robinson, Emmett, 134, *135*, 136
Rockefeller family, 157
Rockefeller Foundation, 17
Rockefeller, John D., Jr., 133
Rockefeller, Laurance, 157
Rogers, George, *152*
Roosevelt, Eleanor, 123–124, 207
Roper House, 155
Rosengarten, Theodore, 181, 183–184
Routh, Josephine Duell (daughter of Charles Halliwell Pringle Duell), 131, 205, 239, *246*, 257
Rubenstein, David, 229
ruins of Middleton Place. *see* destruction of Middleton Place
Rush, Benjamin, 44
Rutledge, Edward, 38, 39, 40–41, 43, 45, 47, 52
Rutledge, Henrietta Middleton, 38, 39, 40
Rutledge, John, 39
Rutledge, Sarah, 166

— S —

S.C. Conservation Bank, 238–239
S.C. Department of Archives and History, 189
Sackville-West, Vita, 122–123
sailing, 4–5, *6*
Saint Andrew's Church, 190
Saint Andrew's Hall, 62
Saint Giles House (U.K.), viii, 254
Saint James Goose Creek, 40
Saint Philip's Church, 10
Saint-Georges, Chevalier de, 228
Sandlapper magazine, 135
Sanford, Mark, *248*
Sanna (enslaved person), 70
Sarry (enslaved person), 51
Schadow, Rudolph, *76*
schooner, Middleton, 70–71, 212–213
Sciences Po, 19
Scipio (enslaved person), 226, *227*
Scott, Walter, 222
Scully, Vincent, 171–172, 174
secession, 60–63. *see also* Civil War, U.S.
Second Continental Congress, 40
Second Great Awakening, 190
Seger, Chris, 8, 15, *15*, 16, 163, 253
1772 Foundation, 196
Shaffer, E.T.H., 120, *121*, 122
sheep, 118
Sheppard, Mary Washington, *13*, 124, 136, 137–138, *137*, 141, 164, 166, 207, 216, 232
Sheppard, Thomas, 137
Shick, Tom, 81
Silvia (enslaved person), 51
Simons, Albert, 153
Simons, Lapham, Mitchell and Small, 156
Sinkler, Michelle, 257
1619 Project, 211
slave badge, *49*
slave trade, 27, *29*, 223, *227*
slavery, vii. *see also* African Americans; African Americans associated with Middleton family; enslaved people; history, African American; interpretation of African American history; slaves, Middleton
  defense of, 60–62, 190
  economy based on, 27–30, 41–42,

48–51, 57, 64–65, 69–71
end of, 213
exhibits on, 197–198, 204, 205, 206, 213–214, 217
in historic interpretation, 138, 219, 224–234. see also interpretation of African American history
National Summit on Teaching Slavery, 229
slaves, Middleton, 231–232. see also African Americans associated with Middleton family; *Beyond the Fields: Slavery at Middleton Place*; enslaved people; interpretation of African American history
after emancipation, 75–77
building of gardens and, 104
during Civil War, 66, 71, 73–74
identity of, 205
list of names, 197–198, 206
researching, xii, 189, 193–195, 205, 225–226
in Revolutionary period, 41–42, 49–51
schooner and, 70–71, 212–213
Sloan, Earle, 94
Sloan, Samuel, 9
Slotchiver, Irvin, 139, 257
Small, Jimmy, 141, 149
Smalls, July, 74
Smalls, Mary, 138
Smith, Alice Ravenel Huger, *94*, 95–96
A Carolina Rice Plantation, 204, 225
on earthquake, 93
"Miss Josephine Smith in Oak with Peacock", *95*
"The Point-Flow", 204
"View Overlooking the Butterfly Lakes and Mill at Middleton Place", *70*
Smith, Benjamin, 206
Smith, Daniel Huger, 95
Smith, Edward, *144*
Smith, Eliphas, 75
Smith, Emma Rutledge (great-grandmother of Charles Halliwell Pringle Duell), 113, 115
Smith, Fred, 68
Smith, Greg, *230*, 231
Smith, Heningham Lyons Ellet "Ha Ha" (grandmother of Charles Halliwell

Pringle Duell), 9, 12–13, *12*, *114*, 232, 251, 254
background of, 113–114
death of, 16, 129
on first years at Middleton Place, 114–116
gardens and, 13, 105, 116–120, 123–126
Smith, Henry Augustus Middleton "H.A.M." (great-grandfather of Charles Halliwell Pringle Duell), 7, *23*, 25, 105, 113, 254
estate of, 129–131
generation skipping trust established by, 130
map and article, "The Ashley River: Its Seats and Settlements", *front endsheet*
ownership of Edmondston-Alston House, 131
ownership of Middleton Place, 23–24, 118, 129
on Williams' work on gardens, 111
Smith, J.J. Pringle (brother-in-law of Williams), 63
Smith, John Julius Pringle "Gramps" (grandfather of Charles Halliwell Pringle Duell), *7*, 9, 12–13, *12*, 16, *114*
death of, 24
gardens and, 105, 116–118
inheritance of Middleton Place, 22–24, 113, 114, 115
life tenancy at Middleton Place, 24, 25, 129
Smith, Josephine (mother of Charles Halliwell Pringle Duell). *see* Duell, Josephine Scott Smith
Smith, Josiah, 46–47
Smith, Mason, 206, *246*
Smith, Peter, 38
Smith, Robert, 11
Smith, Susan Pringle (wife of Williams). *see* Middleton, Susan Pringle Smith
Smith, W. Mason III, *246*, 256
Smythe, Harriet, 153
Snyder, Stephen, iii, xiii, 14, *15*, 16, 253
social justice, 222–224
South Carolina. *see also* Carolina colony
boycott of British goods, 38
in Revolutionary period, 39–51

wealth of, 41
South Carolina Historical Magazine, 100, 109, 117, 126
South Carolina Historical Society, 113
South Carolina National Bank, 24, 131
South Carolina National Heritage Corridor Program, 195
South Carolina Secession Convention, 60–63
South Carolina: A History (Edgar), 28. *see also* Edgar, Walter
South Carolina: A Yankee View (Collier), 150–152
south flanker, 36, *37*, *56*, 81–83, *93*, 139, *156*. *see also* house museum
    dining room, *147*
    Duell family at, 131, 149
    earthquake damage to, 92
    music room/red room, *122*, *145*
    restoration of, 85, 140–142
    under Smiths' stewardship, 114–116, 119
Southern Christian Leadership Conference, 135
Southern Food Symposium, 167
southern studies, 247–248
spirituals, 216–217, 228
Spoleto arts festival, 157
spring house/chapel, 189–190, *191*, *192*, 216
Springville, S.C., 77
stableyards, *119*, 132–134, 137, 159, *160*
Stanton, Gary, 181
Stephen (enslaved person), 51
Stephens, Zoe L., *246*, 257
Stier Kent and Canady, 174
Stone, Dottie, 226, 253
Stoney, Thomas, 123
storms, 54. *see also* Hurricane Hugo
"Story of English, The" (documentary), 216
Suffolk University, 212
Sullivan, Mary Edna, 146, 242, 253
    on *Beyond the Fields*, 197–198
    on candlesticks, 147
    DeWeese family and, 214, 216, 217
    "Moment in Time" exhibit, 232
    research by, 193–195
Sullivan's Island, 223
Summerville, S.C., 68, 82, 238

— T —

tabby, *73*
taxes
    after Civil War, 59
    conservation easements and, 236
    estate/inheritance taxes, 22, 24, 25, 130
    Middleton Inn Associates and, 175–176
    Middleton Place Foundation and, 160
tea room, 163–165
Thatcher, Margaret, *248*
theater, 134–135
Theory and Practice of Gardening, The (d'Argenville), 106
Thomas (enslaved person), 70
Thompson, Jim, 18
timber, 97, 167–168, 179, 242
Tinker, Anne Gaud, 207, 246, *246*, 256
tobacco companies, 7
Todd, M. Tracey, *119*, 162, *225*, 242, 253, 255, 256
    background of, 240–241
    on demonstration rice field, 201
    digital programming and, 222
    in discussions about slavery, 223
    Barbara Doyle History and Archives Center and, 247
    on Duell, 240
    at Edmondston-Alston House, 241
    on enslaved workers, 36
    on gardens, 107
    on interpretation of slavery, 219
    on joint reunion, 206
    on Arthur Middleton's return to South Carolina, 37
    on pandemic, 220, 221
    research by, 193–195
    on slavery, 232, 234
    on South Carolina delegation to Continental Congress, 39
    visiting scholar/internship program and, 212
    on wedding business, 220
    work by, 251
Tom (enslaved person), 51, 70
tomb, family, 37, *75*, 77, 177
Tombee (Rosengarten), 184
tourism, 86–88, 99–100, 123, 131, 167
Town and Country magazine, 170
Trapier, Paul, 191

trees. *see also* timber
   destroyed by Hugo, 177–179
   Middleton Oak, *116*, 177
Trumbull, John, *44*, *45*, 105
trustees of Middleton Place Foundation, 245–247
   Brock, Olivia Mitchell, 256
   Burton, E. Milby, *132*, 133, 136, 141, 257
   Carter, Jane, 257
   Carter, T. Heyward, Jr., 161, 236, 257
   Chrystie, Thomas L., 257
   Dawson, C. Stuart III, 257
   deButts, Jane Pinckney, 257
   di Lapigio, Ascanio Serena, 256
   Dintersmith, Ted, 257
   Duell, C. Holland, 186, *195*, 239, 257
   Duell, Carol Wood, 20–21, *130*, 257
   Duell, Caroline Middleton, 239, 246, 256
   Duell, Charles Halliwell Pringle, 256. *see also* Duell, Charles Halliwell Pringle
   Duell, Roderick, 174, *246*, 254, 257
   Duell, Sallie McPherson, 205, *225*, *234*, 243–245, *243*, *246*, 253, 255, 256
   Ferguson, James L., 257
   Gray, Rachel MacRae, 257
   Green, Jonathan, 224–226, *225*, 228, 256
   Harwood, Lee, 257
   Holliday, Hank, 245, 256
   Hollifield, S. Colby, 257
   Kuyk, James, 256
   Lader, Philip, 170, 257
   Laughlin, Michael, 245, *246*, 256
   Leadem, Richard A., 245, 246, *246*, 256
   Manigault, Peter, *20*, *152*, 247, 257
   Manigault, Pierre, 246–247, 255, 256
   Mayland, Tina, 257
   McMillen, Earl III, 256
   McMillen, Elizabeth Wright, *246*, 257
   Middleton, Earl, 257. *see also* Middleton, Earl
   Middleton, Francis G. "Frank", 206, *210*, 257
   Middleton, Henry Enrico B., 257
   Middleton, Kenneth E., 205, *246*
   Middleton, Lane, 257
   Moore, B. Allston III, 257
   Morgan, Heningham Anne Duell, 9, *10*, *13*, 24–25, 118, 130, 257
   Palmer, Caroline T., *246*, 256
   Pringle, Lee, *225*, 226–230, *227*, 256
   Routh, Josephine Clark Duell, 131, 205, 239, 257
   Sinkler, Michelle, 257
   Slotchiver, Irvin, 139, 257
   Smith, W. Mason III, *246*, 256
   Stephens, Zoe L., *246*, 257
   Tinker, Anne Gaud, 207, 246, *246*, 256
   Todd, M. Tracey, 240–241, 251, 253, 255, 256. *see also* Todd, M. Tracey
   Waterman, June Duell, 131, 239, *246*, 256
   Waters, Charles H., 141, 257
   Young, J. Rutledge III, 257
   Young, J. Rutledge, Jr., 175, 176, 257
Tubman, Harriet, 71–74

— U —

United Timber Company, 97
Upheaval in Charleston (Hoffius and Williams), 91
Uxbridge, 239

— V —

Van Wyck, Charles, 75
Vansina, Jan, 184
vegetative buffers, 235, 236
Venturi, Robert "Bob", 172
Vesel, Cameron, 207
Vesey, Denmark, 190
visiting scholar program, 212. *see also* Bellinger, Robert
visitor experience
   broadening, 159
   digital programming, 221–222
   fine-tuning, 161–163
   food, 163–167
   Living History experiences, 231. *see also* interpretation

visitors to Middleton Place
  after Civil War, 86, 88
  dignitaries, viii, 19, 52, 123–125, *248*
  under Duell's stewardship, 136, 157
  Duncan, 102–105
  gardens opened to, 118
  increase in, 136
  Lowell, 100–102
  during Lillie Middleton's stewardship, 98, 99
  number of currently, 240
  under Smiths' stewardship, 118, 123–125, 129
volunteers, 142, 240, 251

— **W** —

Walker, H., 191
Walker, Stuart, *4*
Wall Street Journal, The, 205
Warney (enslaved person), 51
Washington Race Course, 168
Washington, George, 40
Washington, Mary Leas. *see* Sheppard, Mary Washington
Washington, Monday, 71
Waterman, June Duell (daughter of Charles Halliwell Pringle Duell), 131, 239, *246*, 256
Waters, Charles H., 141, 257
Watson Hill, 237, 239
weddings, plantation, 219–220, 223
Weingarten, Charles Annenberg, 197
Wells, Julian, 95
West, Benjamin, *26*, *38*, 42, 45, 143, *144*, *145*
WestRock, 239
Weyeneth, Robert, 153
Weymouth, Frolic, 170
Whaley, Ben Scott, 153
Whaley, Emily, 153
Wheeler-Bennett, John, 19
White House, 210
Whittier, John Greenleaf, 91
Will (enslaved person), 51
Williams, Arthur Middleton, 136
Williams, John, 34, 189
Williams, Mary (wife of Henry). *see* Middleton, Mary Williams
Williams, Roger, 142

Williams, Susan Millar, 91
Williamsburg, Virginia. *see* Colonial Williamsburg
Williamson, Elizabeth Viola, 112
Wilson, Breanna, 214, *215*
Wilson, Melvin, 214, *215*, 216
Wilson, Troy, 214, *215*, 216
Wilson, Viola, 214
windsurfing, 4, 5
Woltz, Thomas, 245
women, inheritance by, 34–35, 48, 63, 85
Wood Nymph statue, *76*, 77
Wood, Peter, 184
Woodle, Jim, 141, 179, 202
Woodward, Betty Gadsden, 8–9
Woodward, Charles, 8–9
Woolson, Constance Fenimore, 86
Wright, Dye, 206
Wright, July, 85, 92, 206
Wulf, Andrea, 245

— **Y** —

Yale, 8, 14–16, *15*, 18, 171, 172
Yeadon, Richard, 53
Yeamans Creek, 29. *see also* Goose Creek
Yeamans, John, 29
Young, J. Rutledge III, 257
Young, J. Rutledge, Jr., 175, 176, 257

— **Z** —

zoning, 235, 236, 237